THE REVEREND MARK TWAIN

THE REVEREND MARK TWAIN

Theological Burlesque, Form, and Content

THE OHIO STATE UNIVERSITY PRESS

Columbus

Library of Congress Cataloging-in-Publication Data
Fulton, Joe B., 1962–
The Reverend Mark Twain : theological burlesque, form, and content / Joe B. Fulton.
p. cm.
Includes bibliographical references and index.
ISBN-13: 978-0-8142-1024-6 (cloth : alk. paper)
ISBN-10: 0-8142-1024-4 (cloth : alk. paper)
ISBN-13: 978-0-8142-9101-6 (CD)   ISBN-10: 0-8142-9101-5 (CD)
1. Twain, Mark, 1835-1910—Criticism and interpretation. 2. Religion
and literature. 3. Theology in literature. I. Title.
PS1338F85 2006
818'.409—dc22
2005033137

Cover design by Jason Moore.
Text design and typesetting by Jennifer Shoffey Forsythe.
Type set in Adobe Apollo.
Printed by Thomson-Shore, Inc.

9 8 7 6 5 4 3 2 1

FOR HALLIE
AND OUR CHILDREN RORY, FELICITY,
ALDER, AND FIONA

Animae dimidium meae.
—Horace, *Odes, Book I, iii*

{ CONTENTS }

CONTENTS

{ LIST OF ABBREVIATIONS }

Bakhtin's Works

AH	"Author and Hero in Aesthetic Activity"
CMF	"The Problem of Content, Material, and Form in Verbal Art"
DN	"Discourse in the Novel"
MHS	"Toward a Methodology for the Human Sciences"
PDP	*Problems of Dostoevsky's Poetics*
PN	"From the Prehistory of Novelistic Discourse"
RW	*Rabelais and His World*
SG	"The Problem of Speech Genres"

Twain's Works

AMT	*The Autobiography of Mark Twain*
CS	*Christian Science*
HHT	*Hannibal, Huck, and Tom*
MMM	*More Maxims of Mark*
MTE	*Mark Twain in Eruption*
MTHHR	*Mark Twain's Letters to Henry Huttleston Rogers*
MTHL	*Mark Twain—Howells Letters*
MTL	*Mark Twain's Letters* (University of California Press)
MTLP	*Mark Twain's Letters to His Publishers*

MTMB *Mark Twain's Travels with Mr. Brown* (*Alta California* Letters)

MTNJ *Mark Twain's Notebooks and Journals* (University of California Press)

Other Works

LE   *Literary Environment* (Eichenbaum)
MTHF *Mark Twain and Huck Finn* (Blair)
MTLS *Mark Twain and Little Satan* (Tuckey)
MTPD *Mark Twain in the St. Louis* Post-Dispatch (McWilliams)
SJ   *A Sentimental Journey* (Shklovsky)

FOR A VARIETY of reasons, few substantive formal analyses of Mark Twain's works have been produced. Yet Twain was always conscious of the creative potential afforded by traditional literary forms. "There is only one right form for a story," Twain wrote in his autobiography, "and if you fail to find that form the story will not tell itself" (AMT 267). Twain's comment applies to his work generally, but the specifics of his comment are telling. Twain was referring to *Personal Recollections of Joan of Arc,* a work that builds on the traditions of fairy tale, epic, and hagiography; Twain exploits these forms, both critiquing, and conforming to, their ideological concomitants. When searching for the elusive "right form," Twain often selected theological genres—saints' lives, epistles, catechisms, psalms, hymns, creeds, Sunday-school books, tracts, and prophetic works. These forms provided Twain with familiar genres to use as literary forms in their own right, and always to burlesque or parody, often for the purpose of ecclesiastical and social criticism. This study examines Twain's use of theological literary genres and the resulting interplay of form and content in his works.

Methodologically, this study is an organic approach, adopting the Russian philosopher Mikhail Bakhtin's attempt to unify formal and ideological approaches to literary analysis. Readers will note that both the New Criticism and Russian Formalism play a significant role in the analyses contained in this book. The Formalists' attempt to create a *science* of literary analysis is as crucial today as it was during and following World War I, in part because it enforces a discipline so often lacking in the ideological approaches to literature that still predominate. Victor

Shklovsky expresses the practical implications of Formalist ideas for criticism: "The formal method is fundamentally very simple—a return to craftsmanship" (SJ 232). In terms promulgated by René Wellek and Austin Warren, the present study is an "intrinsic" study of some of Twain's works and examines genre, structure, and style, rather than an "extrinsic" approach considering aspects of Twain's life, psychology, or historical era. The study is "organic" in that it adheres to the definition proffered by Cleanth Brooks that an organic approach confronts "the interpenetration of the form and matter" (568).

That said, to the extent that "form and content in discourse are one," as Bakhtin asserts, this study also considers religious *content* (DN 259). When Twain draws on theology for terms like "providence" and "pre-destination," it is important to define what he may have been talking about. Because one cannot understand religious content outside of context, one might assert that form and *context* in discourse are allied organically, as are form and content. Hence, when letters or biographical details inform the discussion, they are included. A fundamental assumption of this study is that comprehending how religious content is immanent in forms like catechisms, jeremiads, and hagiography is of far greater importance than discussing elements of biography. At times, authoritative works such as Calvin's *Institutes of the Christian Religion, The Westminster Catechism,* or the creeds of the church provide important clarification for the discussion. Whether speaking of certain theological terms Twain used or the theologically inflected genres he chose, the discussion of the content—understood as including context—is provoked by the intrinsic interpretive demands of the works themselves.

This study ignores Samuel Langhorne Clemens's religious beliefs, instead considering Mark Twain's manipulations of theological form and content. Where Twain's eternal mail should be forwarded is an unanswerable question that leads nowhere, except perhaps in circles. Exploring how this great literature works *as* literature is self-evidently important and needs no other ideology to strengthen its value. In these days when many critics ostensibly employed by their institutions to study literature spend more time writing about spoons, greeting cards, and the ideologies of shirt collars in the 1870s, one should take Boris Eichenbaum's exhortation to heart: "It's time to start talking about literature" (LE 65). With the advent of neoformalism, many serious scholars have started doing just that, and the author hopes that this study will contribute to the renewed debate over the relationship of formal and ideological attributes of literature.

Before such talk commences, however, I will exercise the author's obligation and prerogative to acknowledge those who have made this study a rewarding and joyous endeavor. Baylor University has provided marvelous support for this study through reduced teaching loads, summer sabbaticals, and an excellent research assistant, Lori Tubbs. Departmental secretaries Lois Avey and Amber Adamek helped with a myriad of details associated with this project, and I am grateful for their assistance. I sincerely appreciate, too, the support of Maurice Hunt, English Department chair; Wallace Daniel, past dean of the College of Arts and Sciences; and David Lyle Jeffrey, past provost of Baylor University, in securing funding for research and travel. The Lilly Foundation and Baylor University's Institute for Faith and Learning also provided a substantial travel grant for study at the Mark Twain Project at the University of California at Berkeley. Baylor's University Research Committee provided travel funds for research in Hannibal, Missouri, Twain's boyhood home. I would like to express my gratitude to curator Henry Sweets, for his assistance and hospitality. I am grateful as well to the University of Notre Dame and the Cushwa Center for the Study of American Catholicism for a generous travel grant that allowed me to work in the Hesburgh Library Archives. Portions of chapter 6 were originally published in *Essays in Arts and Sciences,* Volume 32. They are reprinted here with permission of Essays in Arts and Sciences, University of New Haven. The Center for Mark Twain Studies at Elmira College provided travel funding and delightful accommodations at Mark Twain's summer home, Quarry Farm. My friends Mark Woodhouse and Gretchen Sharlow have made my stays at Quarry Farm personally delightful and professionally productive.

Among Mark Twain scholars, I would especially like to thank Alan Gribben, whose encouragement with this and other projects has been invaluable. It was Gribben's scholarly work *Mark Twain's Library* that revolutionized my understanding of the writer; it will always be required reading for any Twain scholar. The late, great Hamlin Hill provided significant support early in my studies of Twain, for which I will always be grateful. I feel privileged, too, to have as a Baylor colleague one of the great Twainians, J. R. LeMaster; for his colleagues and students alike he is a model of the patient, meticulous scholar. Finally, my serious study of Twain began many years ago in a seminar taught by Leland S. Person, whose close readings still inspire me in my own work.

I thank also my family for their unstinting encouragement and support of this project. My parents, Blaine and Phyllis Fulton, have shown an ongoing fascination with Twain's work that helps propel me forward on the sometimes trying days of research and writing. My wife, Hallie, has been my steadfast partisan, helping me keep alive all my initial enthusiasm. My children show signs of great character, for they enjoy Mark Twain nearly as much as their father. Once, after hearing "The Blue Jay Yarn," my daughter Felicity asked a question the great writer himself would have enjoyed: "Papa, is Mark Twain dead?" For all of us who love the work of this wonderful writer, the answer is clearly a resounding "No!" This book is affectionately dedicated to my wife Hallie and our four children, Rory, Felicity, Alder, and Fiona. Their love and support make the dedication from the Roman poet Horace seem stingy for allotting them only half of my soul; *they have it all.*

{ CHAPTER 1 }

"I WAS EDUCATED, I WAS TRAINED, I WAS A PRESBYTERIAN"

Conformity and Critique in Mark Twain's Religious Dialogue

The most violent revolutions in an individual's beliefs
leave most of his old order standing.
—WILLIAM JAMES (*Pragmatism* 29)

In the work of art, there are, as it were, two ruling powers and
two lawful orders . . . that of content and that of form.
—MIKHAIL BAKHTIN (CMF 284)

IN 1867, AS Twain told the story in the San Francisco newspaper the *Alta California,* he approached the organizer of the *Quaker City* expedition to the Holy Land by having a colleague introduce him as Mark Twain, the *Reverend* Mark Twain. One might reasonably doubt that this really happened, but historical accuracy is in this case beside the point. More apropos is Twain's use of the incident in the *Alta California* letters that he later revised for *The Innocents Abroad* (1869). It was a typical sort of joke for Twain—one with a barb to it. The *Quaker City* expedition was a high-minded expedition with a number of gatekeepers to expel riffraff, and Twain lamented in *The Innocents Abroad* that the "character and standing of every applicant for passage had to undergo the strictest assay by a Committee" (113). By masquerading, even if only in his writing, as the Reverend Mark Twain, "a clergyman of some distinction," Twain springs a practical joke on the committee that, like all such jokes, contains an element of hostility (MTMB 114).

1

This is a *literary* practical joke, however, and not just a personal one. Twain used the cruise to create the occasion for parody and burlesque. The noted author of the tall tale "The Celebrated Jumping Frog of Calaveras County" (1865) and such hoaxes as "The Petrified Man" (1862) and "Bloody Massacre Near Carson" (1863) would accompany a flock of wealthy, psalm-singing Easterners, ostensibly with the design of assisting the Reverend Henry Ward Beecher with his preacherly duties on shipboard. Twain's literary masquerade as the Reverend Mark Twain, like his use of the cruise in his writing, is best understood as a parody of a genre. James Cox suggests that the "invention of 'Mark Twain' had been to impose a character upon a form" (129). One could say, too, that Twain's genius imposed this form on literary forms, reinvigorating those forms through parody, burlesque, and creative revision. The Europe and Holy Land trip was, and remains, for many people a certain *type* of journey infused with a number of expectations. Twain's recitation of the itinerary is telling. In the *Alta California* letters, Twain parodies the itinerary more aggressively than in *The Innocents Abroad* and blends his own words with those of the original, so that we have such sentences as these:

> A stop of four or five days will be made at Alexandria, in Egypt, and the Ruins of Caesar's Palace, Pompey's Pillar, Cleopatra's Needle, the Catacombs, the site of ancient Memphis, Joseph's Granaries, and the Pyramids. They don't go to Cairo, but I do not mind that, because I have been to Cairo once (in Illinois), and that was enough for this subscriber. (MTMB 113)

Even without Twain's humorous interpolations, the text already shows signs of parody. The insistent use of the passive voice makes a spectacle of the reverential language so typical of what we might term a commercial litany, and one knows that it is only a matter of time before Twain breaks through the text to parody it with even greater force. In his revisions of the *Alta California* letters for *The Innocents Abroad*, Twain sets off the passage in a variety of ways to make the point very clear that the itinerary is something separate and apart from his own text; that the boundaries between the inserted text and Twain's text are crystalline. The announcement begins just as an authentic broadside would, with the heading clearly demarked with bold caps, the date in italics, and the text in smaller font. The end of the inserted text is demarcated by the signing of the names of the organizers, and even with a P.S. appended at the bottom. Through these formal means, Twain introduces the inserted text as a competitor with his own. Twain includes the piece in toto, he says, for "[i]t is almost as good as a map. As a text for this book, nothing could be better" (18). Twain makes his own point best: the original text, a devout itinerary provided by the organizers, provides the plan for his own book. The original text is a "map" that suggests the subgenre of Holy Land travel narratives. The broadside embodies the memory of the genre, providing Twain with the text for his book *The Innocents Abroad*. Despite their differences, both the letters for the *Alta California* and *The Innocents Abroad* bear the same functional relationship to the original: both create, in Bakhtin's conception of parody, "images" of the original and so become "parodic doubles" (PN 51). In order to parody the original text, as Bakhtin notes, a writer must "re-create the parodied language as an authentic whole, giving it its due as a language possessing its own internal logic" (DN 364). Twain's parodies express, as Maria Marotti suggests, "a double perspective, that of literary model and burlesquing subject" (34). The result of such a doubleness, however, is unpredictable. In his insightful analysis of Twain's use of the travel genre, Jeffrey Melton sees the writer as both "conforming" and "rebelling," both "following form and snubbing it" (46). Twain's texts parody the original text *and* constantly respond to it, both implicitly and explicitly. Similarly, Twain's introduction to the tour master as the *Reverend* Mark Twain is of a piece with his own plans to write letters from the trip and ultimately to compose a book that will parody the genre. Twain is an imposter, just as the work resulting from his presence on the trip will be an imposter. But not an imposter precisely. Twain's work is not, in Jeffrey Duncan's phrase, "a *counterfeiting* of the referential" (202; original italics), but exists in constant dialogue with the literary models with which the author works. Parody demands that the writer adhere to the formal demands of the genre, so much so that the original and the parody resemble horses in separate fields running parallel to each other, their paths always on the point of convergence.

A parody is a formal acknowledgement of, and deviation from, an established text, but the parodied text is not necessarily the *object* of the parody. Narrowly defined, a parody responds to a particular text, but the parodic work can, as Gary Saul Morson suggests, parody "the genre as a whole" (75). Morson calls such works "anti-genre," though "burlesque" is the more usual term for works that adhere to and diverge from a recognized text or set of texts. Sander Gilman, in his superb study of the parodic sermon, notes that "parody cannot be defined by the ends which it is thought to achieve," but must involve issues of "form" (2–3).

Such a distinction is crucial, for Twain's use of parody is frequently mis-
understood. Obenzinger rightly observes that *The Innocents Abroad* is "a
parody of religious genres" (212) and notes Twain's use of William Hone,
the English parodist. He seriously misunderstands the relationship of
the parody to the original, however, citing the equally confused John
Marsh, who states, "Parody cancels Scripture; only Literature remains"
(39). In fact, parody preserves the form it parodies, for parody embodies
the form, its own deviations necessarily suggesting the original. Were a
parody to truly "cancel" the aesthetic object it parodies, one would witness a formal literary murder/suicide. "Parody is viable only in so far as
what is parodied is still alive," observes Jurij Tynjanov (70). That is, the
text that is parodied must be alive to begin with and the parody must
not kill it, in fact *cannot* kill it. Twain's masquerade as the Reverend
Mark Twain burlesques the straitlaced pilgrims, but does not spell an
end to preaching, pilgrimage, or holy travelogues.

More seriously, both Obenzinger and Marsh elide the difference
between the parodied form and the object of parody, suggesting that the
parodied form is necessarily the target. Quite the opposite is frequently
the case. Twain parodied the Apostles' Creed in his April 16, 1867, letter for the *Alta California:*

> Even Church congregations are organized, not on religious but on politi-
> cal bases; and the Creed begins, "I believe in Abraham Lincoln, the Mar-
> tyr-President of the United States," or, "I believe in Jefferson Davis, the
> founder of the Confederate States of America." The genuine Creeds begin
> that way, although to keep up appearances they still go through the
> motions and use the ancient formula, "I believe in Jesus Christ," etc.
> (MTMB 142–43)

Clearly, Twain parodies the sacred text, but uses it as a vehicle for social
criticism, rather than as the recipient of that criticism. Neither burlesque
nor parody always aims at the form itself, which is often used to critique
some aspect of society; this is particularly true when Twain uses religious literary genres. Through his parody, Twain reveals the difference
between what people say they believe and how they really believe,
drawing a line between the "genuine Creeds" that people think and the
"ancient formula" that is truly genuine. In doing so, Twain honors the
ancient formula, elevating it as the standard by which contemporary
society may still be judged. One sees here the truth that *parodia sacra,*
the parody of sacred texts, is infused with a carnival sensibility, a spirit

of topsy-turvy that debases the elevated for the purposes, as Bakhtin suggests, of "renewal" (RW 83). In his 1817 trial for having published such parodies as "The Late John Wilkes' Catechism," "The Political Litany," and "The Sinecurist's Creed," Englishman William Hone, whose edition of the Apocrypha Twain had read in 1867, successfully defended himself against charges of irreverence and blasphemy. In his defense, Hone stated that parodies of established religious texts, such as the catechism or the Athanasian Creed, are in essence "political" and that "the ridicule which the authors of the parodies attempted to excite, was not always intended to fix on the production parodied" (35). Such a distinction is crucial to understanding Twain's use of parody, for a parodist's use of established religious forms often honors those creeds and catechisms, using them for the purposes of social criticism. Hal Bush rightly reminds critics that Twain's parodies often follow the "rhetorical stylings of the jeremiad" that oppose the "social injustice" of the Gilded Age (83–84). Incorrectly, many critics see the target as the text itself, when frequently the parody champions the cause of the religious text. Twain adheres to the genre in order to create a parody of it, frequently making the original the *"hero of the parody,"* in Bakhtin's words (PN 51).

The irony of the original text becoming the "hero" of the parody is obvious but frankly inevitable. Consider *The Innocents Abroad*. The Holy Land trip is a subgenre of the travel narrative, and many of those who made the trip wrote books about their experiences. Twain's parody of these texts, however, is an example of *parodia sacra,* for he makes light of the serious subject matter and devotional intensity of what are in essence the records of pilgrimage. By quoting and referencing previous Holy Land texts, Twain makes "heroes" of them, however ironically. Seeking to contrast his own realistic view of the Holy Land with the romantic view of his predecessors, Twain repeatedly takes to task books such as "Tent Life in the Holy Land" and "The Land and the Book" (409). Twain even quotes a long passage of a work by "William C. Grimes" as he discusses the beauty of the "Madonna-like" girls of contemporary Nazareth (423). In *The Innocents Abroad,* Twain quotes at length from this author, but provides the spurious name above and the manufactured title, "Nomadic Life in Palestine" for the book. Twain does this, he says, to spare the author, but also because

> I am aware that this is a pretty voluminous notice of Mr. Grimes' book. However, it is proper and legitimate to speak of it, for "Nomadic Life in Palestine" is a representative book—the representative of a *class* of

Palestine books—and a criticism upon it will serve for a criticism upon them all. (426)

Identifying the book as representative of an entire *"class,"* Twain focuses on the traits of the genre, noting quite plainly that his own book will adapt this form, infusing it with a burlesquing attitude. One of Twain's central criticisms is notable: "Our pilgrims have brought *their* verdicts with them. They have shown it in their conversation ever since we left Beirout. I can almost tell, in set phrase, what they will say when they see Tabor, Nazareth, Jericho and Jerusalem—*because I have the books they will 'smouch' their ideas from"* (406; emphasis in original). The predictability of the pilgrims' comments on the Holy Land extends as well to the authors of the books from whom they "smouch." It is necessarily true of Twain, too, for the writer of parody is compelled to take account of the stale original and adheres to the genre closely enough to allow parody to occur. "Form is content as imagined, not merely received: transfigured, not mimed," suggests Dennis Donoghue (13). The truth is that neither form nor content is passively received and that every artist manipulates both. In his excellent analysis of Twain's use of parody, Pascal Covici notes that the "common knowledge of the standard" allows parody, at the same time suggesting that readers are forced by the form to, "almost unthinkingly, participate in Twain's desecration of what the reader himself might not be quite ready to abandon" (139).

Literary forms do not acquiesce in their own parody, however. A dialogue between the aesthetic object and its parodic image ensues, with the original reasserting its own *rejuvenated form.* Time and again, Twain attacks, adopts, and finally adapts literary forms that have become worn out and trite. The staleness and popular awareness of religious literary genres attract Twain, calling him to freshen the form, most frequently through burlesque. "The world grows tired of solid forms in all the arts," Twain opined in 1900 ("Henry Irving" 193–94). Twain's "desecration" actually breathes new life into the literary forms he uses. As Twain quotes the lengthy passages from the work of others, and follows closely the biblical itinerary that has been largely *predetermined* for him by the genre, one begins to ask the question: on whom is the joke? In order to parody any action or artifact, one must invoke the original. In his notebook entries for the trip, Twain establishes a "biblical itinerary" that joins biblical texts with geographical locations (see especially MTNJ 1: 458–79). Parodying the subgenre of theological travel books, Twain becomes a student of the established form and resurrects its importance, making it the object of learned studies like the present one. Thus, he simply must write about the Holy Sepulcher, for instance, as every other writer about the Holy Land does. Twain quotes and parodies their work and so must follow in their footsteps, a fact that one feels in the very structure of *The Innocents Abroad*. "A genre lives in the present," Bakhtin declares, "but always *remembers* its past, its beginning" (PDP 106). Bakhtin and the formalists with whom he debated often discuss the "memory" of genre; a genre has memory in part because people do, but memory exists, too, in the generic structures of narrative. Roman Jakobson suggests that genres are governed by the same "implicational laws" that "are embedded to a great extent in the internal logic of linguistic structures" (*Main* 48). These internal and eternal qualities of a genre exist in dialogue with the present, forcing Twain to take account of the dictates of the genre. The genre insists that certain elements of content will be present and that certain formal traits will shape them, most often with the author's blessing, but inevitably in any case; writers insist, of course, on having their say as well.

In this process, Twain becomes the "image" of the Reverend Mark Twain, if not the genuine article. Leland Krauth sees here "a bounded Twain—the proper Twain who honors conventions, upholds proprieties, believes in commonplaces, and even maintains the order-inducing moralities" (3). Krauth contrasts this "bounded Twain" with the "transgressive Twain" (3), but the dichotomies elide the fact that we experience both identities concurrently. Formally, the transgressive identity may very well serve the bounded identity; that may in fact be the "calling" of the transgressive Twain.

Twain often imagined himself as a preacher, or as the image of one, confessing to his brother Orion that

> I never had but two *powerful* ambitions in my life. One was to be a pilot, & the other a preacher of the gospel. I accomplished the one & failed in the other, *because* I could not supply myself with the necessary stock in trade—*i.e.* religion. I have given it up forever. I never had a "call" in that direction, anyhow, & my aspirations were the very ecstasy of presumption. But I *have* had a "call" to literature, of a low order—*i.e.* humorous. (MTL 1:322)

Called to be a writer, but not a minister, Twain depicted his work as an author in theological terms, humorously describing himself as preacher, prophet, and even saint. Twain's work frequently reminds one of the

Menippean satirists, who drew on traditional genres for their burlesques and "ostensibly improvised sermons," as Gilbert Highet notes, even while developing their own views in response to their opponents (304). In the process, all sides speak up. No longer simply a prop for parody, the figure of the Reverend Mark Twain engages in a dialogue with his fellow reverends, whose intentions may be more high-minded, but whose stories Twain bears in mind while writing *The Innocents Abroad*. The implications of this fact are many, for the Reverend Twain both criticizes and honors the participants in this dialogue, all of those who have employed the genre before him. As a writer of parody, he often critiques, but as a writer of parody he must also, on the level of form and content, conform. These "ruling powers" of narrative, as Bakhtin calls them, are the "old order" left standing after whatever revolutions may have occurred in Twain's beliefs (CMF 284). In sacred parody, Bakhtin observes, "it is often very difficult to establish precisely where reverence ends and ridicule begins," and so it is it with Twain (PN 77). In "A Couple of Sad Experiences" (1870), Twain reflected on the difficulty of writing burlesque, citing specifically his hoax "The Petrified Man" as one example. "To write a burlesque so wild that its pretended facts will not be accepted in perfect good faith by somebody," Twain writes, "is very nearly an impossible thing to do" (388–89). The "body of the burlesque" can catch a reader's attention, deflecting attention from the "nub" or "moral of the burlesque" (389). Marotti is absolutely correct that "[l]iterary models stand for something beyond the purely literary work" and that Twain responds against the genres that embrace "the conventions of society" (51). The interaction is dialogic. A parody can renew a genre, but the interaction is mutual, for the parodic object has to take into account the ideological presuppositions of the genre. *Genre talks back.* After all, Twain follows the same subject matter as countless other pilgrims, and in the same order; he capitalizes the same words; he even uses the same intonations, sentence patterns, and exclamations. His own text becomes a "parodic double," one that institutes a dialogue between the worldviews suggested by these two forms, the original generic object and the parody of it.

TWAIN AND THE FORM OF BELIEF

In the *Alta California* letters, Twain describes listening to the preaching of Edwin Hubble Chapin, who delivers his sermon with a strong, deep, unmistakable earnestness. There is nothing like that to convince people. Nobody can have confidence in cold, monotonous, inanimate utterances, though they were teeming with truth and wisdom. Manner is everything in these cases—matter is nothing. (MTMB 175)

Twain's criticism of vacuous preaching is fairly obvious, but the interesting element here is his fascination with the form the preaching takes: "Manner is everything in these cases—matter is nothing." Even while criticizing the lack of content in the sermons of this very popular preacher, Twain recognizes the power of the sermonic form, registers the power of the genres of belief. This study will make it clear that Twain uses religious genres because manner is "everything." Twain's use of *parodia sacra* engenders in some of his most important works just the sort of dialogue one sees in *The Innocents Abroad*. The works discussed in this study are of two types. On the one hand are the obvious parodies and burlesques of religiously inflected literary genres. Examples of this are Twain's burlesques of Sunday school books in *Roughing It* (1872), his burlesque of church services and hymns in *The Adventures of Tom Sawyer* (1876), and his burlesque life of Christ in "The Second Advent" (1881). On the other hand are works like *Personal Recollections of Joan of Arc* (1896), *What Is Man?* (1906), and *The Mysterious Stranger Manuscripts* (1897–1908). In these works, Twain inhabits the forms of hagiography, catechism, and prophecy creatively, and often with a tone that might seem more serious. Still, Twain burlesques the religious genres in every example, sparking a dialogue between form and content and reinvigorating the genres he employs. The prophetic works are a good example, for in some works, Twain certainly does create a parody to ridicule society, but in some other works the burlesque is more restrained and closer to a literary version of a religious work. The best way to make this point is to compare two works, one the rollicking burlesque "Barnum's First Speech in Congress" (1867) and the other the seething jeremiad "The United States of Lyncherdom" (1901). In both works, Twain employs the prophetic form to comment on racism during and after Reconstruction.

"Barnum's First Speech in Congress (By Spiritual Telegraph)" is an example of the complexity of Twain's response to the genre of prophecy. This genre can be "renewed in new situations," as Bakhtin observes, but it is not freshly created by the author, "just as one cannot invent language" (Notes 153). Certain traits typical of the genre will erupt into the piece, even more so since this particular sketch is on the one hand a hilarious parodic prophecy and is at the same time a serious critique of public discourse, in particular bombastic political language. In 1865, P. T. Barnum, the "Great Showman" and "Prince of Humbugs," was also a Connecticut state legislator. Barnum, best known for creating the American Museum and the "Greatest Show on Earth," was also active in Connecticut politics as part of the Republican party. In 1865, he delivered a speech to the legislature demanding that African Americans be given the right to vote. By 1867, Twain may have accepted Barnum's argument, yet found his political rhetoric reminiscent of his professional patter as a carnival barker luring customers to view the "Fiji Mermaid," "the tattoed man," General Tom Thumb, and the "Ethnological Congress of Savage and Barbarous Tribes." The three-ring circus Twain burlesques conjoins political, religious, and carnival language in "Barnum's First Speech to Congress," published during Barnum's unsuccessful 1867 congressional bid. Twain apprehends this "speech" from the future, reporting that Barnum will cry, "NO! Even as one sent to warn ye of fearful peril, I cry Help! Help! For the stricken land!" (211). Twain patterns the work rather obviously after prophetic form, satirically depicting P. T. Barnum as a prophet, as "one sent," who appears before the "menagerie" of Congress (212). Twain's references may be to bearded women, dwarves, and giants, but he presents them in biblical patterns, such as the repetition of certain phrases, references to "the pride of his strength," the use of introductions such as "O, spirit of Washington!" repeated use of the word "ye," assertions such as "The country is fallen!" and the concluding exhortation, "Rouse ye, my people, rouse ye! rouse ye! rouse ye!" (212–13). The phrase "the pride of his strength" comes straight from the Bible, with the most likely allusion Ezekiel 30:6, "Thus saith the Lord; They also that uphold Egypt shall fall; and the pride of her power shall come down." In the context of Barnum's support for Radical Reconstruction, those Egyptian slaveholders of the allusion are really Southerners attempting to win the peace after having lost the war. Twain's sketch is a frankly hilarious burlesque of a nearly literal carnival congress; the prophecy is pointedly political, and one sees what Bakhtin terms the "parodical prophecy" that follows a theological form closely in order to create a sense of the ridiculous (RW 233). By parodying prophecy in the halls of Congress, Twain makes the leaders appear ridiculous, suggesting, too, that we live in a diminished age, when the prophets are little more than carnival barkers in a national freak show.

Parodic prophecy should not be viewed as just a good joke, for the form, while adaptable to new situations, is not itself new and adheres to its origin. In his *Institutes of the Christian Religion,* John Calvin states that "the common office of the prophets was to hold the Church in suspense," constantly reminding God's chosen people that they were just that *and* calling them to account by virtue of that fact (II: 426). Barnum's speech reduces contemporary politicians to the ridiculous, prophesying in ironic fashion the same destruction that Ezekiel calls down upon the Israelites. Even parodic prophecy, Bakhtin notes, "is a picture of utter catastrophe threatening the world" (RW 237). Like any *biblical* prophet, Barnum criticizes contemporary society. Commenting on the political turmoil during Reconstruction, Twain's Barnum sees Congress's failure to enact Radical Reconstruction as a return of "grim Treason" (212). The phrasing is carnivalesque, as Barnum laments that "once more helpless loyalty scatters into corners as do the dwarfs when the Norwegian giant strides among them!" (212). The serious element is not dwarfed by the hilarity, but rather made larger, grotesque, and unmistakable. "Where is the poor Negro?" queries Barnum, answering his own question by suggesting, "[H]e is free, but he cannot vote; ye have only made him white in spots, like my wonderful Leopard Boy from the wilds of Africa! Ye promised him universal suffrage, but ye have given him universal suffering instead!" (212). Barnum's speech is undeniably comic, but it addresses a rot at the center of society. Twain's presentation encourages us to laugh at the circuslike situation in Washington, but parodic prophecy, as Bakhtin observes, is not "philosophical affirmation" (RW 233). Twain makes a joke of the inflated political language and hyperbole that Barnum was famous for during his years as a legislator, at the same time creating a piece that identifies a real social and political problem: former slaves are now "free," but enjoy only limited political freedom. Twain draws on Barnum's 1865 speech in which he argued for removing the word "white" from the Connecticut constitution. Barnum attacked the one-drop rule that defined a person with any African American heritage as a black and therefore barred from voting. Barnum satirically suggested that Connecticut ought to "let a mulatto vote half the time, a quadroon three-fourths, and an octoroon seven-eights of the time" (Saxon 221). Twain's burlesque version of Barnum's 1865 speech, in which he laments that the law makes former slaves only "white in spots," comically—and prophetically—attacks society. Twain's presentation encourages us to laugh at the carnival scene in which the victorious Northerners are "cowering dwarfs" running in fear from the "Norwegian

Giant" of the South. While rollicking and ridiculous, Twain's parody does make a serious point, for laughter can be regenerative and play some role in the revival sought by prophetic form. Primarily, however, we laugh out of anger and in spite of the fact that the joke cracked in Washington is—once again—on us.

Several decades later, in "The United States of Lyncherdom" (1901), Twain again exploits the prophetic genre as prophecy itself, to create a scathing criticism of contemporary American society. To write this anti-lynching editorial, Twain applied the prophetic form, with all its familiar patterns of syntax, rhythm, and diction, to call America to account for its sins, political and general. The form gives Twain an instant authority that he would not otherwise enjoy. To a great degree, too, the form he chooses contributes to the content. Commenting on the relationship of form to content, Bakhtin asserts that *content follows form* and is not invented by an author, who "only developed that which was already embedded in tradition" ("Toward a Methodology" 166). Twain may choose the form, but that decision enforces a certain adherence to it, fostering the creation of a true jeremiad. Twain begins by stating, "And so Missouri has fallen, that great state!" (479). References to biblical passages are many, for the prophetic works feature many cities that have already fallen or are predicted to; witness Twain's discussion of the prophecy of universal decay in *The Innocents Abroad*. Judging by Twain's use of the word "great" as a qualifier following the identification of the place that has fallen, he may be referring to Revelation 14:8, "And there followed another angel, saying, Babylon is fallen, is fallen, that great city." Twain begins the second section with a formal prophetic invocation, "O, Missouri!" that, again, has many possible biblical sources, but recalls most obviously Jeremiah 4:14, "O Jerusalem, wash thine heart from wickedness, that thou mayest be saved" (see also Jeremiah 22:29 and Matthew 23:37). "O, Missouri" has the unmistakable ring of burlesque to it, as does the title "The United States of Lyncherdom," even if the editorial contrasts to "Barnum's First Speech in Congress" in its formal seriousness. Twain creates "The United States of Lyncherdom" within the Christian prophetic tradition because, like the prophets, Twain delivers judgment on a people who have strayed from the truth. And it is not just political truth. Certainly, Twain criticizes a country that is founded on principles of democracy, that had fought a war over slavery, and that prided itself on the rule of law only to turn away from this grand inheritance; in the work, however, he specifically calls the South to account based on religious principles. As he argues, "in my time religion was more general, more pervasive, in the South than it was in the North, and more virile and earnest, too, I think" (479). Twain immediately brings up the paradox that in this "region of church-es" the citizens "rose, lynched three negroes—two of them very aged ones—burned out five negro households, and drove thirty negro fami-lies into the woods" (480).

Twain ends his antilynching masterpiece with an apocalyptic scene right out of the most vivid passages from the books of Ezekiel and Rev-elation. Discussing the number of lynchings in the United States, Twain suggests we should

> place the 203 in a row, allowing 600 feet of space for each human torch, so that there may be viewing room around it for 5,000 Christian Ameri-can men, women, and children, youths and maidens; make it night for grim effect; have the show in a gradually rising plain, and let the course of the stakes be uphill; the eye can then take in the whole line of twenty-four miles of blood-and-flesh bonfires unbroken, whereas if it occupied level ground the ends of the line would bend down and be hidden from view by the curvature of the earth. All being ready, now, and the dark-ness opaque, the stillness impressive—for there should be no sound but the soft moaning of the night wind and the muffled sobbing of the sacri-fices—let all the far stretch of kerosened pyres be touched off simultane-ously and the glare and the shrieks and the agonies burst heavenward to the Throne. (485)

The nightmarish scene recalls biblical descriptions of the Babylonian captivity, the defeat of the Israelites by enemy powers, and the destruc-tion of Jerusalem. Here, however, no exogenous enemy creates apoca-lypse; the enemy swarms within American souls. Twain's rhetoric of human torches is extreme, but the lynching crisis and the prophetic form itself encourage such extreme rhetoric. Speaking of the prophets, Rabbi Abraham Heschel could have been speaking of Twain: "Their words are onslaughts, scuttling illusions of false security, challenging evasions, call-ing faith to account, questioning prudence and impartiality" (xvii). Twain's American landscape illumined by the burning bodies of lynched African Americans is the fiery social criticism that is a counterpart to his earlier burlesque "Barnum's First Speech to Congress." As different as the two works are, Twain constructs both by burlesquing the prophet-ic form, adapting the genre of prophecy for his own social and religious jeremiad. To apply the distinctions discussed earlier, "Barnum's First

Speech in Congress" is an "image" of prophecy, while "The United States of Lyncherdom" *is* prophecy. This is certainly not to elevate one over the other and implies no value of one over the other; indeed, perhaps the most important comparison to draw here is that there is little *functional* distinction between the two types, for whether burlesquing the genres broadly or adopting them with little burlesque, Twain embraces the original, and his work proceeds according to the dictates of the form. In both works, Twain adopts and adapts prophetic form to criticize and lament a "stricken land."

TWAIN AND THE CONTENT OF BELIEF

Even if "manner is everything" for Twain, "matter" is obviously something, too, and if form engenders content, then content certainly engenders form. Twain's interests and occupations led him to make certain aesthetic choices. The most ridiculous assertion made about Twain and the religious matter in *The Innocents Abroad* is that of Howard Mumford Jones, who suggests that "except for the chapters on Palestine in *Innocents Abroad,* where Twain could not avoid the topic, the name of Jesus scarcely appears in his work" (98). This is hardly accurate, and the chapter "The Second Advent" dispels the folly of his comment on Twain's literary use of the Christ story. Of more concern is Jones's suggestion that Twain discussed the religious matter only because the locale rendered it impossible to avoid. An odd determinism! One thinks of Shklovsky's belief that "a writer's consciousness is nonetheless determined by literary form. The crises of a writer coincide with the crises of literary genres" (*Theory* 171). Such assertions have some validity—after the writer chooses the genre. Twain embraces religious literary form in order to comment on the content such form poses; Jones behaves as though Twain simply happened to stow away on a ship—any ship—at random. Twain embarked on the *Quaker City* cruise to the Old World and the Holy Land to situate himself as an observer and parodist in that environment of devout attention to the geography of religion—it was what he later labeled "health-giving theological travel ("Hellfire Hotchkiss" 184). Twain's impersonation as the Reverend Mark Twain *fashions comedy out of the very situation he created.* No, Twain's deep and abiding interest in religion and the prophets had sources deeper than mere chance and propinquity. Just as Twain chooses religious genres for many works, he chose to go on the excursion for very specific reasons, but doing so created formal obligations that he could not ignore—even if he wanted to.

The present study examines works in which the literary forms of religion and theology play an important structural role, parodically or otherwise. Given the dynamic relationship between form and content, it is useful at this juncture to consider the record of Twain's content of belief; however "extrinsic" such biographical concerns are, the theological ideas immanent in the forms he selects are obviously crucial for literary analysis. Recalling his baptism in "Reflections on the Sabbath" (1866), Twain labeled himself a "brevet Presbyterian," having been "sprinkled in infancy" (40). So insistently did Twain portray himself as a Presbyterian that one must conclude the classification played an important formative role in his literary persona. In a speech entitled "Consistency," delivered on December 2, 1887, to the Hartford Monday Evening Club, Twain stated

> No man *remains* the same sort of Presbyterian he was at *first*—the thing
> is *impossible;* time and various *influences modify* his Presbyterianism; it
> *narrows* or it *broadens,* grows *deeper* or *shallower,* but does not stand *still.*
> In some cases it grows so far beyond itself, upward *or* downward, that
> nothing is really *left of it* but the *name,* and perhaps an inconsequential
> *rag* of the original substance, the *bulk* being now Baptist or Buddhist or
> something. (910; emphasis in original)

Twain never became anything so esoteric as a "Baptist or Buddhist or something," but his literary work charts the ongoing dialogue among different denominations and faiths. Twain carried on a "virtually lifelong engagement with the religious ethos of his culture," observes Stanley Brodwin, a thoughtful scholar for whom the same assertion could be made ("Theology" 221). Still, as admirable as is Brodwin's work, his central description of Twain as a "countertheologian" is untenable, for the term implies a heterodoxy that Twain's writing rarely supports (235). Neither does Twain's work support similar assertions others have made: John Q. Hays's discussion of the "apostasy from orthodox faith" that forced Twain into the "modern position of finding an alternative" (12); J. Harold Smith's discussion of Twain's "anti-orthodoxy" by which the writer "attempts to formulate an independent concept of Deity" (13); and Harnsberger's view of Twain as "unorthodox" (17). The idea that Twain's deity was, in the end, as Albert B. Paine suggests, "a God far removed from the creator of his early teaching" is thus demonstrably widespread (1582). Yet, Twain's work always involves Calvinist orthodoxy, often questioning it, occasionally reinforcing it, and sometimes invoking it in reactionary and chauvinistic ways. Twain's work engages in dialogue with "Baptist or Buddhist or something," that is, with the whole panoply of religious faith, but even his way of expressing the conversation reinforces the orthodoxy at the center of the dialogue. In a notebook entry near the turn of the century, Twain mordantly commented, "What God lacks is convictions—stability of character. He ought to be a Presbyterian or a Catholic or *something*—not try to be everything" (notebook 42, unpublished). Twain was "*something*," but many commentators seem to feel that Twain was "everything." This study will not address the wearisome and unknowable question of whether or not Twain was a Christian, but structurally, at least, "Mark Twain" is an identity that we can know better than Sam Clemens because it embodies and is embodied by literary form; in Twain's work, one is on solid ground to assert that the form and content of belief remain in dialogue. Shurr's study of Calvin's influence on American writers holds true for Twain and orthodoxy:

> From his generalized stimulus come the powerful controlling myths, the stories of our gods, the symbolic tales that express cultural values. It becomes immediately obvious, then, that his influence has not been a totally baneful one. Some of our best productions are given frameworks of steel by his harsh presence. (18)[1]

For Twain, Calvin is part of the "old order" that William James talks about as remaining even after "violent revolutions in an individual's beliefs" (29). According to a contemporary account, one of Twain's fellow *Quaker City* passengers—a real preacher—presented him with a bust of Calvin as a wedding present. Twain dutifully placed Calvin on his writing table, plopped a top hat on the theologian's head, and drew "a pair of spiral moustaches and a fanciful goatee" on his face, making him look "like a French barber" (MTPD 68). Later, Twain reportedly smashed the statue to bits. Whether true or not, the story illustrates both the revolution and what remained standing in the Twain's persona, just as the writer's often explosive use of religious literary genres reveals both iconostasis and iconoclasm. Remove Calvin, and there is no burlesque. A top hat, moustache, and beard are not in and of themselves funny. One needs a straight man. Without Calvin, there would be no Mark Twain.

Calvin's presence on Twain's writing table is symbolic just as his presence in Twain's work is undeniable. In contrast to the fairly common view of Twain as heterodox, his work in fact expresses a particular aversion to what he termed "Wildcat Religions." At times, Twain seems like a comic version of Calvin himself, disparaging Mormons instead of Albigensians. Emerging straight from Twain's experiences in the Western mining camps, the term "wildcat" is a double metaphor, with the first meaning referring to mining. In *Roughing It,* he defines the term:

These were nearly all "wild cat" mines, and wholly worthless, but nobody believed it then. The "Ophir," the "Gould & Curry," the "Mexican," and other great mines on the Comstock lead in Virginia and Gold Hill were turning out huge piles of rich rock every day, and every man believed that his little wild cat claim was as good as any on the "main lead" and would infallibly be worth a thousand dollars a foot when he "got down where it came in solid." Poor fellow, he was blessedly blind to the fact that he never would see that day. So the thousand wild cat shafts burrowed deeper and deeper into the earth day by day, and all men were beside themselves with hope and happiness. How they labored, prophesied, exulted! Surely nothing like it was ever seen before since the world began. Every one of these wild cat mines—not mines, but holes in the ground over imaginary mines—was incorporated and had handsomely engraved "stock" and the stock was salable, too. . . . One would suppose that when month after month went by and still not a wild cat mine (by wild cat I mean, in general terms, *any* claim not located on the mother vein, *i.e.,* the "Comstock") yielded a ton of rock worth crushing, the people would begin to wonder if they were not putting too much faith in their prospective riches; but there was not a thought of such a thing. They burrowed away, bought and sold, and were happy. (285–86)

This lengthy passage provides an admirable definition of what Twain means by "wild cat" mines, but one also sees even here the language of religious enthusiasm, with terms of belief, prophesy, and faith that encourage the writer's metaphorical application of the term to any *religion* that is off the "mother vein," so to speak. In his notes for a speech against Bishop Staley's missionary efforts in Hawaii, Twain criticized the bishop—not for serving as a missionary per se, but for running a "nondescript Church" (MTL 5:331). Twain refers to the bishop's theology as "the wildest of all wildcat religions . . . if there *is* any of the pay rock of saving grace in its main lead, they haven't struck it yet in the lower level" (331). Twain specifically criticized Staley for conforming established religion to the "barbarous" Hawaiian religion (see *Roughing It,* Explanatory Notes 720). Twain uses the term "wildcat" to burlesque religious practices that are anything other than what he views as traditional Protestantism; in his view, they separate themselves from the truth as a wildcat miner separates himself from the known vein of gold. In 1865, Twain saved a comment in his writing notebook: "I've prospected all religions & I like the old Meth. best after all" (MTNJ 1: 78). That bit of (possibly) reported speech expresses Twain's attitudes nicely, for he often casts denominational choices in mining or prospecting terms, but always ends up endorsing the "old" choice after all—though after criticizing all denominations. In his 1866 piece, "The New Wildcat Religion," Twain contrasts the "old legitimate regular stock religions" with spiritualism, again using the metaphor of mining, wondering whether the wildcat "pans out" or not (134). To use the Formalist term, casting denominational politics in such ways "makes strange" the world of denominational politics, again asserting that only traditional forms of worship yield the "pay rock of saving grace."

The original metaphor "wildcat" compares the isolated mines operated by lone miners away from the source of gold to the wildcat, that, in contrast to coyotes, for example, pursues its hunting alone and in isolated areas. The metaphor of this metaphor then is to apply the concept of the wildcat mine to religion, and Twain frequently employs this doubled metaphor to burlesque those who leave the usual denominations for a new religion, or for one that differs significantly from established Protestantism. Twain found his brother Orion a convenient subject for burlesque, for he dabbled in different religions. In "Autobiography of a Damned Fool" (1877), Twain describes the titular fool, clearly based on his brother, as "soft & sappy, full of fine intentions & shifting religions & not aware that he is a shining ass" (MTHL 1: 173). In "Schoolhouse Hill" (1898), the Orion figure is Mr. Hotchkiss, "a diligent and enthusiastic seeker after truth, and a sincere believer in the newest belief, but a man who had missed his vocation—he should have been a weathervane" (190). "His good Presbyterian wife," in contrast, "was as steady as an anvil. She was not a creature of change" (190). In the late work "Which Was It?" (1900–1902), Twain depicts Indiantown as a small village reminiscent of his childhood Hannibal. "Indiantown's Christianity," he notes, "was of the usual Southern breeds—Methodist, Presbyterian, Baptist—and each had a church which was commodious but not architectural" (184). The lone wildcat who does not find the churches "commodious" in a spiritual sense is the Orion figure, here under the name "Hamfat." The name itself seems a parody of traditional biblical names, suggesting someone who is ever chewing over some indigestible theological integument. Hamfat, we are told, is a "fervent disciple and advocate of every frantic 'ism' that had ever come his way" and "he had skirmished under the banner of every religion known to history, including Mormonism, infidelity and Voodoo, and was now 'due to be an Atheist, next revolution of his spiritual bowels,' as Dug Hapgood said" (277). Brodwin suggests that what Twain calls "wildcats" are really just "a riot of conflicting orthodoxies," ignoring the main point of the term "wildcat"—its unorthodoxy (*Myth* 141). Orion was just such an unorthodox figure, and was in fact formally excommunicated from the Keokuk, Iowa, Presbyterian Church, a staid flock that took its theology straight and strong. Having rented a large lecture hall, Orion harangued a paying audience on the subject of his religious views, views considered heretical by his fellow Presbyterians (Lorch 378). In his defense before the Presbyterian Session, Orion announced that each person had "to make up his views satisfactorily to himself" (378). In his literary reworkings of the Orion figure, Twain makes the contrast equally vivid. On the one hand we have the "usual southern breeds" of the church. There is nothing exciting about these "breeds," a fact that Twain depicts as both virtue and defect. Opposing them is the hyperemotionalism of "every frantic 'ism.'" Propinquity is everything in art, as in romance, and by putting "frantic" and "ism" so close to each other, Twain inevitably suggests "fanaticism." Twain's burlesques of "wildcat religions" are both a philosophical attitude and an important structural element of his literature, with the conflict of orthodoxy and heterodoxy creating the structure of many of his works.[2]

If Twain most often depicts deviation from the "mother vein" of the church as foolish, he often depicts it as dangerous, for man "is the only animal that loves his neighbor as himself," Twain writes in "Man's Place in the Animal World" (1896), "and cuts his throat if his theology isn't straight" (85). Through his extensive study of history, Twain achieved a deeper appreciation for the dangerous possibilities latent in all religion, but he most often focuses on the danger of the wildcats. Twain contrasts his own Presbyterianism to wildcats like spiritualism in "The New Wildcat Religion":

> I do not take any credit to my better-balanced head because I never went crazy on Presbyterianism. We go too slow for that. You never see

us ranting and shouting and tearing up the ground. You never neard of a Presbyterian going crazy on religion. . . . No frenzy—no fanaticism—no skirmishing; everything perfectly serene. You never see any of us Presbyterians getting in a sweat about religion and trying to massacre the neighbors. Let us all be content with the tried and safe old regular religions, and take no chances on wildcat. (MTMB 134)

During the composition of *A Connecticut Yankee in King Arthur's Court* (1889), Twain discovered that Presbyterians had, in fact, become dangerously enthusiastic about religion during the Covenanter period of Scots history, but even that knowledge only qualified his opinion; established "tried and true" religions may be confining, but they are at least safe.

The same cannot be said of those denominations that Twain depicts as "wildcats." Twain classes Christian Science with the wildcats, making much of the term "claim," referring to a practitioner's healing through faith instead of medicine.

He calls it his "claim." A surface miner would think it was not *his* claim at all, but the property of the doctor and his pal the surgeon—for he would be misled by that word, which is Christian Science slang for "ailment." (CS 244)

Twain employs the literary device of "defamiliarization" or "making strange" to twist our view of Christian Science practices. Twain defines a "claim" as peculiar to the argot of Christian Science by appealing to a usage peculiar to mining, thus connecting the two on their only real similarity: both the miner and the Christian Science practitioner are looking for gold. The further usage of "claim" as an assertion likewise undermines Christian Science theology, rejecting its central doctrine as only a "claim," a hypothesis.

Throughout his book *Christian Science* (1907), Twain similarly reveals his belief that Eddy's religion was not divinely revealed, but was designed to make money. Like a surface miner, Eddy "is still reaching for the Dollar" (316). In the parlance of the 1860s, "wildcat" also signified illegitimately issued stock for mining operations, and when Joe Goodman, editor of the *Virginia City Territorial Enterprise* labeled Twain a "Puffer of Wildcat," he referred to the common practice of playing up a certain wildcat stock to artificially increase its value (Fatout 44). In "My Late Senatorial Secretaryship" (1868), Twain clearly connects the concept of a wildcat religion with wildcat stock when satirizing a "wildcat" church that would "issue stock" only to have "other denominations . . . 'sell it short'" (258). Four decades later, this was Twain's most serious criticism of Eddy, for her enterprise is like wildcat stock with no real value behind it. Twain considers Christian Science as just a religious version of the business chicanery he has seen before. "Twain constructs a deeply gender-coded opposition," suggests Cynthia Schrager, "one that sets Protestant republican manhood against the feminine despotism of the Christian Science and Catholic Churches" (43). In Schrager's view, Twain's attack on Eddy is really a defense of "autonomous individualism" and a "nostalgia for the (white, male) self-reliant actor" (54). The grounds for Twain's criticisms are quite the opposite. Twain rejects Eddy precisely *because* Eddy embraces individualism over community, innovation over tradition, and because she becomes a wildcat apart from the feminine "mother vein" of the church. Twain's criticisms of the organizational structure of Christian Science center on its rejection of the real ore of religion, a creed. Christian Science began, Twain states ominously, "*without a creed*" (291; original italics), thus allowing Eddy to twist traditional forms of religion to her own ends, creating a "reformed Holy Family" that added her name to the list (287). She also fashioned "The Lord's Prayer—Amended" (316). Twain himself rewrote religious creeds by practicing *parodia sacra,* but he does so either to purify traditional religion or to invoke traditional religion to purify society. However much Twain may criticize orthodox religious beliefs, he never tries to manufacture an alternative to them. The point of his "The Revised Catechism" (1871), for example, is that a new belief in the Dollar has replaced the old beliefs, not that the old has been literally revised. In fact, the literary object requires that the sacred text not be revised at all. Twain invokes the parodic image to criticize an age that has turned its back on the doctrine embodied in the catechism. Twain labeled his late work *What Is Man?* (1906) a "new gospel," but it has much in common with the sacred texts to which it responds. In Twain's view, Eddy perverts sacred text to create what will "be the most insolent and unscrupulous and tyrannical politico-religious master that has dominated a people since the palmy days of the Inquisition" (251).

Similarly, Mormonism, with its "western 'peculiar institution'" of polygamy, was an exotic for Twain, and in *Roughing It* he time and again contrasts the two classes in the West, the Mormons and the "orthodox Americans" (166). His depiction of polygamous practices is voyeuristic—witness his discussion in chapter 15 of Mormon family life—but his work depicts, too, the tyrannical aspects of the new religion, including the tradition of "Destroying Angels," whom he defines as "Latter-Day Saints who are set apart by the church to conduct permanent disappearances of obnoxious citizens" (85). When Twain meets a "Destroying Angel," he finds him more destroyer than angel. Within the book proper, the criticism of the sect is mainly parodic, but Twain refers the reader to two appendixes, "Brief Sketch of Mormon History" and "The Mountain Meadows Massacre." Both appendixes explain Twain's fear of Mormonism, based on both theological and political grounds. Twain derides Brigham Young for usurping the privileges of "apostle" and "prophet," concluding that in the end he "proclaimed himself a God!" (547). Twain's "The Mountain Meadows Massacre" is an example of the writer employing biblical form to criticize a wildcat religion whose use of revelations was, in his view, a manipulation of biblical genre and nearly an implicit parody of it. In 1857 a group of Mormons, dressed as Indians, attacked a group of settlers, killing 120 of them. Twain stresses the fact that the settlers were "gentiles" and that Brigham Young caused the slaughter based on a spurious "revelation" that they ought to do so (551). After describing the horrific massacre, Twain states, "the number of persons butchered by the Mormons on this occasion was *one hundred and twenty*" (552; emphasis in original). The biblical language emphasizes what Twain calls "the coveted resemblance to the Israelitish tribes" seen in Mormon self-representations (550). The burlesque addresses both the Old Testament God and the more contemporary question of those living out that ethos. Twain criticizes misuse of scripture, slavery of women in a "peculiar institution," massacres, judicial intimidation, and threats to federal troops. He poses these problems as existing in a causal relationship to the Mormon deviation from "orthodox" Christianity.[3]

Mormonism was hardly Twain's bête noire, however. In a journal entry written sometime in 1884, sarcasm and incredulity ooze from the line: "Keep *Catholics* & drive out Mormons?" (MTNJ 3: 42). Twain does not call Catholicism a "wildcat" religion, and its dominant features for him seemed to be its visible connection with ancient observances and its historical involvement in politics. Those are hardly the traits of a wildcat, as he defines the term. Yet, in Twain's works, those traits were precisely the attributes that set Catholicism apart from Protestantism as a danger for political, religious, and mental freedom. The idea of "mental slavery" was one Twain considered frequently, and if the "wildcats" are marked by the loss of individual will to the emotion of worship, Catholicism shares, in his view, a subordination of the will to the larger will of the church and its dogma. From the beginning to the end of his career, Twain expressed some interest in Catholicism as a subject, but his discussions are nearly always marked by ignorance, fear, and loathing, both in his public and private writings.

What does it mean to label Twain "anti-Catholic"? Raymond Tumbleson neatly defines anti-Catholicism: "It is the ghost in the machine, the endless, neurotic repetition by self-consciously rational modernity of the primal scene in which it slew the premodern as embodied in the archetypal institution, arational and universal, of medieval Europe" (13). So was the Catholic Church for Twain, for it symbolized for him a "premodern" world of universal tyranny, a world he understood from the sermons he heard in childhood against the Catholic menace. That was the world of tyranny he imagined he opposed when, as a young man in 1861, he heartily recommended the book *Armageddon: or the Overthrow of Romanism and Monarchy* to his brother Orion. In this book, Samuel Davies Baldwin identifies the Catholic Church as the anti-Christ, predicting that the battle of Armageddon would be fought before 1875 in the Mississippi Valley (MTL 1: 120–21; Gribben *Library* 42). The prophetic form in Baldwin's work that Twain was to put to such good use in the *No. 44, The Mysterious Stranger* was imbued with anti-Catholicism, and it is no accident that Twain sets two versions of *The Mysterious Stranger Manuscripts* on the threshold of the Reformation.

At the core of Twain's literature Catholicism remained the "alien Other." When Twain wrote about the great Catholic cathedrals in *The Innocents Abroad,* his anti-Catholic biases were evident to everyone, even to Twain himself. Twain candidly admitted in *The Innocents Abroad* that he had "been educated to enmity toward everything that is Catholic" (479). Several journal entries from the 1880s are telling. Mark Twain's writing notebooks are full of ideas for literary projects that he eventually wrote, but many ideas on these pages remained undeveloped. Here is one of them:

> For a play: America in 1985. The Pope here & an Inquisition. The age of Darkness back again. Pope is temporal despot, *too.* A titled aristocracy & Primogeniture. Europe is *republican* & full of science & invention—none allowed here. (MTNJ 3:45)

Twain wrote this entry in January 1884, many months before he would be handed in a small bookshop the copy of *Morte D'Arthur* by George Washington Cable. That picturesque event is often credited as the genesis of *A Connecticut Yankee in King Arthur's Court*. A month later, in December, Twain would write his famous entry in his notebook, "Dream of being a knight errant in armor in the middle ages," a dream that obviously provided the core to what would eventually develop into his novel (MTNJ 3: 78). These two popular origination fables, while to some degree true, must be qualified. Twain's entry "America in 1885" is arguably one of the germs of *A Connecticut Yankee in King Arthur's Court,* and it is a very anti-Catholic bacillus indeed. Rather than sending a representative from the present into the past, however, for "America in 1985" he would, in a sense, graft the medieval past onto the future. Such a plot embodies Twain's view of the Catholic church as an atavistic survival into the modern era. By writing his comment in 1884, Twain seemed to be thinking along the lines of dystopian fiction, planning to produce his play *1985* in the following year, 1885. The parallels to Orwell's *1984* published in 1948 are inescapable, but the "Big Brother" of Twain's world would be the familiar bugaboo, The Holy Father, the Pope. Similarly, Twain wrote in his journal a short time after recording his "dream of a knight errant" another subject for a dystopian tale: "America in 1985. (Negro supremacy—the whites under foot.)" (MTNJ 3: 88). In 1884, then, Twain conceived of several possible projects involving dystopian time travel. While it is impossible to know how Twain might have developed the two that he left on the pages of his notebook, it does seem fair to say that the subject matter in both cases is so reactionary that it suggests Twain held on to some of the more pernicious of his early bigotries. Throughout his life, Twain wrote comments betraying a fear that "Romanism" or "Popery" would take over the country, just as he had believed it when recommending Baldwin's scurrilous volume to Orion. One sees the traces throughout his fiction, even in *Personal Recollections of Joan of Arc* (1896), as discussed in chapter 5 of this study.

One must justify Twain's dismissive attitude toward wildcat religions, on the one hand, and his championing of the importance of many denominations on the other. Having a few Orions around, shifting endlessly from one denomination to another, is a small price to pay for the political freedom that results from a fragmented church. In *A Connecticut Yankee in King Arthur's Court,* Hank Morgan, while himself a Presbyterian, introduces a variety of denominations because he fears "a united church" and so begins an ahistorical reformation (127). In "The Secret History of Eddypus" (1901–2), the historian, who also mentions one "Mark Twain, the Bishop of New Jersey," suggests that "this multitudinosity of sects was safety" (356).

Parody and burlesque are always double-voiced, however, and Twain's jokes about wildcat religions also comment on more traditional forms of worship and belief. Like the *Quaker City* excursion, Twain's western travels brought him into constant contact with a variety of religious practices. During his years in San Francisco, Twain wrote a number of burlesques of Oriental religions, and his several pieces about the Chinese Temple built by the Ning-Yong Company are good examples of his response. The first of these, written on August 19, 1864, "The New Chinese Temple," introduces the "Josh house, or place of worship," built by the Chinese for "their unchristian devotions" (41). Twain's description of the statue of Josh is both a realistic representation and a xenophobic rejection of the formal aspects of the worship, for after lavishing much attention on the "gold leaf" and the "glaring red" face, Twain concludes that "the general expression of this fat and happy god is as if he had eaten too much rice and rats for dinner, and would like his belt loosened if he only had the energy to do it" (41). Interestingly, Twain puts the Chinese temple to more sophisticated parodic use in the next installment, "The Chinese Temple," using the figure of Josh to comment on his own Calvinist God and the concept of predestination. This "old original Josh" can "bless Chinamen or damn them, according to the best of his judgment" (44). Twain ends the passage by subjecting his own denomination to the treatment: "As far as we are concerned, we don't believe it, for all it sounds so plausible" (44). Twain uses the exotic figure of Josh (his twisting of the proper term "Joss" to become the statuesque materialization of the western "josh" or "joke") to "make strange" the Calvinist God so familiar to his contemporaries. He casts the traditional Christian doctrines into a milieu dominated by a rat-eating God whose celebrations include the "beating of drums, clanging of gongs and burning of yellow paper" (44). Twain's rendering of Buddhist practices here recalls his disparaging rejection of Mormon worship that includes "horns, and cymbals, and trumpets and all the ungodly paraphernalia of their choir service" (MTMB 149). Twain certainly is "joshing" throughout the sequence of essays, and while the burlesque is less pointed than some other examples, it falls into the purview of *parodia sacra*. When Twain suggests with wonderful assonance and alliteration in a third article, "The New Chinese Temple," that he has become "imbued with Buddhism," he is making a rather tasteless and highly humorous joke about the "infernal odors of opium and edibles cooked in an unchristian way" (45). At the same time, he continues the joke, saying that he has started to "imbibe, unasked, Chinese instincts" (45). Precisely what these are he does not say. It does bear pointing out that Twain exploits the environmental determinism for humorous purpose that he uses with such formal brilliance in "The Facts Concerning the Recent Carnival of Crime in Connecticut" (1876), *The Prince and the Pauper* (1881), *Adventures of Huckleberry Finn* (1885), *A Connecticut Yankee in King Arthur's Court,* and many others. While the burlesques about the new temple never rise much above low humor, one should note that Buddhism in the text remains strongly "Other," and Twain employs words with negative theological connotations such as "unchristian" and "infernal." He suggests there is some danger and horror amid what he calls, in yet another piece on the subject, "a sort of Celestial free and easy" ("Supernatural Impudence" 47).

Twain's suggestion that these other denominations and religions are deviant is frequently unfair, but such burlesques are often covertly directed at his own denomination. Sometimes he criticizes directly. In his essay "Reflections on the Sabbath" (1866), Twain notes his own rank of "Brevet Presbyterian," which affords one

the right to be punished as a Presbyterian hereafter; that is, the substantial Presbyterian punishment of fire and brimstone instead of this heterodox hell of remorse of conscience of these blamed wildcat religions. The heaven and hell of the wildcat religions are vague and ill defined but there is nothing mixed about the Presbyterian heaven and hell. The Presbyterian hell is all misery; the heaven all happiness—nothing to do. But when a man dies on a wildcat basis, he will never rightly know hereafter which department he is in. (40)

The passage really becomes a "parodic double" of the sort discussed earlier. Twain implicitly criticizes the wildcat religions, and the form itself asserts the superiority of the "mother vein" of the church, for the wildcats always deviate from that original source. Yet, how should Twain's comment on valuing a faith in hell be read?

This early passage from the San Francisco years resembles Twain's comment decades later in *Christian Science*. Writing this book, he presumably set out to write a text deriding Christian Science and its founder, Mary Baker Eddy. The form asserts this purpose in a myriad of ways, and yet, once again, Twain critiques his own denomination as well, here while discussing the subject of infant damnation.

At the same time, I do feel that the shrinkage in our spiritual assets is get-

ting serious. First the commandments, now the Prayer. I never expected
to see these steady old reliable securities watered down to this. And this
is not the whole of it. Last summer the Presbyterians extended the Calling and Election suffrage to nearly everybody entitled to salvation. They
did not even stop there, but let out all the unbaptised American infants
we had been accumulating for two hundred years and more. There are
some that believe they would have let the Scotch ones out, too, if they
could have done it. Everything is going to ruin; in no long time we shall
have nothing left but the love of God. (317)

No one wants that! This superb burlesque aims at many targets. The reference to "suffrage" links the liberalizing of the church to current and
ongoing political debate over women's suffrage, suggesting the
inevitable relaxing of creeds, political and theological. The language of
Wall Street, with assets, securities, and stocks, hints at the financial
forces often at play in religious enterprises. Twain's criticism of both the
liberalizing forces and also the conservative forces is crucial, and is an
element of content that provides much of the structure for *Christian Science*. In some ways, the book is named inappropriately, for Twain lassoes
many other religious groups into the dialogue. Nathaniel Hope Preston
states that "[i]n later life Twain, as is well known, tried to assuage his
metaphysical anguish through flirtations with Christian Science, 'mental telegraphy' and other religious phenomena outside the main stream
of the orthodox Christianity he could not accept" (71). This is a common
and mistaken assumption, however, for Twain's interests in other religions or phenomena—these "flirtations"—were part of a serious exploration in theology, both of orthodoxy and wildcats. His interests in the
medium "Miss X," for example, were part of his larger interest in traditions of Christian prophecy and are so discussed in chapter 7 concerning *No. 44, The Mysterious Stranger*. Twain engages in dialogue with
both orthodoxy and wildcats, never endorsing either one, for he proposes to establish a dialogue between the two. Twain's burlesques of heterodoxy are most frequently critical both of the religious "wildcats" and
of mainstream Protestantism.

Twain's depiction of wildcat religions is consonant with his use of
the formal aesthetic elements of traditional Christianity. Twain was
above all thoroughly versed in the creeds and the forms of belief of his
particular denomination. In the penultimate chapter of his massive biography of Twain, Albert B. Paine discusses the writer's religion, commenting that "Mark Twain's religion was a faith too wide for doctrines—

a benevolence too limitless for creeds" (III: 1584). If we take Paine's comment to mean that Twain was constantly questioning the doctrines and creeds of traditional Christianity, the biographer is absolutely correct; nothing could be more untrue, however, than the suggestion that Twain was ignorant of, or disinterested in, the Christian doctrines and creeds. In fact, they provide the creative spark for many of his works. Similarly, Paul Baender's assertion that Twain "felt dismayed curiosity at the creeds and disciplines of Christianity" is far too dismissive of the *formal* influence of the creeds and other religious artifacts. An "organic theory of literature," Cleanth Brooks asserts, rejects the "old dualism of form and content" (568). In an organic study like this one, an intrinsic analysis of the works themselves can be buttressed by Twain's autobiographical commentary, letters, manuscripts, marginalia, writing journals, and published works. Reading such material, two facts become clear: the Presbyterian version of Calvinism, its content, provides the theological assumptions for Twain's religious dialogue; conversely, the formal genres of traditional religious belief provide a solid structural framework for Twain's parodies of that religious content and of social issues surrounding them. One sees the unity in the attributed item "The Stock Broker's Prayer" (1863), which parodies "The Lord's Prayer," but with a social target: "Our father Mammon who are in the Comstock, bully is thy name; let thy dividends come, and stocks group, in California as in Washoe" (93). Similarly, in his parody "The Revised Catechism," Twain begins with the form, directing questions at the current political and social climate, and in particular the Tammany politicians. Twain's parody of the *Shorter Catechism* substitutes modern values for the eternal verities of the catechism.

> What is the chief end of man?
> A. To get rich.
> In what way?
> A. Dishonestly if we can; honestly if we must.
> Who is God, the one only and true?
> A. Money is God. Gold and greenbacks and stock—father, son, and the
> ghost of the same—three persons in one: these are the true and only God,
> mighty and supreme; and William Tweed is his prophet. (539)

Along with the twist of the Islamic formula, "There is one God, Allah, and Mohammed is his prophet," Twain creates a parody of the catechetical form, but the form itself is not the object of parody. The trinity substituted for the Father, Son, and Holy Ghost are the trinities of capital: gold, greenbacks, and stock. The parody occurs through the reader's awareness both of the original form and content and of the point of divergence. The original *Shorter Catechism* is static, while the parodic image of it comments on the changing mores of the society. The social critique that ensues could not exist were it not for the history of the catechetical form. Twain directed the piece toward society, but one must point out that the vehicle for his critique, the catechism, is not content to criticize from the outside; inevitably, it advocates its own weltanschauung as the best alternative to this latter-day corruption. Form, particularly when it is parodied, remembers its origins and will have its say. Twain, who so often relied on religious form for his own social criticisms, typically encourages such a complex dialogue; even if he had not, however, the form would have.

The fundamental focus of this study is that Twain conducted for the better part of six decades a theological dialogue in which much of the "old order" of belief remained standing, both in form and content, even in such works as *What Is Man?* and *No. 44, The Mysterious Stranger.* In fact, an analysis of Twain's career shows an increasing reliance on the form and content of religious belief, and Twain uses these elements in traditional, though creative, ways. For example, as mentioned in the discussion of *Christian Science,* Twain wrote frequently on the subject of infant damnation, including treatments of it also in the *A Connecticut Yankee in King Arthur's Court* manuscript, "Aix-les-Bains" (1891), the *Mysterious Stranger Manuscripts,* and *What Is Man?* and marking passages in many books that he read on the subject (See Fulton, *Mark Twain in the Margins,* 41). It was an issue that vexed many during the nineteenth century due to the Calvinist concept of innate depravity and the practice of infant baptism. One can understand some causes of the controversy when reading Calvin's assertion that "even infants bringing their condemnation with them from their mother's womb, suffer not for another's, but for their own defect" (I: 217). For us, a baby is a bundle of joy, but for Calvin a baby is "a seed-bed of sin" (I: 217). Calvinist doctrine thus seemed to assert that unbaptized infants would spend eternity in Hell, a prospect Twain found repugnant. He was not alone, and the debate over infant baptism and infant damnation was, in the words of Kenneth Ross of the Presbyterian Historical Society, "the abortion debate of the nineteenth century" (Interview). Twain dove into the fray, marking passages in books he read that discussed the doctrine, commenting on it in essays he wrote, and writing about it in longer works.

The most effective of such examples is Twain's essay, "Aix-les-Bains." One of the author's most neglected masterpieces of the essay form, "Aix-les-Bains" is a beautiful reflection on eternity and the passing of creeds. It cannot be understood as such without an adequate grounding in the content that creates the form, for as Bakhtin asserts, ideological content can itself be "genre-shaping" (PDP 152). Concerned about the recent vote of the Presbyteries to maintain church doctrine as it had stood for centuries, Twain mentions the fact in the work, but in a larger sense the texts he responds to are the doctrines under debate that imply unbaptized infants would spend eternity in Hell. These doctrines, embodied or implied in the Westminster *Confession of Faith,* the *Shorter Catechism,* and Calvin's *Institutes,* are the ideologies that produce the form of the work. Twain's burlesque of the debate is his own contribution to it, and is a frank prophecy that creeds change and even disappear.

Twain begins his piece by declaring the locale "enchanting," then draws the reader's attention to the word by saying, "It is a strong word, but I think the facts justify it" (1). The word, which Twain repeats elsewhere in the essay, conjures up images of chants and incantations, the religious magic of a bygone era. The essay as a whole adheres to the established tone, for Twain uses the locale to discuss the eternal truths of the human condition. The essay begins with sickness, with the recognition that people go to Aix-les-Bains precisely because they are sick. "All diseases welcomed," an advertisement assures consumers, and a trip to the resort will cure rheumatism, gout, and nerves (1). Far worse than the myriad of minor diseases is the deeper ill experienced by these convalescents, one of whom is diagnosed with "an inflammation of the soul" (10).

Twain depicts the "soul-sickness" as a disease of the modern age, and finds in Aix-les-Bains the perfect locale for his spiritual ruminations. It is a place where one can, as Bakhtin says of Scotland, "see time in space" ("Bildungsroman" 53). There are, Twain tells us, "many layers of race, religion, and government" visible at Aix-les-Bains, and he brilliantly uses the metaphor of a book when describing the geological layers on exposed cliff walls as the "stratified chapters of the earth's history" (2). Reading this "book," Twain finds himself thinking of the procession of history, remarking on the Roman arches of the town, the Christian churches, and the telegraph office. Reminding us of Henry Adams, Twain identifies three eras in the world, all visible at Aix-les-Bains: "So there you have the three great eras bunched together—the era of war, the era of theology, the era of business" (2).

Aix-les-Bains is situated in the era of business, and this serves to develop the context of infant damnation, for Twain focuses on the hellish aspects of this world. One main street is "Rue du Puits d'Enfer—pit of Hell street," a connection Twain makes much of, for it leads directly to two "pleasure resorts—the Cercle and the Villa des Fleurs" (4–5). In them are casinos, and Twain describes the "fashionable gambling hell" to clarify that he is writing more about theology than gambling: "the moment you cross the sacred threshold and enter the gambling hell, off the hat must come, and everybody lights his cigar and goes to suffocating the ladies" (7–8). Structurally, Twain begins with the Calvinist text that he opposes, infant damnation, introduces Aix-les-Bains as a place wherein time is visible, and then proceeds to take us to a hell whose lords are chance and money, developing his presentation with infernal imagery of cigars, fire, and suffocation.

One realizes that had there been no Fall of Man, there would be no Aix-les-Bains, nor any Aches. (For "Aix-les-Bains" has its parodies—this "paradise" is only a paradise for rheumatics, that is, for people with "aches" and pains). This rumination on human ideas about God takes some unexpected turns as it follows not the dictates of parody, but the pull of the original doctrines Twain seemed inclined to refute. Twain soothes his anger that the presbytery voted to leave the doctrine of infant damnation unchanged by creating a burlesque sermon about the changes of our conceptions of God:

It is curious to think what changes the last of the three symbols stands for; changes in men's ways and thoughts, changes in material civilization, changes in the Deity—or in men's conception of the Deity, if that is an exacter way of putting it. . . . Mighty has been the advance of the nations and the liberalization of thought. A result of it is a changed Deity, a Deity of a dignity and sublimity proportioned to the majesty of his office and the magnitude of his empire, a Deity who has been freed from a hundred fretting chains and will in time be freed from the rest by the several ecclesiastical bodies who have these matters in charge. It was, without doubt, a mistake and a step backward when the Presbyterian Synods of America lately decided, by vote, to leave him still embarrassed with the dogma of infant damnation. Situated as we are, we cannot at present know with how much of anxiety he watched the balloting, nor with how much of grieved disappointment he observed the result. (3–4)

It is hardly heterodox for Twain to remind people that "[s]ituated as we are," that is, here on earth, we cannot pretend to know what God thinks when we argue over doctrine. Twain jokes further about the present God being a God of the business era who excels in "successful management of a complex and prodigious establishment" (3). The depiction reveals much about Twain's narrative practice. Frequently beginning with a text that he criticizes or parodies, Twain then revels in the nuances of the debate. Here, he responds to the text of infant damnation and derides the synods that left it in place, more for their hubris than their decision, however. Indeed, the changing conception of God in the business era is itself a parodic double of doctrinal conceptions of God, depicting the deity as a captain of industry, shuffling papers, getting the job done. The "step backward" taken by the synod becomes double-voiced, for Twain almost literally steps backward, moving his own text further and further back in time, as if turning back the chapters of the geological record with which he began. Not unexpectedly, Twain invokes Eden.

The question provoked by a text that seems on its surface to announce the theme of liberalizing Christianity is this: if the changing conception of God and the revision of doctrines fashion a better environment for people to thrive, then why do people still suffer sicknesses of both body and soul, and, more to the *textual* point, why do they come to Aix? The answer is largely a formal one, for Aix becomes the locus of historical change, the one spot in the world that for the moment encapsulates historical change that can never completely destroy the early texts and creeds. The revision of doctrine is both inevitable historically, just as one geologic chapter succeeds the next, but is also, on some level, lamentable. The doctrine of hell Twain criticizes has been replaced by a real hell, and the text asserts a causal relationship may exist. Even though Aix is only a paradise for a fallen world, Twain describes the town and its surroundings as an insular Eden detached from the hell of modernity. Traveling by train to Annecy, Twain is struck by "a garden land that has not had its equal for beauty, perhaps, since Eden; and certainly Eden was not cultivated as this garden is" (12). This prelapsarian land is an imaginary realm, predoctrinal in its purity, where no break between God and humanity has occurred. Twain's description brims with baptismal imagery as he observes bodies of water, imagines bathing in healing waters, and contemplates drinking curative waters. Twain writes that the lake itself is "a revelation, it is a miracle. It brings the tears to a body's eyes it is so enchanting. That is to say, it affects you just as all things that you instantly recognize as perfect affect you—perfect music, perfect eloquence, perfect art, perfect joy, perfect grief" (12).

Twain ends by describing an old abbey that exudes a "mystery of remote antiquity" (13). The details are telling. As a direct correlative to the Calvinist text introduced early in the essay, the "worn-out inscription" on the stone step is a temporal image encompassing the passing of time and written creeds. The worn-out inscription functions to remind the reader that the Calvinist text under debate will likewise be effaced by time, as it eventually was. Inside the old abbey, one of the ancient creeds survives, bearing the "Latin word commanding silence," making the point that "silence" is the only command to which everyone without exception will one day adhere (13). The monks in the abbey are gone, and so necessarily adhere to the command. Two French women operate the abbey as a hostelry, thus connecting it to the third era, the era of business.

Yet, the pull of the past is so strong that it remains alive in the text and at Aix. The effaced text of the conclusion, like the Calvinist text in the process of effacement, exerts constant pressure on Twain's musing. The era of theology cannot come back, but neither has it entirely disappeared. The God of the era of theology stirs within the pages of the text, for Twain's essay becomes a kind of benediction in the end, one that transcends doctrinal dispute. Time flows on, doctrines change, but the curse that separates us from Eden remains to be removed by a court higher than the Presbyterian Synods of America. Ironically, as human ideas about God become more *human,* humans become more haggard and careworn. So these pilgrims strain their eyes, attempting to decipher the "worn-out inscription" on the stone and enter the "dead silence and security and peace of this old nest," happy their return will "heal their blistered spirits and patch up their ragged minds" (14).What begins as a critique of a particular text on innate depravity and infant damnation becomes a reflection on the fallen state of mankind generally. While this essay cannot restore the God of the second era and his creeds, and does not seek to, the third era, Twain concludes, is not the haven humanity seeks.

AN ORGANIC APPROACH TO TWAIN

Scholars must, then, follow in Twain's footsteps, or follow in the footsteps Twain followed, for the form and content that shape his texts in a tug of war are frequently missed by a world of scholarship that has little interest in theology or in rigorous formal criticism. "Aix-les-Bains" shows Twain writing, as he so often did, about a recondite point of theology, responding to particular Calvinist texts. His concern over infant damnation can hardly be called a rejection of Calvinism any more than those Presbyterian synods voting to amend the doctrine rejected Calvinism. Both demonstrably take the issue very seriously. Still, Everett Emerson's suggestion that Twain "judged himself a hypocrite and gave up trying to become a Christian" is a common one (37). Other writers, like James D. Wilson, attempt to show that "during the formative stage of his career, 1865–75, Clemens pursued the 'reasonable religious folly' of orthodox belief, and that his quest was deep, authentic and tied inextricably to his evolving esthetic understanding" (170). Both may be true, but ultimately such attempts to chart the fluctuating state of Clemens's soul offer little for literary analysis. Assertions that Samuel Clemens believed in God, did not believe in God, that he wanted to believe in God but couldn't, or that he did for a time believe in God, or that *he did so* believe in God are all equally useless. Of great damage, too, is the way such approaches obscure the fact that the "old order" still stands in Twain's *work* in the concepts, the genres, and in the personae he employed. Drawing on an author's biography deepens an understanding of the works, but the reverse does not hold. Literary artifacts support no claims whatsoever about the state of an author's soul. One sees in Twain's writing the continuing *literary vitality* of sacred form, both as *parodia sacra* and as literary adaptations of sacred forms. Twain's work retains the forms of belief, and that, more than the man, must be the study of literary scholarship.

Likewise, an organic approach to Twain aims at the dynamic interrelatedness of form and ideology. Twain claimed there is "[o]ne right form for the story" and demonstrated throughout his career a remarkable facility for using a variety of literary forms, yet most scholars of the last decades have ignored the formal constituents of Twain's writing (*Autobiography* 267). Formal analyses without social or biographical context have an inert quality, but ideological analyses ignore the aesthetic artifact. Amy Kaplan's *The Social Construction of American Realism* provides a forceful example, for she begins with an avowed goal: "we can root this fiction in its historical context to examine its ideological force" (8). The litmus test of such criticism amounts to little more than, we shall praise works whose content we agree with and disparage those works whose content we despise. Jane Smiley adopts such a tack, faulting *Adventures of Huckleberry Finn* for not saying the right things. Stowe's *Uncle Tom's Cabin* is superior to Twain's work, in Smiley's estimation, because it contains "the power of brilliant analysis married to great wisdom of feeling"

(65). The editorial page of a decent newspaper will meet that benchmark, yet it is not literature. Shklovsky, in one of his cantankerous moods, exclaims, "Just imagine—Koni asserts that Pushkin's significance lies in his defense of trial by jury!" (*Sentimental* 234). We might adapt Shklovsky's comment to our own discussion: Just imagine, ideological critics believe Twain's significance lies in his opposition to slavery! Jonathan Arac is absolutely correct to admonish contemporary critics who embrace *Adventures of Huckleberry Finn* as a great book *because* it is an antiracist text. To do so is no *critical* advance over John Wallace's judgment that the work is not art because it is "racist trash" (16). Against the backdrop of critics like Steven Mailloux, for whom *Adventures of Huckleberry Finn* is an "ideological drama" (62), Arac rightly asserts that the book should be considered "an aesthetic object" (782). Twain is great not by virtue of what commendable statements he makes, but by virtue of how he embodies those commendable statements in commendable literature. Interestingly, Stacy Margolis, in her response to Arac and Smiley, asserts that "they are making claims not so much about what *Huckleberry Finn* means as about what it does" (329). Margolis is correct. We ought to be talking about how Huckleberry Finn means as a functional constituent of *what* the work means.

If such a turning away from the question of form is a dereliction of duty, other critics justify the move by blaming Twain himself. How could there be any formal concerns worth discussing in work like Twain's that is so haphazard, so contingent, so *formless?* Of the many comments one could cite, perhaps Richard Chase's is the most telling: "There has been a tendency in recent years to overestimate Mark Twain, particularly among those readers who are quick to object to any semblance of difficulty or obscurity in literature" (150). In Chase's view, Twain's reputation has been buoyed by those favoring simple, easy books. (See Tom. See Tom steal jam. See Tom run.) Assuming a writer is simple-minded, one finds simple things to say about the book. The assumption, or illusion, of Twain's simplemindedness provides lazy critics with a means of avoiding the difficult work of interpretation: studying the genres Twain worked with, reading the works Twain read, and taking seriously the theological issues Twain seriously considered. More recent critics follow Chase's lead. Richard Bridgman ostensibly analyzes travel in Twain's work, though the critic hardly mentions the travel genre, and it is not difficult to see why. Twain, according to Bridgman, was simply too dim to illuminate the material, let alone have any sophisticated understanding of form. Instead, Bridgman focuses on the "hazy moments in his travels . . . when Mark Twain encountered or thought of something that was sufficiently compelling for him to want to record it; yet when he translated it onto the page, it remained problematic, for his conscious mind had not yet mastered it" (4). Relying on Twain's misrepresentations of his writing, and ignoring the great deal of real evidence in Twain's work, Forrest Robinson similarly finds a Twain with no "conscious rhetorical strategy" ("Innocent" 43). One could waste a great deal of time proving the fallacy of such arguments, but one can simply cut through the Gordian Knot of the argument and let the works speak for themselves; Twain's works speak so well that they simply cannot be the product of such a hack as the aforementioned critics believe.[4] The present study will demonstrate Twain's appropriation of the genres of religious belief, and his sophisticated rhetorical strategies in using them.

The point is this: Dreadful interpretive consequences result from assuming that Twain was careless and unsophisticated, for such an attitude discourages the kind of analysis scholars should always engage in anyway. Hershel Parker's chapter on Twain's *Pudd'nhead Wilson* in *Flawed Texts and Verbal Icons* is the perfect example of this tendency. Parker believes that "mere literary approaches such as the New Criticism" are not suited for Twain, for his aesthetic practices cannot support such an approach (145). Such ideas amount to self-fulfilling prophecy. For example, of the myriad of articles that have appeared on Twain's great dialogue *What Is Man?* until chapter 6 of this study was published as a separate article, not a single scholar had considered it *as a dialogue.* Why is that? Indeed, as incredible as it seems, more often than not, Twain's dialogue is referred to as an "essay," with *no discussion of the significance of form.* While Twain's *Personal Recollections of Joan of Arc* is obviously written as an experiment in hagiography, no one has conducted an extensive analysis of the formal influence of the Saints' Lives on the work; "Martyrdom covers a multitude of sins," as Twain argues, but it cannot efface the sins of criticism. Twain's *Mysterious Stranger Manuscripts* are similarly read as evidence of Twain's pessimism and despair, but aside from a few isolated comments, they have not been analyzed in relation to prophetic form—despite the fact that Twain compares *No. 44* to the prophet Ezekiel and structures his narrative after Ezekiel, Jeremiah, and Revelation. Twain relied on a variety of literary forms when structuring and developing his own works, and the proof is available in Twain's comments, writing notebooks, letters, and—most importantly—the literary works themselves. A scholar might be excused for ignoring all evidence but the last.

The principal idea of this book is that Twain should be studied with an organic approach that unites formal and ideological awareness. Indeed, the interactions between form and content are the most productive places for scholars to situate themselves. The solution is not the "Neoformalism" some have called for, but an organic approach that engages the dynamic interrelatedness of form and content. The forms Twain employs are ancient, and in choosing them he makes an ideological statement that creates a dialogue with all of those who have used them before, whether the form is travel narrative, catechism, prophecy, creed, or even the Socratic dialogue. It is within this context that a scholar must conduct the analysis, and it cannot be done accurately without taking into account what Bakhtin terms the "two ruling powers" of narrative: form and content (CMF 284). The two exist in constant dialogue and irrepressible conflict.

This study differs markedly from most studies of Twain in that it takes seriously the writer's uses of literary form; by focusing on sacred forms, rather than what Twain's beliefs may have been, this study differs, too, from the handful of works that consider Twain's involvement with theology. It is striking to note the extent to which religious issues have been excluded from serious scholarship of Twain, striking because Twain was more engaged in theological reading and thinking than virtually any other major writer of the 1800s, not excluding Hawthore, Melville, or Twain's Hartford neighbor, Harriet Beecher Stowe. Twain's aesthetic, as distinct from any question of personal belief, exploits form and content to provoke sophisticated theological dialogue. Twain spoke frequently of his vocation to be a kind of preacher, and he certainly did preach to his society by using literary forms associated with religious belief. More significantly, however, his persona becomes a genre, an image of form as the *Reverend* Mark Twain. It is this persona that Twain used for half a century to deliver burlesque sermons and jeremiads. Through these sermons, Twain engaged with his society, and provoked a dialogue between religious form and content. In "Villagers of 1840–3," Twain wrote of his childhood home, Hannibal, Missouri: "In sixty years that town has not turned out a solitary preacher" (33). As usual, Twain told the truth, mainly.

"PROV'DENCE DON'T FIRE
NO BLANK CA'TRIDGES, BOYS"

God, Grotesques, and Sunday-School Books
in Mark Twain's Roughing It

This species of humor is certainly grotesque, and hardily extravagant. . . . As Irving stands, without dispute, at the head of American classic humorists, so too precedence in the unclassical school must be conceded to Mark Twain.
—*OVERLAND MONTHLY*, Review of *Roughing It*

Nothing that glitters is gold. (*Roughing It* 188)

THE *OVERLAND MONTHLY* was hardly alone in its repeated estimation that *Roughing It* (1872) was a "grotesque" production ("Anonymous Review" 580, 581). In the years following the book's publication, many reviewers noted the presence of the grotesque in *Roughing It*. Writing in *Appleton's Journal,* George Ferris lauded the "grotesque and irresistible form" present in Twain's work (17). B. B. Toby, reviewing the book for the *San Francisco Morning Call,* criticized the illustrations as "even more grotesque than the text," yet found the "grotesqueness and absurdity" of the text strangely appealing (1). As for Twain's most perceptive critic, William Dean Howells applauded the "grotesque exaggeration and broad irony" as peculiarly fitting for depicting the West, "for all existence there must have looked like an extravagant joke, the humor of which was only deepened by its nether-side of tragedy" (754). Twain himself similarly summed up life in the West: "It was a wild, free, disorderly, grotesque society!" (*Roughing It* 392). In fact, when *Roughing It* first appeared, however wildly their estimations of the book's literary qualities varied, reviewers agreed on one assessment: It was new; unexpected; *grotesque*.

This "big California & Plains book," as Twain called it, is often viewed as the writer's bid for membership in Irving's "classical school" (MTL 4:309). Twain attempted to adhere to Eastern models, in such interpretations, more than it stood against them. If *Roughing It* fails to achieve "classical form," then, it is not for want of trying on Twain's part, but rather from want of talent. This "modern" view began with Van Wyck Brooks, who saw Twain's book as part of his effort to become a "conventional citizen" (82). Hamlin Hill, too, states that "In part at least, *Roughing It* was a personal act of contrition on its author's part for the life he had led prior to coming under the refining influence of his bride, her family, and the entire cluster of Eastern values they represented" ("Mark Twain's *Roughing It*" 10). Most famously, Justin Kaplan decreed that Twain's "*Roughing It* was his first application for membership to join the social order" (81).

If *Roughing It* was such an application, it was rejected as far as the literary world went. Those who endorsed Twain's work in the 1870s did so either because they found it grotesque or in spite of that fact. No one denied it. An anonymous reviewer writing in the *Manchester Guardian* for March, 6, 1872, disapproved of *Roughing It* on precisely these grounds, complaining that Twain suffers "an inability to distinguish between the picturesque and grotesque" ("Anonymous Review" 7). Time and again, reviewers of *Roughing It* contrasted Twain's "grotesque" aesthetics with the aesthetics of "the Irving school," "the classical school," or more generally "the picturesque." The dichotomy between Irving and Twain is probably ill-considered, for the earlier writer certainly made prosperous use of the grotesque; one need only recall Irving's description of Ichabod Crane at the supper table. Nevertheless, the reviewer correctly implies that while Irving and Twain belonged to the same family of writers—that is to say humorists—they are properly classed as belonging to different branches of that family.

Early reviewers rightly labeled *Roughing It* "grotesque," for it burlesques classical conceptions of imagery and form. *Roughing It* differs from the "classical school" by employing what Mikhail Bakhtin terms "grotesque realism," whose "essential principle . . . is degradation, that is, the lowering of all that is high, spiritual, ideal, abstract" (RW 19). The grotesque provides Bakhtin with a major element of his theory of

"Carnival," celebrations and actions that turn the world topsy-turvy, creating unexpected opportunities for the creation of "something more and better" (RW 21). Grotesque images admirably serve that purpose. Distortions of our idealized and abstract views of the world typify grotesque realism's images: "they are ugly," Bakhtin asserts, "monstrous, hideous from the point of view of 'classic' aesthetics, that is, the aesthetics of the ready-made and the completed" (RW 21).[1] How many examples of such degraded images could one find in *Roughing It!* All in the work is "degraded": the "Noble Red Men" are "prideless beggars" (127); the tea is "slumgullion" (24); the preacher is a "gospel-sharp" (311), and even the narrator himself suffers from a "native imbecility" (403). Everything in the book undermines the ends and means of classical aesthetics. An unsympathetic reader of *Roughing It,* if one can even imagine such a *monstrum horrendum,* might assert that the book brims with unrelated anecdotes, inexplicable events, and a general disorderliness. A sympathetic view of the form is that *Roughing It* embodies the landscape of the West: *Roughing It* lopes along like a coyote then darts away in a flash; gusts like the Washoe Zephyr; slides from one story to the next like Tom Morgan's ranch; and finally bucks readers three counties away like the Genuine Mexican Plug or an exploding silver mine. The old prospector in chapter 28 informs the narrator, *"nothing* that glitters is gold," and the dictum holds true for the entirety of *Roughing It.* Twain's rewriting of the old proverb presages his revision of the "golden" aesthetics of the "classical school" to the grotesque realism of the "unclassical" school.

There is plenty of evidence that Twain himself feared his book would be a "grotesque" production even as he wrote it. On April 26, 1871, Twain wrote to "Mother" Fairbanks, "I am pegging away at my book, but it will have no success" (MTL 4:381). Later, he wrote to Orion that it "will be a tolerable success" and commented to his publisher, Elisha Bliss, that at least it will be "pretty readable" (MTL 4:386, 389). Calling *Roughing It* "pretty poor stuff," Twain feared negative reviews, so he ordered his publisher to keep a lid on advertising for the book until the subscriptions had been accomplished. (MTL 5: 76; See also MTL 5: 308–9). Even as grotesque realism was his early forte, Twain feared the label. Writing to Thomas Bailey Aldrich on January 27, 1871, Twain seemed almost defensive, pleading that Bret Harte had "trimmed & trained & schooled me patiently until he changed me from an awkward utterer of coarse grotesqueness" (MTL 5: 316). Most significant, however, is Twain's statement in a letter to William Dean Howells, after reading his review of *Roughing It:*

> Since penning the foregoing the "Atlantic" has come to hand with that
> most thoroughly & entirely satisfactory notice of "Roughing It," & I am
> as uplifted & reassured by it as a mother who has given birth to a white
> baby when she was awfully afraid it was going to be a mulatto. I have
> been afraid & shaky all along, but now unless the N.Y. "Tribune" gives
> the book a black eye, I am all right. (MTL 5: 95)

Twain's fear that *Roughing It* might turn out to be a "mulatto" or to
get a "black eye" provides a carnival embodiment for his book, highlighting its grotesque attributes and elevating them above classical aesthetics. *Roughing It* is not a "white baby," to adopt Twain's analogy. In
fact, it is in a sense a "mulatto" of a work, not a "tragic mulatto," but a
"comic mulatto," a carnival combination of high and low. Typical of all
grotesque images, Twain's "mulatto" combines death and life, the birth
of a baby with a black eye and perhaps black blood. The harsh humor
of the comment certainly has racist undertones, and from that perspective it degrades precisely that which his age elevated and idealized:
white motherhood.

Considering his misgivings, Twain's elation at Howells's review is not
surprising. Twain found the composition of *Roughing It* unexpectedly . . .
rough, as it turned out. The work was difficult for precisely the reasons
that Twain had once thought it would be easy; Twain began, not from a
tabula rasa, but rather by compiling the book in part from previous articles he had written as well as history and statistics gleaned from other
sources. How could one achieve a unified book through such methods?
Could one hope for authenticity or anything approaching Irving's "classical school"? The eminent historian of the West Walter Prescott Webb
observes that, "The realities of the West, the far country, have created
an illusion of unreality. The West was not a land where anything could
happen; but rather, it was a place where the unexpected was sure to
happen, where the Eastern traditions and conventions would not hold
out, and where Eastern practices would no longer work" (481). During
much of the composition, however, Twain was unable to see the justice
of such claims and still measured his success by Eastern models, models
that would assay as grotesque or mulatto anything less than the "glit-
tering gold" of the "classical" school. Beset by doubts about the quality
of his work and his method of composition, Twain wrote again to "Mother" Fairbanks, "This book has been dragging along just 12 months, now,
& I am *so* sick & tired of it" (MTL 4: 418–19).

Shortly thereafter, however, a new tone emerged. "I wrote a splendid chapter today, for the middle of the book," wrote Mark Twain to his wife, Olivia. "I admire the book more & more, the more I cut & slash & lick & trim & revamp it" (MTL 4: 443). The date was August 10, 1871. What had changed Twain's attitude on August 10? Significantly, the "splendid chapter" he had written that August day was chapter 53, "The Story of the Old Ram."[2] One of the book's most celebrated passages, this chapter features the narrator Jim Blaine, whose stories deviate from the classical mold. As Twain wrote in later years:

> The idea of the tale is to exhibit certain bad effects of a good memory: the sort of memory which is too good, which remembers everything and forgets nothing, which has no sense of proportion and can't tell an important event from an unimportant one but preserves them all, states them all, and thus retards the progress of a narrative, at the same time making a tangled, inextricable confusion of it and intolerably wearisome to the reader. (MTE 217–18)

Grotesque characters abound in chapter 53, their stories strangely united by a grotesque lack of plot. The story is a tour de force of the seemingly pointless story, going nowhere but delighting readers even as the narrator never quite gets around to telling "The Story of the Old Ram." Writing *Roughing It* by relying on his own memories, his previous publications, letters provided by his brother Orion, and the guidebooks and works of history he always used, Twain himself may have feared becoming one who "forgets nothing" and who has "no sense of proportion" (MTE 217). Twain made comedy out of the notion that *Roughing It* might resemble Jim Blaine's story, using the grotesque to take real fears and, as Bakhtin asserts, turn them into "amusing or ludicrous monstrosities" (RW 47). As John Bassett maintains, *Roughing It* is "a kind of literary manifesto" (93), and it is achieved largely through the organic synthesis of grotesque form and content, the manifesto in miniature, "The Story of the Old Ram."

ROUGHING IT AND "THOSE FINE MORAL HUMBUGS"

Indeed, "The Story of the Old Ram" is a microcosm of *Roughing It,* for it reveals the aesthetic order and logic beneath the delightfully disordered and illogical surface; moreover, in chapter 53, Twain's "grotesque realism" is a form of *parodia sacra,* responding to the subgenre of "Providence Tales," stories that chronicle Providence's rewarding of the just and punishment of the wicked. Central to the story is Jim Blaine's assertion, "Prov'dence don't fire no blank ca'tridges, boys" (366). Throughout the passage, Jim Blaine explains the mystery of "Prov'dence," arguing that "[t]here ain't no such thing as an accident" and "ain't anything ever reely lost" (366), a theological concept Twain burlesques in *Roughing It* near the start of his career and in "Letters from the Earth" (1909) at the tail end of it when Satan discusses why the fly had been allowed to survive on Earth: "Providentially. That is the word. For the fly had not been left behind by accident. No, the hand of Providence was in it. There are no accidents. All things that happen, happen for a purpose" (424). Through Jim Blaine in *Roughing It,* Satan in "Letters from the Earth," and from a myriad of characters in between those works, Twain restates in parody the definition of Providence asserted in chapter 5 of Presbyterianism's foundational text, the *Westminster Confession of Faith:* "God, the great Creator of all things, doth uphold, direct, dispose, and govern all creatures, actions, and things, from the greatest even to the least" (178/6.024). Calvin, in the *Institutes of the Christian Religion,* similarly asserts that "all events whatsoever are governed by the secret counsel of God" (I:173). These texts provide the original for the genre of Providence Tales—and for Twain's burlesque of them. "The Story of the Old Ram" is rightly classed with such antigenre works as "The Christmas Fireside for Good Little Boys and Girls," known also by its subtitle, "The Story of the Bad Little Boy That Bore a Charmed Life" (1865). The title of the work announces its form and content, but like other examples of this type of story, this one explicitly establishes itself in relation to the genre of what Twain calls "Sunday-school books" (407). These "mild little books with marbled backs" are constructed with a number of traditional elements, including periodic structures featuring a series of narratives strung together to reveal how God's providence operates in the world (408). In his sketch "Christian Spectator" (1865), Twain responds specifically to a periodical that contains "one of those entertaining novelettes, so popular among credulous Sabbath-school children, about a lone woman silently praying a desperate and blood-thirsty robber out of his boots" (395). This is precisely the sort of thing Jane Tompkins defends in her influential book *Sensational Designs* when arguing that "their sensationalism ultimately lies not so much in the dramatic nature of the events they describe as in the assumptions they make about the relation of human events to the spiritual realities that make them meaningful" (154). Tompkins blames the widespread distaste among modern readers for such tracts and Sunday-school books on the notion that the "theological assumptions are different from ours" (154). In fact, the theological assumptions contained in those works were difficult for many people to accept back then, and Tompkins finds herself in the untenable position of trying to defend what was, even in its own era, viewed by many people as contrary both to reality and, if one may make the distinction, to doctrine. Job, after all, was a good man who suffered. Twain burlesques the works Tompkins lauds, criticizing them as aesthetically bad in part because they were ethically and theologically wrong. Twain rightly calls the *Christian Spectator* "one of those fine moral humbugs" (395) that misleads readers with its Providence Tales. Simply put, in this popular distortion of Providence, the good are always protected and rewarded while the bad are always either redeemed or punished. One thinks of such distortions in Increase Mather's *An Essay for the Recording of Illustrious Providences* (1684) and Cotton Mather's *Magnalia Christi Americana* (1702), both of which helped to establish in the popular mind the idea of Providence as a destiny that is manifest, rather than the "secret counsel of God." Twain cribs his structure for "The Christmas Fireside" from literary descendants of these books. He inverts the structure, so that the opposite happens, and when his protagonist fished on Sunday, he "didn't get struck by lightning" (409). The series of actions becomes a chain of expected actions that *do not happen,* so that even when the boy steals a rifle and goes hunting on the Sabbath, he "didn't shoot three or four of his fingers off" (410). This structure, similar to what Edgar Branch calls the "genre of the 'missed item,'" is constructed of absences, nullities, and stories-that-aren't and had a tremendous influence on the structure of *Roughing It* (Introduction 21).

"The Story of Mamie Grant, the Child Missionary" (1868) is one of the most amusing of these broad burlesques of the genre of Providence Tales, and Franklin Rogers identifies it as a "condensed burlesque of such temperance literature as that written by Timothy Shay Arthur" (Introduction 32). Twain names Arthur in the text, when his protagonist Mamie hopes that one day her missionary efforts may appear "in a beautiful Sunday School book, and maybe T. S. Arthur may write it. Oh, joy!" (39). "The Story of Mamie Grant, the Child Missionary" follows the parodic pattern in that Mamie's proselytizing is the ruination of her family, as she distributes religious tracts to bill collectors instead of paying them what is owed. Ultimately, Mamie's family loses their home. Structurally, this story adheres to the pattern employed by T. S. Arthur in *Ten Nights in a Bar-Room and What I Saw There* (1855). Episode by sentimental episode, Mamie tells stories of the depraved and wicked, just as in Arthur's narrative each visit to the barroom reveals further depravity. With each tale Mamie relates, her father gets into more and more trouble. Just as the miller in Arthur's narrative becomes "bloated" and "disfigured" and eventually is killed by his own son (172), Mamie's father is brought down by his daughter's actions.

These stories, drawn from periodicals like the *Christian Spectator* or books published especially for the Sunday school audience, provide typical content and form of the Providence Tale, and it is that genre that renders Mamie insensible to the demands of reality—that a mortgage must be paid, for example. One of the tracts Mamie distributes is "The Blasphemous Sailor Awfully Rebuked," depicting a sailor who is immediately punished by thunder and lightning after cursing (37). This example of a "special providence" in which God's judgment is visited upon an individual was one of Twain's particular disagreements with how the concept of Providence was popularly employed. When Mamie reflects on the sailor's story, she asserts, "Imagine, Oh, imagine that wicked sailor's position! I cannot do it, because I do not know what those dreadful nautical terms mean, for I am not educated and deeply learned in the matters of practical every-day life like the gifted theological students, who have learned all about practical life from the writings of other theological students who went before them, but O, it must have been frightful, *so* frightful" (37). The burlesque of the "Sunday-school book with a marbled back" rests on this fundamental disjuncture between reality and theology. The theological concepts, notably Providence, illustrated by these marble-backed books are inherently "bookish" and divorced from a close connection to the "practical life" Mamie refers to. These "gifted theological students" know of Providence from other books because they cannot know of it in the same way from reality, for in reality, it is obvious that good people do not always prosper nor are bad people always punished. In the Sunday-school books, however, that is often precisely what does happen. Bearing titles like the anonymously written *Willy Graham; or, The Disobedient Boy* (1844) and *The Polite Boy. With Illustrations. By Uncle Madison* (circa 1860), these books inculcated social and religious virtue through stark contrasts of angelic and fiendish behavior, and the rewards and punishments thereof. Ironically, "Grandfather Twain" does learn from writers like "Uncle Madison," for he adopts their literary models for parodic purpose and to reconnect Providence with reality. The grotesque form of *Roughing It* so often commented on is a twisting of these Providence Tales, just as "The Story of the Good Little Boy Who Did Not Prosper" (1870) responds to "all the Sunday-school books" as a model but explodes into burlesque with Twain explaining that in his Providence Tale, "there was a screw loose somewhere, and it all happened just the other way" (374–76).

Similarly, in such works as *The Adventures of Tom Sawyer* (1876), "About Magnanimous-Incident Literature" (1878), and "Edward Mills and George Benton: A Tale" (1880), Twain burlesques the entire genre of Sunday-school books, inverting the typical structure, so that even as he adheres to the episodic structure of the Providence Tale, the actions do not illustrate what they are seemingly designed to, the beneficent working of "a bountiful Providence," as phrased in the latter tale (748). One sees in the *parodia sacra* of *Roughing It,* too, just such an adoption and distortion of the narrative plan of the Sunday-school book. A drunken silver miner seems an unlikely spokesperson for Providence, arguing to the larger world that "everything that people can't understand and don't see the reason of does good if you only hold on and give it a fair shake" (366). The *parodia sacra* in this passage is the perfect example of Bakhtin's assertion that one sees in such writing "the entire spectrum of tones—from reverent acceptance to parodic ridicule—so that it is often very difficult to establish precisely where reverence ends and ridicule begins" ("Prehistory" 77). Twain cannot be accused of reverence, for burlesque is at once a criticism of popular literary distortions of Providence and a rejection of classical aesthetics. Yet, Twain's burlesque of the genre returns the concept of Providence to its original explanation that defines it as a "mystery." The story, then, is both a formal and ideological burlesque of the Providence Tale. Ironically, the restored definition of Providence provided Twain with an explanation of how a writer brings order to chaotic materials, making the grotesque beautiful, even as he makes the idealized concept of Providence grotesque.

"SH—! DON'T SPEAK— HE'S GOING TO COMMENCE"

All around the cabin, everyone has quieted down to listen to Jim Blaine's story. The narrator awaits expectantly, having long desired to hear this "stirring story" and "wonderful adventure" (361, 367). Chapter 53 is a frame story, featuring a frame narrator who introduces "The Story of the

Old Ram." One of the most familiar narrative structures in the writer's repertoire, the frame story has long been a common feature of world literature and has been a particular favorite in this country since the advent of dialect stories like "The Big Bear of Arkansas." Readers love the illusion that as they read they are *listening* to a good story from a good storyteller. A frame story creates that intimacy and immediacy, as a speaker directs the story toward the "you" of the audience. Convinced that "The Story of the Old Ram" is a "stirring story," the frame narrator watches Jim Blaine closely for weeks, hoping to catch him "satisfactorily drunk" and in the perfect condition to tell the story (361). The anticipation he feels is nearly palpable as Blaine holds forth on the empty powder keg. Jan Harold Brunvand calls chapter 53 "the old greenhorn hoax of a 'sell,' the long-winded, pointless narrative that makes a laughing stock out of a poor dupe who expects to hear a legitimate funny story" (61). The laughing at the end of the story is of the conspiratorial sort. "The tears were running down the boys' cheeks—they were suffocating with suppressed laughter—and had been from the start, though I had never perceived it," the green Twain informs the green readers who have likewise been "sold" (367). Twain used this form many times. In "A Reminiscence of Artemus Ward" (1867), he portrays himself as tricked by the complicity of Ward and the other fellows. The difference between the Artemus Ward sketch and chapter 53 of *Roughing It,* however, is that Ward was complicit and aware of the trick, unlike Blaine who truly is oblivious to the plot being hatched. Just as in "The Story of the Old Ram," there is a moment of epiphany in "A Reminiscence of Artemus Ward" when Twain announces, "Then I saw that I had been sold" (233).[3]

It is well to remember that "The Story of the Old Ram" is, in fact, an aesthetic object. What with the believable dialect characters and the effective frame story, one might just believe it was *recovered* by Twain and not *created* by him, just as some critics are still "sold" by Twain's claim that his 1874 masterpiece, "A True Story," really was "repeated word for word as I heard it" (578). As Jim Blaine's audience quiets down, the reader anticipates hearing a "story" that follows the classical formal dictates of a story, featuring narrative, plot, and characters that relate to the action. Grotesque realism, as Bakhtin defines it, is "hideous and formless" and rejects the "aesthetics of the beautiful" (RW 29). Reading Twain's story, one expects a narrative adhering to the aesthetics of the beautiful, but one finds an aesthetics of the grotesque. One should qualify this immediately, for even the violation of the form acknowledges it; there can be no grotesque realism without classical aesthetics, so it only seems "formless." Twain's "The Story of the Old Ram" is one of the most grotesque examples of American writing ever produced, and one of the most delightful.

Blaine's first sentence, even in dialect, adheres to the classical mold: "I don't reckon them times will ever come again" (361).The narrator will focus, as such narratives so often do, on times past, on "them times." But, as the narrator observes later, "the mention of the ram in the first sentence was as far as any man had ever heard him get" (367). In the beginning of chapter 53, Twain labels the story "stirring." At the end of the chapter, Twain calls the story that is never told "a wonderful adventure." These descriptions sound like nineteenth-century ad copy for a narrative well within the bounds of traditional aesthetics, reminding one, too, that Providence Tales are often adventure stories, packed with "stirring action." While the story begins and ends with a nod toward the conventions, in between the "stirring" and the "wonderful," the expected traditional narrative fails to materialize. Like the parodic Providence Tales, this sketch is notable for what is missing and for what does not happen. The expected story that Twain does not tell in chapter 53 of *Roughing It* is the much applauded "The Story of the Old Ram." Had we actually been told the story of the Old Ram, it would have been both "stirring" and "wonderful," we are assured, but Jim Blaine has *never* told the story, and so it remains "a dark mystery" (361, 367, 368).

The absent story is always present, however, for the form such a narrative would have taken is the means by which we measure what in fact transpires. Perhaps, then, those critics who insist that Twain's *Roughing It* has much in common with eastern models are, in some sense, correct. Robert Edson Lee, for example, in his book *From East to West,* charts the changes Twain made in material he reused, terming the end result "a washed and weakened version" (109). Joseph Coulombe, too, asserts that the book proves "Twain subdued his blunt western vernacular voice, endorsed many stereotypically eastern values, and moderated his impulse for harsh social satire" (238). Twain responds to classical and traditional form, but his very acknowledgment violates its central tenets, creating antigenre. Perhaps, as Formalists would argue, the new form is born simply because the old form is moribund. Likewise dead is the ideology immanent to the genre, the popular distortion of Providence itself. The Providence Tale is the target, in the inseparable totality of its ideological and formal aspects. Michael McKeon suggests that the Providence Tale contains within it the germ of the "tall tale," for by its very nature, the form seeks to explain inexplicable events (101).

Thus, Twain finds an element of the ludicrous in the form itself, an element he extends to the extremes of absurdity.

"YOUR GAME EYE HAS FETCHED LOOSE, MISS WAGNER DEAR"

The story Jim Blaine *does* tell is one that "always maundered off, interminably, from one thing to another" (367–68). Providence Tales do maunder off, but they tend to maunder off from one *event* to another, just as Twain focuses on his "variegated" travels, not from one *character* to another as happens in Jim Blaine's narrative. In "How to Tell a Story" (1895), Twain differentiates between two types of stories, asserting that the "humorous story depends for its effect upon the *manner* of the telling; the comic story and the witty story upon the *matter*" (201). The "high and delicate art" of the humorous story involves the method of delivery, but in written work, one may say it relies on the form that Twain devises to approximate the "manner" (201). Formally, Twain's "Story of the Old Ram" is an antigenre and responds at every point to the "Sunday-school book." Like "The Story of Mamie Grant, the Child Missionary," this sketch is episodic, as are the models they burlesque, but it "makes strange" the Providence Tales once so popular. No form is blank, and in reality *Roughing It* constantly burlesques established texts, particularly the Sunday-school books with their flawed definitions of Providence. If we think of the point or nub of the story as a bullet and the reader as the target, Jim Blaine is no threat to anyone, for a "blank cartridge" is a cartridge containing plenty of gunpowder, but no shot. Such a cartridge appears normal on the outside, but lacks what really makes a firearm dangerous. With a blank cartridge, as with Jim Blaine's story, there is noise but no conclusion. Blaine populates his story with one grotesque character after another. Rather than focusing on the ram, or the story of the ram, Blaine moves from one recollection to the next easily, as each person reminds him of another. However grotesque, the situation is realistic, and one that many people have experienced when speaking to older relatives; one day we, too, perhaps will tell such stories. While Blaine himself maintains that "Prov'dence don't fire no blank ca'tridges," the speaker himself does. He develops a story with a "charge," so to speak, but with no bullet/thesis to hit the target. He reminds one of Twain's self-description in "Old Times on the Mississippi": "my memory was never loaded with anything but blank cartridges"

(341). Symbolically sitting on an "empty powder-keg," Blaine is himself a "blank ca'tridge" (361). He "draws a blank" and forgets to actually tell the story he has announced, leaving—it would seem—only a blank page in his wake.

With Blaine, Twain creates the perfect storyteller. In "How to Tell a Story," Twain asserts that "the teller does his best to conceal the fact that he even dimly suspects that there is anything funny about it" (201). Blaine, of course, is truly unaware that there is anything funny about his story, or nonstory. He is the perfect unself-conscious narrator. When Twain revised the yarn for performance on the platform, he accentuated this aspect of the story, drawing the narration out so long that Blaine even seems unaware of the passing of time from "them times" to "these times" (see MTE 218–25).

Similarly, the characters whose stories he does relate are themselves "blank ca'tridges," so much so that one must conclude blankness is the thematic point of the story, just as formally the work is a burlesquing antigenre of Providence Tales. There is the one-eyed Miss Wagner, for example, who borrows an ill-fitting and ill-matched glass eye from Miss Jefferson, "to receive company in" (363). Miss Wagner strives for an aesthetic completion, a sense of classical beauty that others would applaud. Instead, the eye, too small for Miss Wagner, "would get twisted around in the socket, while t'other one was looking as straight ahead as a spyglass" (363). Of course, the eye frequently fell out, so Miss Wagner unknowingly turned "her old dead-light on the company empty" (363). With her blank expression, Miss Wagner, too, is a sort of "blank cartridge." The focus on incompleteness, emptiness, and blankness permeates the description; like Blaine's story, Miss Wagner's eye goes off in diverse and inappropriate directions; there is no motive force behind the eye, and it, too, "maunders off." As the description continues, we discover that Miss Wagner is also bald and missing one leg. Miss Wagner qualifies as grotesque to begin with, and she renders herself even more so with her attempts at completion. By embracing a classical aesthetic that she cannot possibly attain, Miss Wagner embodies Bakhtin's notion that grotesque images illustrate the "eternally unfinished" nature of reality (RW 256). Miss Wagner is an American version of Gogol's Collegiate Assessor Kovalyov, who awakens one morning to discover that his nose is missing, leaving only "a completely empty, flat place" in its stead (207). The story charts Kovalyov's grotesque attempts to regain his nose, which has gone on to live a life of its own, a life of some celebrity. Miss Wagner, too, is ever in a state of incompletion. Even her glass eye refuses to stay put. She responds by being always "considerable on the bor-row" in her attempts to find prosthetic limbs, wigs, or glass eyes (364). For Twain's revision of classical aesthetics, Miss Wagner is the grotesque Beatrice to his silver-mining Dante, Jim Blaine.

The coffin-peddler Jacops is another such character. A despicable old buzzard, he camps outside of "old Robbins's place" with a coffin, hoping to earn the ailing man's trade (364). His narrative, like the oth-ers, is incomplete, for he hopes to conclude by making his sale and bury-ing his customer. Old Robbins, however, deceives him and buys the cof-fin with the agreement that if he does not like it after trying it out, he will get his money back and more. Robbins figures that "if he missed fire he couldn't lose a cent" (365). To "misfire" is again to be a sort of blank cartridge, something that is incomplete, but in this case even the gun-powder does not fire: *nothing* happens. As it turns out, Robbins is only in a trance, not really dead at all, and so the character sketch ends with the coffin as empty as Miss Wagner's eye socket. The grotesque imagery presents the reader with a death-in-life scenario that makes light of what ordinarily one fears.

Just as Robbins's coffin is empty, there is nothing to put into William Wheeler's. Wheeler was pulled through the machinery in a carpet fac-tory and "his widder bought the piece of carpet that had his remains wove in" (367). The body has, in a sense, disappeared into fourteen yards of three-ply carpet. Since the days of Homer, the carpet has served as a symbol of aesthetics, just as the female figure has, and one leaps at the chance to categorize William Wheeler's mishap in the mill as a "yarn." The storyteller is a weaver of stories, one who fashions a work of art out of many narrative strands. Howells nodded to this concept in his review of *Roughing It:*

> A thousand anecdotes, relevant and irrelevant, embroider the work; excursions and digressions of all kinds are the very woof, as it were; everything far-fetched or near at hand is interwoven, and yet the complex is a sort of 'harmony of colors' which is not less than triumphant. (755)

Howells is certainly correct that there is deeper level of "harmony" in *Roughing It*. Still, grotesque imagery, actions, and people dominate the work and must play a role in whatever "harmony" emerges. All the dis-parate elements of the book are interwoven in Twain's complex imagi-nation, but as an example of grotesque realism, *Roughing It* retains an unfinished, grotesquely harmonious quality. Incompletion, and not the "finished" quality of the "aesthetics of the beautiful," provides *Roughing It*'s aesthetic power, for the harmony cannot be understood without considering the relation of Twain's text to the Providence Tales it burlesques. While tempting, the idea that *Roughing It* responds to the new "content" of the West is untrue, for the book's new form is born not to express new content, but because the old form is dead. Henry James would not count the unfortunate Wheeler's story as the inspiration for his own metanarrative, "The Figure in the Carpet," although in that story, too, the "primal plan, something like a complex figure in a Persian carpet," is the answer to "the thing we were all so blank about" (290). In short, Blaine's assertion of providential order is on one level not borne out by the seeming lack of order in his story, a story populated with blanks, absences, and grotesques.

"THERE AIN'T NO SUCH A THING AS AN ACCIDENT"

There are no accidents in "The Story of the Old Ram," however, and one should not overlook Twain's satirical "Prefatory" at the beginning of the book:

> This book is merely a personal narrative, and not a pretentious history or a philosophical dissertation. It is a record of several years of variegated vagabondizing, and its object is rather to help the resting reader while away an idle hour than afflict him with metaphysics, or goad him with science. (n. pag.)

Similarly, in 1885, Twain warns that those "looking for a moral" in *Adventures of Huckleberry Finn* would be "shot." Just as there is a "moral" in *Adventures of Huckleberry Finn, Roughing It* contains the occasional "philosophical dissertation," albeit very humorous ones, and "afflicts" the reader with metaphysical questions. Bassett claims that chapter 53 is "an attack on interpretation," for "[n]ot only does it omit any signified for the ram, it hides or indefinitely defers the signifier" (98). However true Bassett's statement is, like so many comments focusing solely on linguistic aspects, it misses the point. Similarly, one should not accept Twain's opening rejection of metaphysics at face value, as does Bruce Michelson, for whom Twain was "playful and game-loving" and not a "metaphysician" ("Ever Such" 28). Since when are the two mutually exclusive? Michelson argues that *"Roughing It* depends for its success on being an act of play itself, taking full advantage of play's temporary dominion over truth" (39), but it is well to remember that play, like humor, is serious business and does not exclude truth. Flannery O'Connor might have been thinking of Twain in "The Grotesque in Southern Fiction," when she writes that "In nineteenth-century American writing, there was a good deal of grotesque literature which came from the frontier and was supposed to be funny; but our present grotesque characters, comic though they may be, are at least not primarily so" (817). The dichotomy between humorous and serious writing is impossible with Twain, however, and he writes with a seriousness and humorousness of purpose few other writers attain. Truth and humor happily cohabitate in the sketch when Blaine announces that "there ain't anything ever reely lost; everything that people can't understand and don't see the reason of does good if you only hold on and give it a fair shake; Prov'dence don't fire no blank ca'tridges, boys. . . . There ain't no such a thing as an accident" (366).

To support his view of Providence, Jim Blaine relates the story of his Uncle Lem whose back was broken when a drunken Irishman carrying a hod of bricks "fell on him out of the third story" (366). Blaine's interpretation of the event is, again, an appeal to Providence to explain why bad things happen to reasonably good people like his uncle. The answer is clear: Uncle Lem was there as a special providence to break the Irishman's fall; the Irishman in turn broke Uncle Lem's back in several places. The interpretation is stultified, however, by the presence of Uncle Lem's dog, which might have served to save the Irishman's life at his own expense, rather than Uncle Lem's. Blaine's explanation is classic:

> Why didn't the Irishman fall on the dog? Becuz the dog would a seen him a coming and stood from under. That's the reason the dog warn't appinted. A dog can't be depended on to carry out a special providence. Mark my words it was a put-up thing. Accidents don't happen, boys. (366)

James Caron argues that "A tale designed to illustrate the workings of providence ought to tell how Uncle Lem was miraculously saved at the sacrifice of a stranger. Faith in the plan of God, in his wisdom and mercy, would naturally flow from such a wondrous event" (162). That is indeed the form Twain parodies, and Caron would be correct if this were a Providence tale and not a burlesque of that form. Twain's story can only be understood by what it burlesques. Jim Blaine's tale responds at all levels to those "marble-backed Sunday-school books" with their tales of good rewarded and evil punished. Those books do not jibe with reality, nor even do they jibe with theology. The Providence Tales themselves are inaccurate depictions of doctrinal definitions of Providence, and take the "secret counsel" Calvin described and attempt to render it manifest; moreover, Calvinist definitions of Providence make no claim that good acts are rewarded on earth. Calvin defines a "special providence" as simply the belief that "particular events" are designed by God for a specific end, citing the whirlwind that plunges Jonah over the side of the ship as an example (I: 78). When one considers the many instances of "special providences" in the scriptures, it becomes clear that quite frequently human pain results, and not the blissful narrative Caron describes. Ironically, Jim Blaine's Providence Tale is truer to theology and reality, for even if he claims to see a pattern that by definition must always remain a mystery, at least his tale recognizes that we live in a world where tragic things happen: a world where people, like Uncle Lem, have their backs broken; where people, like William Wheeler, are killed in industrial accidents; and where people, like Miss Wagner, sometimes lose eyes, limbs, or even hair. In "Man's Place in the Animal World" (1896), Twain makes the following comparison:

> For style, look at the Bengal tiger—that ideal of grace, beauty, physical Perfection, majesty. And then look at Man—that poor thing. He is the Animal of the Wig, the Trepanned Skull, the Ear Trumpet, the Glass Eye, the Pasteboard Nose, the Porcelain Teeth, the Silver Windpipe, the Wooden Leg—a creature that is mended and patched all over, from top to bottom. If he can't get renewals of his brickabrac in the next world, what will he look like? (89)

Just as with the stories in *Roughing It*, Twain makes readers laugh at their own "human condition." Twain's genius is that he turns the "dark and terrifying" elements of reality into "ludicrous monstrosities" (RW 47), liberating readers for a time from the terrors of living in the world. In Twain's world, fear becomes laughter; Providence explains the everyday "roughing it" that people experience, and Twain's grotesque parody of those providential explanations helps us to laugh at a joke that sometimes seems to be at our expense.

Twain often criticized those who explained miraculous or catastrophic events by invoking the theological concept of "special providences." In his version of the Apostles' Creed, written sometime in the

1880s, Twain followed his positive assertion "I believe in God the Almighty" with a qualification: "I do not believe in special providences" ("Three Statements of the Eighties" 56). Similarly, in such works as "Letter From the Recording Angel" (1887), *Pudd'nhead Wilson* (1894), "As Concerns Interpreting the Deity" (1905), and the "Little Bessie" dialogues (1908–9), Twain embedded in various literary forms his rejection of special providences. His novels, too, contain such references, with one of the best presentations being the dialect discussion of special providences in *The Refuge of the Derelicts* that occupies all of chapter 11 (1905–6). The characters Aunty Phyllis and 'Rastus argue about how it was that 'Rastus happened to be on hand to save a young girl from a runaway horse:

> "You is de man dat's allays sayin' de' ain't no sich thing as special providence. If 'twarn't for special providence, what would 'a' went wid dat buggy en harness? Who put you in dat road, right exackly in de right spot, right exackly at de right half-a-second?—you answer me dat, if you kin!"
>
> "Who de nation sent de *hoss* down dah in sich a blame' fool fashion?" (238)

The chapter ends with that core question, for Twain does not reject providence, per se, but human presumption. This is particularly so when the term is used as a cover-up for human incompetence. For just that reason does Mary in "The Man That Corrupted Hadleyburg" (1899) deride the "designs of Providence," exclaiming: "Ordered! Oh, everything's *ordered*, when a person has to find some way out when he has been stupid" (400). One of Twain's undated proverbs states, too, that "There are many scapegoats for our blunders, but the most popular one is Providence" (MMM 946).

If Twain saw human stupidity as one motive for appealing to Providence, an inflated sense of human worth is another. In a notebook entry in 1886, Twain imprinted this diatribe:

> Special providence! That phrase nauseates me—with its implied importance of mankind & triviality of God. In my opinion these myriads of globes are merely the blood-corpuscles ebbing & flowing through the arteries of God, & we but animalculae that infest them, disease them, pollute them: & God does not know we are there, & would not care if he did. (MTNJ 3: 246–47)

Twain's rejection of the special providence really reinforces the general concept of Providence. Criticizing the aggrandizement of humans and the concomitant trivialization of God, Twain lambastes the hubris of humans in presuming to explain divine purposes. It is left to Jim in *Tom Sawyer's Conspiracy* to give the orthodox view: "*You* can't relieve Prov'dence none, en he doan need yo' help, nohow" (164). Providence, in Twain's view of the world, is simply a given. Those who try to explain Providence are stultified, just as in the book of *Job* God speaks from the whirlwind, chastising those who would presume to explain His ways. The correct human response to the mystery of Providence is the blank of language, silence.

Time and again, Twain invokes providential explanations as a catch-all term that people employ to bring order out of chaos, but at its heart the term cannot explain the inexplicable, as it seems designed to do. "Providence leaves nothing to go by chance," Twain informs us in *Roughing It*'s chapter 38. "All things have their uses and their part and proper place in Nature's economy: the ducks eat the flies—the flies eat the worms—the Indians eat all three—the wild-cats eat the Indians—the white folks eat the wild-cats—and thus all things are lovely" (247). Until the introduction of the list, Twain's statement is a typically providential one, but then there is "a screw loose," just as in "The Story of the Good Little Boy Who Did Not Prosper." All things are not lovely, of course, they are grotesque, but that, Twain argues, is reality. The most typical image in *Roughing It* is that of the lone tree growing on the Mono Lake island, surrounded by "venomous water," "scorched and blasted rocks," and "jets of steam" (251). Conjoining life and death, the "small pine of most graceful shape and most faultless symmetry" seems to Twain "like a cheerful spirit in a mourning household" (251). In *Roughing It,* Providence is the point d'appui of Twain's grotesque realism; even the imagery surrounding the fate of William Wheeler suggests that the grotesque warp and woof of the universe has a place for humankind within it, even if it is a design with "a screw loose."

What is at stake in *Roughing It* is, then, quite a serious game after all. In the context of the burlesque of Providence Tales, the pervasive imagery of blankness and degradation might well seem a nihilistic vision. Grotesque imagery of blankness, death, and destruction might suggest a world in which there is no beautiful master text, just as there is no real "story" in Blaine's drunken recollections. The master text, however, is always present in the parodic response. One should not assume that a burlesque of Providence destroys the original text, for quite the contrary is true; it reconnects it with reality and so rejuvenates it, just as Twain's "Colloquy between a Slum Child and a Moral Mentor" (1860s/1880s) shows the vast gulf separating theological terms and practical reality, particularly the gritty reality of a slum child. Twain provides a footnote for this work: "Respectfully recommended for the Sunday School books" (109). In his fine analysis of Twain's translation of Heinrich Hoffman's *Struwwelpeter,* or "Slovenly Peter," J. D. Stahl concludes that Twain "adds a strong flavor of fascination with the absurd, grotesque, and violent to his rendition" (177). Stahl notes Twain's use of "Puritan theology" (177), and one might reasonably claim that Twain's translation of the text amounts to a parody of it. Hoffman's texts, with titles like "The Story of Cruel Frederick," "The Dreadful Story of Pauline and the Matches," and "The Story of Augustus Who Would Not Have Any Soup," are as didactic as any of the Sunday-school books, but become, in Twain's translations, parodies of the original. Paula Uruburu connects the development of the American Grotesque to the Puritan "plain style," an attempt to use rhetoric of the commonplace in sermons. Citing Thomas Hooker's comparing Grace to "a great Onyon" that hangs in a house, growing bigger and bigger, seemingly by its own volition, she traces the use of grotesque imagery to convey religious ideas to the later development "by our writers to infuse everyday objects, things of the most mundane and often ugly reality, with an 'inner life' of their own, in fact, to rely upon the use of the familiar in order to illuminate that which appears unknowable or unfamiliar" (33). Her brilliant study convincingly traces the influence of the plain style on Edward Taylor, Mary Rowlandson, Edwards, and others down through the twentieth-century development of the American Grotesque.

Significantly, in this regard, Twain took time out from his "California & Plains book" to write his occasional piece "About Smells" (1870). In this work, he roasts the Reverend T. De Witt Talmage, a Presbyterian minister who had complained about the odor of working men attending church, a subject Twain later burlesques in "The Second Advent" (1881), as discussed in chapter 4. In "The Indignity Put upon the Remains of George Holland by the Rev. Mr. Sabine" (1871), Twain likewise castigates a minister, calling him a "freak of Nature" for refusing to officiate at the funeral of an actor (517). One might suggest Twain saw Mr. Sabine as a "grotesque" because of his adherence to a "picturesque Christianity" that violated the fundamental principles of its namesake. Conversely, Christ, in fraternizing with sinners and tax collectors, was from a pharisaical viewpoint a grotesque.

Just as Twain delighted in correcting Talmadge and Sabine, he must have delighted in having Jim Blaine tell of the missionary who was eaten by cannibals, for through this burlesque he suggests that only by becoming grotesque can one bring life.

> That there missionary's substance, unbeknowns to himself, actu'ly converted every last one of them heathens that took a chance at the barbacue. Nothing ever fetched them but that. Don't tell me it was an accident that he was biled. There ain't no such thing as an accident. (366)

A parodic Christ figure, the missionary contains both death and life, as the imagery of grotesque realism does. Having the cannibals eat the missionary degrades the oh-so-high-and-mighty and illustrates in fiction the same sense Twain expressed in his journalist pieces that those who would minister to people must not stand apart from them. The consuming of the missionary by cannibals is really a burlesque of transubstantiation as they partake of the body of Christ through the missionary who sought to bring them into the body of Christ, the church. The symbol of communion becomes real. We laugh at the absurdity of the situation, at the indignation of the missionary's relatives, and at Blaine's insistence that it all makes sense. Still, Twain makes his point with humor and hostility that true mission work means, in some sense, sacrificing oneself as the Reverends Sabine and Talmadge most demonstrably did not. Symbolically, mission work means empathizing with those to whom one would minister, rather than pushing away day laborers, theater folk, and man-eaters.

Lest one deduce from these examples that Twain simply disliked the clergy, one should note that during the composition of *Roughing It* Twain likewise leaped to the defense of deserving ministers; in "Mr. Beecher and the Clergy" (1869), for example, Twain defends the Reverend T. K. Beecher, who had been expelled from the Ministerial Union of Elmira, New York. His crime? He held popular and well-attended meetings in an "opera house" (291). Looking at these and other occasional pieces that Twain wrote during the *Roughing It* years, one notes that Twain consistently champions those who bring the gospel down to the common person. In chapter 47 of *Roughing It,* the famous meeting between the minister and Scotty Briggs has as its main theme the translation of the gospel of Christ into the language of the people. Twain tells us pointedly that "Slang was the language of Nevada. It was hard to preach a sermon without it, and be understood" (309). For this reason, the "spirituel new fledgling from an eastern theological seminary" has to learn the new language and bring the gospel to the people who need it (309). There is some truth, then, to Julian Markels's assertion that "*Roughing It* is rhetorically assured and consistent in its deflation of establishment religion" (144), so long as we understand that Twain is using the grotesque to bring religion down to the "reproductive lower stratum," as Bakhtin phrases it, in order to provoke rebirth (RW 21). Structurally, at least, with his burlesque of Providence Tales, Twain criticizes popular American theology, purifying the definition of Providence and restoring to it its dominant sense of mystery.

"The Story of the Old Ram" differs from Twain's journalistic pieces in that it is a literary piece, but the message is similar: the very idea of Providence exists *because* the world is grotesque. The finished and the beautiful have no place in *Roughing It* precisely because they are not real. In *Roughing It,* the grotesque becomes the norm. Beginning with the assumption of a fallen world populated with fallen people, there is nothing surprising in the reality depicted in *Roughing It*. Rather than depicting the West, then, as a sort of exception to the rule, Twain uses the West to depict the reality of a world in which everything is grotesque; the new form is not called into being by new content, but rather by the dead literary form that never did adequately express the old content. Creating a story without the typical appeal to classic aesthetics, Twain connects grotesque images of the body and Providence in a "carnival mesalliance" that unites, Bakhtin asserts, "sacred with the profane, the lofty with the low" (PDP 123). Elevated to an almost meaningless panacea for any ill, Providence as a term is a "blank cartridge," in the sense that William James deems any philosophical term too abstract to be useful as a "blank cartridge." "Pragmatically, then, the abstract word 'design' is a blank cartridge," James argues. "It carries no consequences, it does no execution" (52). Similarly, Twain finds Providence, as used popularly, too abstract to provide solace amid earthly ill, so he brings the concept down to earth. Even the gun-slinging metaphor begins the work of degrading the abstract theological concept to street-level reality. With the metaphor, Twain reminds his readers in very graphic ways how violent reality is, how blank and incomplete the world is, and reminds us just why people appeal to Providence in the first place.

Not surprisingly, the vast majority of critics view Blaine's story as Twain's rejection of the theological concept, rather than a burlesque of a literary form and a clarifying of a theological term immanent to that form. Tom Towers, for example, provides a typical summary of the book's argument: "there is no scheme in myth or science which will account for the awful facts of human life" ("Hateful" 15). Likewise, Lee Clark Mitchell contends that *"Roughing It* lives up to its title and, like the drunken story that Jim Blaine tells of his grandfather's old ram, never quite succeeds in getting to the point" (69). Simply put, *Roughing It* asserts the truth that Providence *does* explain everything, but that we cannot know what that explanation is; as Calvin reminds us, Providence is "the secret counsel of God" (I:173). Twain's sketch is so brilliantly done, so *designedly* done, it supports the argument that there truly are no accidents, but it does not assert the beauty of the result. Throughout his career, Twain portrays chaos and confusion as givens of human life, as fundamental law. As Lawrence Berkove observes about the content that produces the form of *Roughing It,*

> [Twain] saw postlapsarian life as designedly hellish, marked by man's Sisyphean efforts to escape God's curse of Adam: that he would earn his bread by the sweat of his brow. *Roughing It*'s underlying unity—and the book is far more unified than has been generally recognized—is largely accomplished by the thematic operation of Twain's bitter belief not in the justice of this view of existence but in its empirical accuracy. (23)

In short, Twain may or may not have "liked" his Calvinist inheritance, but it orders his work nevertheless, particularly in his burlesque of popular theological stories in *Roughing It.*

Twain certainly had plenty of evidence that reality was grotesque and not picturesque even as he wrote his book. Some facts of Twain's life during the composition of *Roughing It* support a view of the world—not just the West—as a place where everything happens all the time, or as Webb says, where "the unexpected was sure to happen" (481). During 1870–71, Twain experienced the birth and illnesses of children, the visit of Olivia's closest friend, Emma Nye, who would then contract and die of typhus in the Clemens home, and the subsequent severe illness of Livy herself. All of these facts provoked Twain to write Elisha Bliss,

> I had rather die twice over than repeat the last six months of my life. . . .
> If I *dared* fly in the face of Providence & make one more promise, I would say that if I ever get out of this infernal, damnable chaos I am whirling in at home, I will go to work & amply & fully & freely fulfill some of the promises I have been making to you—but I don't dare! Bliss—I don't dare! (MTL 4:365–66)

One must be careful of making too much of this letter, but Twain's attitude does seem almost fearful, evincing a certain canny wariness that Providence truly fires no blank cartridges, but live ammunition. A universal plan may exist, but it is not our plan, and Twain often links Providence with fear. One recalls that Huck is slapped by Providence and that Captain Wakeman in *Roughing It* has a "hand like the hand of Providence," suggesting a threatening force (425). In the letter, too, one sees Twain dwelling amid chaos, the chaos of everyday life, yet stating that there is some order or plan to the universe; there is, not coincidentally, the very real fear that God's plan may not necessarily be *our* plan. In contrast to the Providence Tales he responds to, Twain defines Providence not as something desirable but as something factual; the term asserts a trinity of violence, sovereignty, and mystery. Providence simply *is,* and no human opinion about it or explanation of it is likely to be helpful, useful, or accurate. In "Reflections on the Sabbath" (1866), Twain rejected the idealizations of the "Sunday-school books" with their ubiquitous "good little boys . . . who always went to heaven, and the bad little boys who infallibly got drowned on Sunday," vowing: "I hold that no man can meddle with the exclusive affairs of Providence and offer suggestions for their improvement without making himself in a manner conspicuous. Let us take things as we find them—though, I am free to confess, it goes against the grain to do it, sometimes" (39).[4]

How Twain reacted to grotesque reality outside of his literature is telling. Twain remembered the days of Emma Nye's illness and death as "among the blackest, the gloomiest, the most wretched of my long life" (MTE 251). His response to the horror, however, was to seek shelter in the grotesque. "The resulting periodical and sudden changes of mood in me, from deep melancholy to half-insane tempests and cyclones of humor," Twain reflected, "are among the curiosities of my life" (MTE 251). During that time, as he tells it, Twain made his famous "crude and absurd map of Paris" that grotesquely distorted the real map of France's capital (MTE 251). Time and again in Twain's writing, one sees the use of the grotesque to make light of reality during times when reality horrifies, turning the monsters of real life, as Bakhtin suggests, into "amusing or ludicrous monstrosities" (RW 47). Twain retreated into the grotesque, finding it more comforting than the Sunday-school books that were obviously untrue.

Certainly, there is heavy irony in having the symmetrically inebriated Blaine deliver a sermon on Providence; the fools in Shakespeare get all the best lines, too. That Blaine is "symmetrically" inebriated suggests a grotesque mesalliance of order and disorder, just as systematic theology is used to explain chaotic reality. Even the setting, with all the miners gathered around Blaine while he delivers his "sermon," suggests a burlesque of a church service, "a grotesque degradation of various church rituals and symbols and their transfer to the material bodily level" (RW 74). Blaine's first statement "I don't reckon them times will ever come again" restates in parody "In the beginning." What follows is a church service decidedly not divine, where whiskey, not wine, is shared, in which transubstantiation is a form of cannibalism, and in which one is unsure if the Reverend Twain's gunslinger God is a lawman or a badman. The sermon argues that the Lord moves in mysterious ways, at times using odd instruments. Perhaps even very odd instruments like the poor Uncle Lems of the world. As David in *The Refuge of the Derelicts* observes, "sometimes the methods employed by Providence seem strange and incongruous" (189).

The blanks, the gaps, the events that do *not* happen, even the central assertion, "Prov'dence don't fire no blank ca'tridges, boys," with its double or even triple negative, connects chapter 53 back to Twain's burlesques of Providence Tales. Just as "Sinful Jim" in "The Christmas Fireside" does *not* lose fingers when firing a rifle, is *not* struck by lightning, and does *not* go to jail, the Jim in *Roughing It* does *not* tell a story, but tells about people who do *not* have legs, arms, eyes, and so on (410). The moral of these burlesques of Providence Tales is always the same: mystery. "How this Jim ever escaped is a mystery to me," readers are told in "The Christmas Fireside" (409). In chapter 53 of *Roughing It,* too, the story the narrator hopes to hear remains "a dark mystery" (368). Twain's Providence Tale inverts the usual structure of the Sunday-school book and so returns the term to its original theological definition, classically expressed by Calvin as "the secret counsel of God" (I: 173).

Indeed, however grotesque it may be to have the drunken Jim Blaine deliver a sermon, time and again in Twain it is the vernacular character who bears satirical truth. Certainly, there are characters in *Roughing It* like the parson who talks to Scotty Briggs. And there are characters like Briggs himself whose honest vernacular provides "no mean timber whereof to construct a Christian" (317). A long line of dialectal characters in Twain deliver sermons that are a part of the deep penetration of Calvinism into folk consciousness. Consider Roxy in *Pudd'nhead Wilson,* for example, whose sermon on grace is a model of orthodoxy: "dey ain't nobody kin save his own self—can't do it by faith, can't do it by works, can't do it no way at all. Free grace is de on'y way, en dat don't come fum nobody but jis de Lord" (931). While putting theological language into the mouths of dialectal characters develops an honestly realistic fiction, their effect on the reader as grotesques is to create a carnival rebirth for these ideas, not to destroy them. In *Roughing It,* Twain proves himself to be of a like mind with William James, who was in 1872 formulating these ideas that he would set down decades later in his work *Pragmatism:* "The prince of darkness may be a gentleman, as we are told he is, but whatever the God of earth and heaven is, he can surely be no gentleman. His menial services are needed in the dust of our human trails, even more than his dignity is needed in the empyrean" (34–35). Just as Twain endorsed the Reverend Thomas K. Beecher for his popular sermons in opera houses, the actor George Holland for his "theatrical ministry," or even his own character Scotty Briggs for his sermons in slang, he uses the grotesque in the character of Jim Blaine to bring Providence down from the empyrean to the human world of dust. Jim Blaine's sermon renews understanding of just what the term Providence implies, explains why temporal disorder creates a desire for a godly order, and fosters a community of those united by laughing at our common condition.

With his use of theological language, Twain also pleas for the providential writer. With his work *Roughing It,* he admittedly composes a book out of many sources and of a subject matter that is chaotic and "variegated." If Twain does treat metaphysics, he also brings to the fore questions about both the story and the story writer who must "cut & slash & lick & trim & revamp it." In Blaine's story, nothing *is* lost. Each character brings to mind another character and another story. Blaine, viewed this way, has "no sense of proportion," just as Twain said. Blaine, that is, had no *artistic* sense. *His* story is a blank cartridge and fails to hit its target. Without any sense of authorial control, his story belies his own assertion that "Accidents don't happen, boys" (366). Indeed, he proceeds accidentally. Twain's story, however, is another story. In "The Story of the Old Ram," Twain's authorial control is at high pitch and, appropriately, it is nearly invisible.

Readers' appreciation for chapter 53 in particular and *Roughing It* generally is directly related to its seeming artlessness; the more it violates classical aesthetics, the more readers love it. Beidler's assertion that chapter 53 has "little to do with any plan of overall design" would have delighted Twain, for it proves that even a professor could be "sold" (46). The record of "variegated vagabonding," the alliteration of which is a coy wink at the "classical school," is a manifesto of grotesque realism.

The central role played by the grotesque in *Roughing It* undermines Dieter Meindl's assertion that there is a "fundamental lack of affinity between realism and the grotesque" (106). On the contrary, where reality is grotesque, anything else would be insufficiently representational. A school of "grotesque realism" would demand writers whose greatest success lies in purposeful artlessness as they reveal reality through the grotesque. Moreover, the constant coupling of death and life, of negation and affirmation, is both a rejection of classical aesthetics and liberation from our fear of the rough world we live in. Twain makes the concept of Providence itself grotesque to further dispel the earthly terrors people try to explain as part of a sensible design of a God who oversees "all creatures, actions, and things, from the greatest even to the least" (*Westminster Confession* 178/6.024). There is much evidence within *Roughing It* and in Twain's life suggesting the Calvinist concept of Providence was deeply engrained in his ways of thinking about the world, yet Twain's grotesque parody of Providence illustrates the fundamental human impulse to laugh at funerals, to whistle in cemeteries, and to crack jokes when we are under the gun, so to speak. Flannery O'Connor defends the grotesque on precisely these grounds, saying that such literature must be "violent and comic" (816). The Sunday-school book Providence Tale tries to explain away fears of chaos, but human fears are too much a part of this "dusty" world to be satisfactorily explained by an appeal to the empyrean. *Roughing It* is also a manifesto calling for a regeneration of our understanding of literary providence. Like God, the writer of grotesque realism "fires no blank cartridges"; the degree to which reality achieves no classical beauty is the very context that demands grotesque realism. In the beginning, Twain feared he might not produce literary gold, and in the end, he recognized that "*nothing* that glitters is gold" (188). *Roughing It* and its grotesque aesthetics are the only ore worth mining. With *Roughing It,* Twain achieves a new sort of literature that becomes a "classic" in its own right, all the while without becoming an exponent of the classical school.

MARK TWAIN'S HYMNS IN PROSE:

Doxology and Burlesque in The Adventures of Tom Sawyer *and* Adventures of Huckleberry Finn

It is a slander to suppose that God can enjoy any congregational singing.
—MARK TWAIN (MTNJ 2: 338)

Parody is a road that leads to something else.
—BORIS EICHENBAUM ("O. Henry and the Theory of the Short Story" 268)

GIVEN SOME of Mark Twain's comments about his novel *The Adventures of Tom Sawyer* (1876), it is somewhat surprising that the *structure* of the work has been the focus of many substantive articles. "Since there is no plot to the thing," Twain wrote William Dean Howells, "it is likely to follow its own drift, & so is as likely to drift into manhood as anywhere—I won't interpose" (MTHL 1: 87–88). Of course, Twain made other comments belying this disingenuous assertion, and beyond his claims of artlessness stands the novel itself; scholarly commentary, too. Considering the tendency to neglect or even deny Twain's literary competence, one is inclined to think that the number of analyses addressing the novel's structure says something about the power of a successful work to command respect. John Seelye finds himself in the uncomfortable position of arguing both that the work "testifies to the unconscious artistry that was [Twain's] greatest gift" *and* that the novel is "one of the most carefully controlled (and contrived) of his fictions . . . nearly neoclassical in rigidity" (419, 413). Even Forrest Robinson, who generally portrays Twain as an incompetent hack, finds it possible to "attempt to adumbrate and defend a plot structure for the novel" (*Bad Faith* 19). Traditionally—and correctly—the novel is also viewed as a burlesque of the Sunday-school book, much in the way the previous chapter explores the influences of that form on *Roughing It*. Walter Blair suggests that "Tom Sawyer then is a humorous—though not burlesque—version of 'The Story of a Bad Boy Who Did Not Come to Grief'" (MTHF 66).[1]

A comment Twain made after the book's publication deserves closer analysis than his earlier claim about the work's lack of plot. In 1887, when approached by a producer hoping to dramatize the book, Twain declined with this telling statement: "Tom Sawyer is simply a hymn, put into prose form to give it a worldly air" (Mark Twain's Letters, Paine edition II: 477). Such language might, of course, simply be the conventional praise of youth, but the identification of the work as a "hymn" resonates with a number of the book's structural elements. Twain's comments on *The Adventures of Tom Sawyer* underscore a compelling peculiarity of the novel and its companion *Adventures of Huckleberry Finn* (1885). Notable for their burlesque depiction of religion as the last refuge of hypocrites, both works contain a single instance of pure, undefiled worship involving the singing of a particular hymn, the Doxology. In *Adventures of Huckleberry Finn,* this unique point in the narrative occurs during the Peter Wilks funeral, a scene "all full of tears and flapdoodle," as Huck tells us (213). Yet, within this hypocritical church service, the Doxology is sung spontaneously with remarkable, even singular, effect in the novel:

> And the minute the words was out of his mouth somebody over in the crowd struck up the doxolojer, and everybody joined in with all their might, and it just warmed you up and made you feel as good as church letting out. Music *is* a good thing; and after all that soul-butter and hogwash, I never see it freshen things up so, and sound so honest and bully. (213)

The ironies of the passage are many, for the "doxolojer" restores Huck's soul, one might say, to a post-Sabbath condition; he feels as "good as church letting out" when singing the song, and in a sense church *has* let out. Singing the Old Hundred forces a cessation of the "soul-butter and hogwash" that make church services in the novel deceitful and hypocritical. Singing the hymn on the spur of the moment restores the spontaneity of worship, for it is an honest and uncalculated worship that—for a moment—supplants the plotting hypocrisies of the king and duke.

The genetic link between *Adventures of Huckleberry Finn* and its prequel is most profound in the singing of the Doxology. In *The Adventures of Tom Sawyer,* another congregation spontaneously sings the Doxology at a funeral, and if music can "freshen things up" in *Adventures of Huckleberry Finn,* here the music suggests rebirth. In *The Adventures of Tom Sawyer,* the Doxology is truly a hymn of rejoicing after Tom Sawyer, Joe Harper, and Huck Finn materialize at their own funeral service. In Tom's case, the hymn plays an even more important role, for in *The Adventures of Tom Sawyer,* the chapter in which the hymn is sung is central to the thematic concerns of the novel. Clark Griffith views the novel as having a five-tiered structure and notes that "of Tom's five principal feats in *Sawyer,* two (winning a Bible, attending his own funeral) take place inside the village church, while a third (prophesying for Aunt Polly) stresses religious terminology and raises Biblical echoes, and the two others (rescue from the cave, finding buried treasure) either begin as churchly activities or result in celebrations that lead back to the church" (131). The church is indeed central to the novel's structure, but it is also a looming presence that any healthy boy wishes to avoid—until the funeral. Only at that point is Tom truly anxious to go to church. Fittingly, the preacher takes his funeral text from John 11:25, "I am the resurrection and the life." Like the funeral in *Adventures of Huckleberry Finn,* in which the primary mourners impersonate a relationship to the deceased, the funeral in *The Adventures of Tom Sawyer* is fundamentally dishonest, a swindle, for no one has even died. Tom is culpable, but more significant than the *boy's* dishonesty is the hypocritical behavior of the congregation who can remember only the boys' "sweet, generous natures" and utterly forget their "rank rascalities, well deserving of the cowhide" (140–41). Forrest Robinson suggests that the singing of the Doxology at this moment is a "happy brand of hypocrisy . . . in which the suspension of disbelief is proportional to the perceived social dividends of knowing gullibility" (*Bad Faith* 41). Harold Aspiz, too, sees Twain as "taunting" his readers and coming close to "sacrilege" (145). Is the singing of the hymn just a wink at the hypocrisy of the characters and a taunt to readers, or is something more transcendent occurring?

The boys' return to the church shocks the community, especially the preacher, who first catches sight of them:

There was a rustle in the gallery, which nobody noticed; a moment later the church door creaked; the minister raised his streaming eyes above his handkerchief, and stood transfixed! First one and then another pair of eyes followed the minister's, and then almost with one impulse the congregation rose and stared while the three dead boys came marching up the aisle, Tom in the lead, Joe next, and Huck, a ruin of drooping rags, sneaking sheepishly in the rear! (141)

As the shock deepens, the preacher exhorts the congregation, "Praise God from whom all blessings flow—SING!—and put your hearts in it!" (141). A "triumphant burst . . . shook the rafters" as the congregation, perhaps for the only time, sings the old hymn with gusto and honesty (141). Albert Stone observes that while the passage "begins as a prank on sentimental townspeople" it ends by resurrecting not boys who were never dead at all, but a "sense of community" (82).

The singing of the Doxology is part of the parodic funeral in the novel, an example of carnival grotesque that, in Bakhtin's words, "permit[s] the combination of a variety of different elements and their rapprochement" (RW 34). The parodic funerals in both works do celebrate deaths, not of Tom or even the really dead Peter Wilks, but of the hypocritical worship services. The singing at the parodic funerals represents a *temporary* cessation of hostility between the artificial world of adults and the natural world of children, allowing temporary harmony between civilization and nature. In *The Adventures of Tom Sawyer* in particular, the text actually suggests such a union immediately before the funeral: "When the Sunday-school hour was finished, the next morning, the bell began to toll, instead of ringing in the usual way. It was a very still Sabbath, and the mournful sound seemed in keeping with the musing hush that lay upon nature" (140). This alliance between the world of people and the natural world is further developed by the funeral text from John: "And whosoever liveth and believeth in me shall never die" (11:26). In characters like Tom Sawyer, Twain separates the idea of "living in me" from the concept of "believing in me." Twain's allusion to John is an important one, for it occurs within passages discussing baptism, resurrection, and also "Thomas Didymus," or "Thomas the Twin," which suggests perhaps Tom's duplicity in the scene (11:16). In any event, children like Tom and his playmates contrast to the world of adults, where *profession* of belief is paramount, in that they unreflectively, spontaneously *live*. The words of the hymn are simple and powerful.

Praise God from Whom all blessings flow,
Praise Him all creatures here below,
Praise Him above ye heavenly host,
Praise Father, Son, and Holy Ghost.

Singing the Doxology, whose ancient words remind us of the difference between God and humans, the "creatures here below," endorses the spontaneous world of "creatures" over the complex world of adults. Twain interweaves the plot, the Doxology, and the text from John to imagine a parodic funeral service for dead forms of worship that dominate religious life in *The Adventures of Tom Sawyer.* Implicitly, the hymn recognizes that people are "creatures here below" and should have forms of worship that recognize that fact.

Why these singular moments in the two novels should both involve this old hymn in strikingly similar ways might be due to some biographical explanation. Twain did enjoy singing hymns, even assisting with the group singing on the *Quaker City* excursion. For Twain, hymns were synonymous with joy, and he wrote Livy in 1873, during the years that he composed *The Adventures of Tom Sawyer,* that "I feel as gay as a hymn" (MTL 5: 358). The Doxology is specifically important, however, not just generically, for it is an important part of the order of service in the Presbyterian and other churches. It is summative, providing a précis of Christian doctrine and obligation. It is a creed. The Doxology expresses theology simply and clearly. Compared to abstruse points of Calvinist doctrine like predestination, parodied in *Adventures of Huckleberry Finn* as "preforeordestination," the Doxology is unsullied by doctrinal dispute (147). In terms of content, the hymn very plainly asserts the Trinitarian view of God, Christ, and the Holy Spirit, outlining in almost archetypal terms the obligation that the creatures down here have to the God up there.

In *The Adventures of Tom Sawyer,* the Doxology contributes to the sabbatical structure of the work, for the book insistently focuses on the days of the week in such a way as to highlight the religious calendar— Sunday is always in the offing, always the inevitable threat to a boy's natural freedom. With very few exceptions, the reader always knows where the action is relative to the Sabbath, and many chapters gain their thematic significance from their position relative to the Sabbath. While *The Adventures of Tom Sawyer* is often viewed as having no serious thematic concerns, in fact the entire structure of the book looks toward a redefinition of worship, moving toward the Doxological moment visible in the funeral scene. Centering on the weekly calendar with the first day of the week as Sunday, the novel's structure insistently contrasts the natural, spontaneous worship of children with the formalized, hypocritical worship of adults. As Tom Towers suggests, "In nature the children intuit a spiritually vital world which seems to oppose that of adult society at every point" ("Never" 512). Joseph Coulombe notes the use of nature in the book, but seriously understates its structural importance by arguing that Twain "sought to capitalize on current trends, and he made occasional use of romantic notions of nature as a moral sanctuary" (123). These "notions" are not simple stylistics, but provide the work's "dominant," a term Jakobson defines as "the focusing component of a work of art: it rules, determines, and transforms the remaining components" ("Dominant" 41). The contrast between natural worship and formal religion is the central and pervasive determinant of the novel's ethical force. One should, then, take seriously Twain's description of *The Adventures of Tom Sawyer* as "a hymn, put into prose form," for like hymns, the book anticipates a communal outpouring of worship. While Twain often burlesques congregational singing, moments such as the singing of the Doxology demonstrate an acceptance of Calvin's defense of such singing: "In this way the God whom we serve in one spirit and one faith, we glorify together as it were with one voice and one mouth" (II:181). In select, central moments, Twain's texts support such ideas. Twain's burlesque of the Doxology in the 1863 piece "A Sunday in Carson," in which he heard "the Rev. Mr. White give out a long-metre doxology, which the choir tried to sing to a short-metre tune," contains a description that seems pure fun (222). Yet Twain, writing in the tradition of *parodia sacra,* makes the point that "this rendered the general intent and meaning of the doxology considerably mixed, as far as the congregation were concerned, but inasmuch as it was not addressed to them, anyhow, I thought it made no particular difference" (222). In this burlesque, one can see that the reason a hymn like the Doxology can unify is that the focus is on praise of God, not on self-aggrandizement and jockeying for social position that one sees so much of in *The Adventures of Tom Sawyer* or the attempts to bilk believers out of their money in *Adventures of Huckleberry Finn*. While Twain observes that the "meaning of the doxology" was disturbed, in reality the fact that the Doxology was addressed to God *is* the meaning.

One could argue that Twain does envision a structure to *The Adventures of Tom Sawyer* much like the structure of the hymn itself, for initially, at least, Twain had sketched out a four-part plot for the novel:

I, Boyhood & youth; 2 y & early Manh; 3 the Battle of Life in many lands; 4 (age 37 to 40,) return to meet grown babies & toothless old drivellers who were the grandees of his boyhood. The Adored Unknown a [illegible cancellation] faded old maid & full of rasping, puritanical vinegar piety. (Gerber, Introduction, 8–9)

Although Twain discarded this particular plan, many scholars have commented on the quaternary structure of the narrative. Most famously, Walter Blair has argued that Twain founds his structure on four "units of narrative" (Tom and Becky, Tom and Muff Potter, Tom on the island, and Tom and Injun Joe), each of which begins with childish behavior and ends with a "mature sort of action . . . directly opposed to the initial action" ("Structure" 84). Thus, by book's end, Tom is more adult than child having, in Blair's memorable estimation, "gone over to the side of the enemy" (88). Albert Stone notes a similar structure, but with satirical force: "each escapade is rounded out with a mock moral" (61). Although he identifies different elements, John C. Gerber sees as well an "interweaving of four oppositions" in the book ("Adventures" 14). The four-line structure of the Doxology and the presence of the fourth commandment, "Remember the Sabbath day and keep it holy," are central to *The Adventures of Tom Sawyer*, but one need not look for stanzaic structure and repeated chorus in the novel. If there is a chorus and response in the narrative, it is an embedded dialogic structure that constantly compares Sunday with the other days of the week; the structure embodies a search for a resurrected definition of hymn and worship. The boys' attitude at the end of church, at least when school is not in session, is to exult that they face a week of freedom. The Sabbath is the primary *temporal* determinant of the culture depicted in the novel. This fact is ironic, because the Sabbath is not the primary *spiritual* determinant of the culture.

The insistent contrast between Sunday and other days provides the basic structure of the novel and, along with the burlesque of the Sunday-school books, one can see how much *The Adventures of Tom Sawyer* owes to discussions of what true worship is. Twain himself states in his preface that the character Tom Sawyer, and presumably his novel, "belongs to the composite order of architecture." Such a structure is no accident, but has its roots in the earliest manuscript of *The Adventures of Tom Sawyer*, the "Boys Manuscript," begun around 1870. Byers observes that "in setting up the 'Boy's Manuscript' as a diary with the day of the week preceding each entry, Twain foreshadowed the form of

Tom Sawyer" (81). John C. Gerber calls the manuscript "almost a dress rehearsal" for the novel he eventually did write (Introduction 7). In *Mark Twain's Burlesque Patterns,* Franklin Rogers contends that

> He has used the plot of 'The Boy's Manuscript' for his 'running narrative-plank' and inserted episodes and subplots, a number of which are burlesques or near-burlesques, to make his novel. Structurally the result is quite like *Roughing It* in that the inserted material is neatly fitted into place and connected to the frame plot. (109)

The roots are perhaps even deeper, for in the "Boy's Manuscript," Twain adheres to the essentially chronological diary form he burlesqued in chapter 59 of *The Innocents Abroad* (1869), in which he compares a notebook he kept while at sea with an earlier notebook he kept as a boy. In both instances, the records were dismal failures and Twain gets some humor out of the absurdity of recording mundane details inherently unworthy of recording. In the boy's diary, he records the following:

> *Monday*—Got up, washed, went to bed.
> *Tuesday*—Got up, washed, went to bed.
> *Wednesday*—Got up, washed, went to bed.
> *Thursday*—Got up, washed, went to bed.
> *Friday*—Got up, washed, went to bed.
> *Next Friday*—Got up, washed, went to bed.
> *Friday fortnight*—Got up, washed, went to bed.
> *Following month*—Got up, washed, went to bed. (508)

Once Twain has the weekly order established, he uses the last three entries to indicate both having little to say and forgetting to record even such minimal entries. One difference between his adult journal and the boy's diary is worth mentioning, and that is the insistent imposition of Sunday into the adult calendar. Indeed, while Sunday is entirely absent from the boy's diary, it dominates the journal Twain suggests he kept aboard ship, providing in fact the first entry:

> *Sunday*—Services as usual, at four bells. Services at night, also. No cards. (507)

Both journals are of particular importance to the structure of *The Adventures of Tom Sawer,* begun just a few years after the publication of

Chapter/Day	Sunday	Monday	Tuesday	Wednesday	Thursday	Friday	Saturday
1							
2							
3							
4							
5							
6							
7							
8							
9							
10							
11							
12							
13							
14							
15							
16							
17							
18							
19							
20							
21	Examination	Day					
22	Summer	Vacation					
23	Summer	Vacation					
24	Summer	Vacation					
25							
26							
27							
28							
29							
30							
31				Cave?	?	?	
32							
33	Two Weeks	After	Cave				
34							
35	Three	Weeks	Later				

Figure 3.1 Days and chapters in *Tom Sawyer*

The Innocents Abroad. Both chart the essentially boyish character of the journal keeper for whom "[s]tartling events appeared to be too rare" (509). Dominoes and the Lord's day dominate the adult shipboard journal, which records an essentially dreary existence. One sees in *The Innocents Abroad* the same craving for excitement that marks Tom's character in the later work, but one sees as well the emphasis on Sunday as an especial chronological marker in the week. In *The Adventures of Tom Sawyer,* Twain adapts the diary form fruitfully for the larger thematic point. Tom attempts a diary of the sort Twain burlesqued in *The Innocents Abroad:* "He attempted a diary—but nothing happened during three days, and so he abandoned it" (165). Twain did not abandon the structure, however, for the insistent progression from one day to the next, visible in the "Boy's Manuscript" as "Tuesday—Wednesday—Friday—Saturday—Tuesday—Tuesday Week—Tuesday Fortnight—Saturday" is essentially the same type of structure Twain employs in his novel. One signal difference is striking. Twain adds Sunday to the calendar, a day that plays the same role in *The Adventures of Tom Sawyer* as it does in the burlesque calendar of *The Innocents Abroad.*

One can see the debt, then, that Twain owed to these early forms, but the divergences are perhaps more significant. Twain rejects first-person narration and exploits the temporal structure to much greater ends. The structure in *The Adventures of Tom Sawyer* moves beyond the prosaic description of a boy's life to a structure that has embedded within it the significant thematic concern of contrasting natural and artificial forms of worship that are attached to the weekly calendar. Looking at the chart (Figure 3.1) for *The Adventures of Tom Sawyer,* one can see the movement from the regimented life of chapters 1–21 through the change in the experience of time that accompanies summer vacation. The shift from one understanding of time to another is accomplished by changes in how chapters are introduced.

The chart reveals some intriguing structural aspects of the book. One point made immediately obvious is the progression from day to day that Twain adheres to very closely throughout the work. The days marked in black correspond to chapters where Twain precisely indicates what day or days are included. The gray marks indicate chapters that do occupy specific days, but in which Twain does not say it is a "Tuesday" or "Friday," for example. One notes, too, in the novelistic structure that chapter 21, "Examination Day," marks a decisive break between two different conceptions of time in the work. Moving from chapter 1 through chapter 21, Twain progresses day by day from Friday—Saturday—Sunday—Monday—Tuesday by chapter 11. Chapters 12–15 are not linked to named days, but are specific, and when Twain picks up the temporal markers in chapter 16, it is as if only one day has gone by. Chapters 12, 13, 14, and 15 thus function as exemplary days, specific but unnamed. Chapter 12 features the "Pain-Killer" episode. Chapter 13 tells of "Tom Sawyer, the Black Avenger of the Spanish Main" as he retreats to Jackson's Island (115). Chapter 14 details Tom's adventures on the island. Chapter 15 has Tom swimming to town to overhear Aunt Polly and Joe Harper's mother commiserating. Twain begins specifying the days again in chapter 16, and chapter 17 is Sunday, the funeral sermon where the Doxology is sung.

Strikingly, the days Twain does not specify correspond to the days the boys spend on the island after escaping from civilization. It is as if time has ceased to have meaning, for the meaning of time is imposed by civilization. While on the island, the boys hear the sound of a cannon attempting to make their presumably drowned bodies float to the surface. The boys become gradually aware of the sound, "just as one sometimes is of the ticking of a clock which he takes no distinct note of" (123). One should note the contrast of time in these chapters, for it parallels the change in time after examination day and the onset of summer. With the exception of the island chapters, the first twenty-one chapters of the novel are quite specific about time.

After the boys return to St. Petersburg, time resumes its normal course. The chapters between their return in chapter 17, the funeral Sunday, and chapter 21, Examination Day, occur on Monday after their return. With Examination Day in chapter 21, the school year ends and summer begins. With the arrival of summer, however, comes a fundamental shift. Chapters 22, 23, and 24 cover many days and many weeks, creating the impression of a much longer narrative time than they actually account for. Twain employs markers like "for three days," "[d]uring two long weeks," and "[t]he next day and the day after" to show the fundamentally different conception of time when school—and to a surprising degree church—is out of session (165, 169). "The slow days drifted on," Twain concludes chapter 24, "and each left behind it a slightly lightened weight of apprehension" (174).

Even after these three chapters, one notes the acceleration of the plot, contrary to the idea that these are "slow days." Such acceleration is visible on the chart's quick saltatory black lines that contrast with the drawn-out treatments early in the book. Before Examination Day, for example, Twain slows the pace, spending five chapters (6–10) discussing one single Monday. A single Sunday in chapters 4 and 5 is so drawn out, (delightfully so) that it threatens to become the "Sabbath that has no end" Satan derides in "Letters from the Earth" (1909) as the eternal counterpart to the earthly Sabbath people "quickly weary of" (410). After Examination Day, Twain *reverses* the procedure, designing several chapters that cover multiple days instead of multiple chapters covering single days. The acceleration is most notable in chapter 28, which covers four entire days.

One would rightly anticipate that during these summer months, the onerous activities of Sunday would continue even though the onerous activities of school had ceased. In surprising ways, Twain creates the contrast between the two sections of the book by reducing Sabbatical activities after chapter 21. While chapter 21 is specified only as Examination Day, it resembles earlier church services, even featuring "a sermon so destructive of all hope to non-Presbyterians that it took the first prize" (162). After this the Sundays simply cease in all but name. "There was no Sabbath school during day-school vacation," Twain's narrator informs us (205). Even that central symbolic chore is removed, as if to protect the purity of the summer as a counterpoint to the rest of the year. The chart indicates, too, that Twain plays tricks on the reader to remove Sabbath from the weekly structure after chapter 21. In chapter 26, Tom goes to sleep on a Saturday night, only to wake up the very next day in chapter 27—on a Monday! This is truly a boy's summer dream!

The resumption of temporal markers in the latter half of the book coincides with Injun Joe's return to the plot in chapter 26. Injun Joe kills Dr. Robinson in chapter 9, a chapter in which Tom hears "the ghastly ticking of a death-watch" and begins to believe that "time had ceased and eternity begun" (92). With the resumption of the temporal markers indicating specific days, one sees a similar quickening of the plot. As Joe's plot line increases in importance, time is both demarcated and confused. While in the cave, for example, Tom and Becky lose track of time, thinking "it must be Wednesday or Thursday or even Friday or Saturday" (216). Injun Joe's "half-breed" identity places him between two definitions of time, and the plot lines in which he appears exist between measured and unmeasured time.

To recap, then, the book begins in a regimented way during the school year, where the tyranny of the weekly calendar is most felt. The regimentation ceases precisely with Examination Day. Even Sabbath school stops. In the summer months, time wallows around and becomes almost atemporal. Twain then resumes temporal markers with the assertion of justice for Injun Joe and the confused identification of time in the cave. These temporal markers function, in Eichenbaum's expression, as an "endeavor to predicate a unity of device over a diversity of material," a difficulty Twain addressed with *Roughing It* as well ("Formal Method" 10).

To comprehend this structure, one must understand what John Byers calls the "author's almost obsessive notation of the passage of time" (81). "If Twain did attempt to use any controlling scheme in the novel," Byers suggests, "it is the often slow but steady progression of the days of the weeks and the weeks of the months of a very long Hannibal summer" (86–87). In fact, Twain creates such an impression by his creative use of temporal markers after Examination Day, but in reality the bulk of the book occurs before summer. Not until the end of chapter 21 does vacation begin. In both sections, Sunday is the crucial day, the essential temporal marker in the work, particularly when Twain notably curbs its influence in the second section. Sunday is as notable in its presence in chapters 4, 5, and 17 as it is in its absence in chapter 27. Numerous writers have noted the binary distinctions in the work, light and dark, life and death, youth and adult, and these are part of the essential structure of the novel that sets Sunday against the rest of the week.[2] Sunday, as the day set apart for worship, becomes the temporal structural unit that embodies other binaries and other criticisms, for Sunday is the world of adult obligation and is the centrally onerous task required of children. It is the vehicle for the novel's social satire.

Twain links the two definitions of worship with two different conceptions of time. In his exemplary analysis of *Adventures of Huckleberry Finn*, John Bird concludes that "we can read the whole novel as Huck's failed attempt to escape the confinement of time's pervasiveness" (263). Susan K. Harris suggests, too, that "[o]ut on the river Huck in effect abandons human time" (*Escape* 71). Spiritual time in *Adventures of Huckleberry Finn* occurs in the natural world, always in stark contrast to the regimented sense of time in the social world of religious hypocrisy. Structurally, the work oscillates between the hypocrisy of organized religion with natural worship. The sermon Huck hears at the church where the Grangerfords and Shepherdsons hold a very temporary truce in their deadly feud is on the subject of "brotherly love and such-like tiresomeness" (147). The situational irony is followed immediately by the famous reverie of chapter 19, with Huck and Jim adrift on the raft. Huck's desire to gain freedom from social conceptions of time is apparent in many details in the scene, as John Bird discusses, but the sense of time is also connected with a renewal of worship. Huck and Jim find themselves discussing "spirits," leading to an even more theological conversation.

> It's lovely to live on a raft. We had the sky, up there, all speckled with stars, and we used to lay on our backs and look up at them, and discuss

about whether they was made or only just happened—Jim he allowed they was made, but I allowed they happened; I judged it would have took too long to *make* so many. Jim said the moon could a *laid* them; well, that looked kind of reasonable, so I didn't say nothing against it, because I've seen a frog lay most as many, so of course it could be done. We used to watch the stars that fell, too, and see them streak down. Jim allowed they'd got spoiled and was hove out of the nest. (158)

The moment is one of very few moments in the work associated with theological discussion in a positive way. In the Grangerford's church, sermons were hypocritical, but also involved doctrine that Huck could not begin to follow. One recalls his reference in that previous chapter to "preforeordestination" (147). The theology of chapter 19's raft scene is really akin to the Doxology, with the natural world creating within the "creatures here below" a natural desire to discuss the deity, doing so in the most natural of terms, such as frogs and bird eggs. Twain makes the contrast obvious by sandwiching the scene between the Grangerford's church and the arrival of the king and the duke. The king specializes in "workin' camp-meetin's; and missionaryin' around" (161), and in the Pokeville Camp-meeting of chapter 20, he takes over the meeting in a scene that, for a moment, proffered a rapprochement between the worlds of religion and nature. The outside service with the singing of hymns is, as Huck says, "kind of grand," but devolves into groaning, shouting, and becomes "just crazy and wild" (171–72). The "wildcat" religion is obviously no substitute even for the hypocrisy of the church attended by the Grangerfords and Shepherdsons. The discussion of stars on the raft is a moment when "the whole world was asleep" and the days and nights "swum" by (156). Nature, Time, and Childhood form a trinity of worship in *Adventures of Huckleberry Finn*.

In *The Adventures of Tom Sawyer*, a similar thematic function of time governs the novel. "In a very real sense," argues Louis Rubin, "Tom Sawyer arrests the progression of time, holds onto childhood instead of conforming to the values and habits of adults" (214). To accomplish this, Twain employs different conceptions of time, undermining through his burlesque the usual definition of Sabbath as a spiritual-idyllic time. Bakhtin's use of the term "chronotope" to describe the connectedness of space and time is useful, for clearly *The Adventures of Tom Sawyer* is, as so many have suggested, a kind of idyll in which one experiences time as a "dense and fragrant time, like honey . . . a time saturated with its own strictly limited, sealed-off segment of nature's space" ("Forms of

Time" 103). "The chronotope," Bakhtin argues, "is the place where the knots of narrative are tied and untied" ("Forms of Time" 250). In Twain's St. Petersburg, the time is of two sorts, on the one hand the spiritual-idyllic time and on the other quotidian time. Twain's aptly named city is the gateway between these two conceptions of time, the locus of dialogue between the spiritual and the mundane, between *aevum* and *tempus, kairos* and *kronos*. Twain reverses the usual definitions, however. One thinks of the theological distinctions between the special observances of Advent, Christmas, Lent, and Easter, and what is known in the liturgical calendar as "ordinary time." Usual definitions proclaim that Sabbath provides privileged access to transcendence, but in this burlesque, the Sabbath is governed by oppressive ordinary or quotidian time with transcendent moments restricted to the young while in the natural world. The only exception is the spontaneous singing of the Doxology. Indeed, two different types of time provide the structure of the novel, which can be interpreted as a dialogue between two types of time and the types of worship associated with them. The clearest example of this is the beginning of chapter 4. The first paragraph of the chapter contains two sentences, one describing natural worship, the other, formal worship. The first line introduces the inherently worshipful aspect of nature: "The sun rose upon a tranquil world, and beamed down upon the peaceful village like a benediction" (57). It is Sunday, and one should point out the irony in *beginning* the day and beginning the Sabbath with the benediction. This *parodia sacra* inverts the usual temporal associations with the order of service, implicitly suggesting the order of service and the natural order are not the same. In the order of service, the benediction, of course, is given at the end as a formal blessing on a congregation; it is, one might say, the reward one gets for sitting still for the sermon. In contrast, Twain's line stands alone at the *beginning* of the chapter, implicitly asserting that one need not attend services to obtain the blessing—it is given freely by God through nature.

Against this backdrop, we have the second sentence of the chapter: "Breakfast over, aunt Polly had family worship; it began with a prayer built from the ground up of solid courses of Scriptural quotations welded together with a thin mortar of originality; and from the summit of this she delivered a grim chapter of the Mosaic Law, as from Sinai" (57).[3] Twain brilliantly equates lack of originality with lack of real feeling in this sentence, illustrating it stylistically through carefully selected mixed metaphors. He also contrasts the building of the prayer "from the ground up" with the benediction that "beamed down" from above in the first sentence (57). Aunt Polly's prayer is "grim," bereft of the joy inherent to the natural benediction. Twain characterizes quotidian time as divorced from any sense of joyous worship by associating it with Mosaic law. "Remember the Sabbath day and keep it holy," states the fourth commandment, but Twain's fourth chapter examines just what "keeping it holy" might mean. One might suggest that Twain here associates a Calvinist church service with an Old Testament sense of obligation dating back to the Decalogue. Calvin notes that observation of the Sabbath "was abolished with the other types on the advent of Christ" (II: 339), but then provides various reasons for continuing to set aside one day for the Lord. Twain depicts Aunt Polly's sermon delivered "as from Sinai," that is, as belonging to a different age and not to the new covenant. Christ has come to the world, been crucified, risen, and yet, Twain seems to suggest, the form of worship has remained as exacting as before. This disjuncture fascinated Twain. In an unpublished notebook entry, he contrasts the two: "God, so atrocious in the Old Testament, so attractive in the New—the Jekyll & Hyde of sacred fiction" (unpublished notebook 47, 18). Twain's depiction of the shift from Old to New Testament is similar in *The Prince and the Pauper* (1881) when Edward Tudor reacts to the law that an Englishman can be sold as a slave. Proclaiming "Thou shalt not!—and this day the end of that law is come!" he uses Old Testament language to herald the arrival of a New Testament leader (197). Calvin suggests that the Lord's Day is associated with rest, creation, and resurrection, but it is clear in *The Adventures of Tom Sawyer* that "the end of that law" is not yet come to St. Petersburg (II:343).

In Chapter 2, Twain similarly associates nature and the natural world of children with a spontaneous form of worship. "Saturday morning was come, and all the summer world was bright and fresh, and brimming with life," Twain writes. "There was a song in every heart; and if the heart was young the music issued at the lips" (46). A natural outpouring of song marks spontaneous and youthful worship, just as in spontaneous congregational singing, and Twain connects the play of the young with the progress of pilgrims toward Bunyan's "Delectable Mountains" through his allusion of describing Cardiff Hill as a "Delectable Land, dreamy, reposeful and inviting" (46; see also "Explanatory Notes" 471; see also the "Explanatory Notes" section in the California edition of *The Adventures of Tom Sawyer*). Similarly, John Halverson connects Tom's retreat to the forest in Chapter 8 as a reenactment of the Man in Black in Chaucer's *Book of the Duchess* (51). While there certainly are some parallels to Chaucer's text and to the Christ story, Halverson misses the point of the retreat to the woods, in that the location is used to discuss Tom's relationship to the church as much as it is a place to explore alternatives to it. Tom hears Joe Harper's horn, for example, and reacts by grabbing a wooden sword and preparing to play Robin Hood. Halverson argues that "Tom's reaction to the sound of the horn is that of a faithful Christian" (54), but it seems more reasonable to suggest that Tom's retreat to the woods and his play there is set in contrast to the world of regimented time and Sabbath obligations. Bakhtin's comment is apropos: "In the provincial novel, as in the idyll, all temporal boundaries are blurred and the rhythm of human life is in harmony with the rhythm of nature" ("Forms of Time" 229). Once summer arrives, the temporal markers are present, but they are far less regimented. As mentioned earlier, Twain even has Tom go to sleep on Saturday night in chapter 26 but wake up on Monday morning in chapter 27. Sunday's mysterious disappearance, whether an intentional device or not, brilliantly contributes to the spiritual-idyllic chronotope.

The burlesque structure of the novel, then, disassociates church time from the spiritual-idyllic chronotope. One goes to church, if one does, in order to enter the spiritual idyll, but consider the depiction that occurs in chapter 5. Beginning with the ringing of the "cracked bell," Twain creates a carnival grotesque description of a church service. Twain's strategy is to "make strange" a very ordinary situation, so ordinary in fact that his description of the church service seems very familiar to Presbyterians even today, from the minister who falls into "a peculiar style" of rising and sharply falling intonation as he sings, to the same character turning "himself into a bulletin board" to read announcements before the sermon (67). This carnival metamorphosis shows the truth of the church service, for the preacher is not a bearer of gospel, the good news, but a bearer only of news. Twain makes his satirical point clear by musing that "the less there is to justify a traditional custom, the harder it is to get rid of it" (67). While there is a great deal of comfort in reading about what one still experiences in church services, there is also a great deal of humor in the scene as readers recognize the truth of Twain's burlesque. Desiccated form dominates the service and, as comforting as the usual, expected order can be, Twain points out the absurdity of turning what should be spiritual-idyllic time into quotidian time. This church service is *not* a special or spiritual time. Twain's depictions in *The Adventures of Tom Sawyer* resemble his description of the services in "The New Wildcat Religion" (1866):

I do not take any credit to my better-balanced head because I never went crazy on Presbyterianism. We go too slow for that. You never see us ranting and shouting and tearing up the ground. You never heard of a Presbyterian going crazy on religion. Notice us, and you will see how we do. We get up of a Sunday morning and put on the best harness we have got and trip cheerfully down town; we subside into solemnity and enter the church; we stand up and duck our heads and bear down on a hymn book propped on the pew in front when the minister prays; we stand up again while our hired choir are singing, and look in the hymn book and check off the verses to see that they don't shirk any of the stanzas; we sit silent and grave while the minister is preaching, and count the waterfalls and bonnets furtively, and catch flies; we grab our hats and bonnets when the benediction is begun; when it is finished, we shove, so to speak. No frenzy—no fanaticism—no skirmishing; everything perfectly serene. You never see any of us Presbyterians getting in a sweat about religion and trying to massacre the neighbors. Let us all be content with the tried and safe old regular religions, and take no chances on wildcat. (134)

Twain's piece on spiritualism as a wildcat religion criticizes the wildcat as well as his own denomination. His humorous depiction of the Presbyterian church service suggests a lack of real religious feeling, and his metaphorical comparison of Presbyterians to horses in a harness creates a visual image that really gets at one of his favorite terms, "training." Like horses, Presbyterians know what they are supposed to do, for it is all routine. These mundane elements of the service proceed in a thoroughly unexceptional way, as the parishioners make themselves comfortable by propping the hymn books up, catching flies, and most significantly, ticking off the verses one by one—in order. Twain suggests by these details that the main virtue of Presbyterianism consists in certain traits that are absent: emotion, feeling, and vitality. That is, Presbyterianism has the defect of its virtue and vice versa; bound by confining tradition, Presbyterianism is also "safe" and "tried and true."

In *The Adventures of Tom Sawyer,* Twain accentuates the profane activities such as catching flies that are mentioned in "The New Wildcat Religion," using such obviously inappropriate activities to pursue his definition of worship. The natural world of boys and girls contrasts to the forms that bore and the prayers that damn. Tom, for example, waits impatiently for his chance to catch a fly, which he does "the instant the 'Amen' was out" (68). Following this, Tom takes out a captive pinch-bug which, true to its name, first pinches him and then a dog who becomes "a woolly comet moving in its orbit with the gleam and speed of light" (69). Tellingly, the parishioners suppress their "unholy mirth," and it "was a genuine relief to the whole congregation when the ordeal was over and the benediction pronounced" (70). The structural ironies are obvious, with nature's benediction, ordinarily given at the end of service, coming at the beginning of chapter 4—*before the church service starts*. At the end of the formal church service in chapter 5, the congregation receives the benediction with relief, not joy. The contrast between the long, tortuous road to the benediction at the end of chapter 5 and the brief, natural benediction at the beginning of chapter 4 illustrates the structural-thematic point Twain makes in the novel. The "all creatures here below" worship best when they worship naturally.

If the novel as a whole has its roots in *The Innocents Abroad* and "The Boy's Manuscript," the important chapters 4 and 5 have their roots in Twain's 1871 letter to Livy while on the lecture circuit in Paris, Illinois. That day, Twain had attended services at a small country church. In this remarkable letter, Twain begins simply, telling Livy that "[i]t was the West & boyhood brought back again, vividly" (MTL 4: 527). Twain captures the order of service seen then and today, from the opening hymn to the announcements, prayers, and closing benediction. Twain singles out the choir for burlesque, calling it "a grand discordant confusion . . . & finally a triumphant 'Oh, praise the L-o-r-d!' in a unison of unutterable anguish" (MTL 4: 528). Grudgingly, Twain grants that the hymns, if "honestly & sincerely" sung are "approved in heaven" (MTL 4: 529), but the contrast between the "unison of unutterable anguish" and Calvin's "one voice and one mouth" is delightfully grotesque; both may be in unison (literally, in one voice), but there the comparison ends. Twain's suggestion that "it was Herod's slaughter of the babes set to music" is hilarious, but in a way true, given his description of the children who suffer through the service (MTL 4: 528). Much of the letter contributes directly to the novel, including long sermons of a decidedly Calvinist flavor. In the church described in the letter, the effervescent energy of youth fizzes over, disturbing the sacred service. Describing not so much the sermon as the life that carries on during the sermon, Twain focuses on a particular "engaged couple" who are unable to repress the life welling up within them.

> These two did nothing but skylark all through the sermon, & I really took just as much comfort in it as if I had been young & a party to it. Only— it was such a pity to think that trouble must come to that poor child, &

her face wither, & her back bend, & the gladness go out of her eyes. I har-
bored not a critical thought against her for her un-churchlike behavior.
Lord! It was *worship!* It was the tribute of overflowing life, & youth,
health, ignorance of care—it was the tribute of free, unscarred, unsmitten *nature* to the good God that gave it! I think it must have been recorded
in heaven, above even the choir's "voluntary." And when these two giddy
creatures stood up & bowed the head when the blessing was invoked, I
made easy shift to believe that as fair a share of the benediction
descended upon them from the Throne as upon me, who had been decorous & reverent & had only picked flaws in the minister's logic and
damned his grammar. (MTL 4: 529–30)

Here, "decorous & reverent" and doubtless with some caricature,
Twain becomes the "model boy," behaving just as Aunt Polly would
have her Tom behave. Yet in this letter, Twain works toward a redefinition of worship—by burlesquing the worship service itself. The "un-
churchlike behavior" of the young woman becomes not blameworthy,
but praiseworthy as worship from "free, unscarred, unsmitten *nature* to
the good God that gave it!" In *The Adventures of Tom Sawyer,* Twain rad-
ically redefines worship, suggesting in the novel, as well as in this formative letter, that true worship is the natural expression of joy, as when
the congregation rises to sing the Doxology "with one impulse."

The structure Twain devises in his novel serves the theme by relating
church services to quotidian time and by drawing out the church-dom-
inated time even through the churchy Examination Day of chapter 21.
Twain emphasizes the artificial nature of the worship, linking it to the
"smothery" world of adults. Perhaps because *Adventures of Huckleberry
Finn* is rightly viewed as a book with so much to say about race in America, *The Adventures of Tom Sawyer* suffers by comparison and is viewed
as the "boy's book" that some thought it was. Twain, it should be
remembered, did not so view the book, explaining his view in a letter to
William Dean Howells: "It is not a boy's book at all. It will only be read
by adults. It is only written for adults" (MTL 6: 503). Alan Gribben has
shown with his usual meticulous study that the book does owe much to
the boy book genre ("Wish" 149–50). For these reasons, perhaps, some
critics have a simplistic view of the book. Bernard DeVoto labels the
book "the supreme American idyll" (304) and Jeffrey Holland calls the
novel "a kind of religious reverie" (24), but both minimize the structural complexity of such an achievement. It would be more accurate to say
that the novel proposes these states so visible in childhood as attainable

by adults. Perhaps most illustrative of this critical strain are the comments of Tony Tanner: "In Tom Sawyer where Clemens is recreating in
idyllic form his own childhood, the latent challenging rebelliousness of
Huck is allowed little scope. Writing rather whimsically and indulgent-
ly from an adult third-person point of view, Clemens allows the idealized
cosiness of his childhood village and the safe pranks and naughtiness of
Tom, who is basically a respectable youth, to dominate the tone of the
book" (139). Tom, in this view, is the ultimate conformist, and the book
in which he appears necessarily endorses the "soul-butter and hogwash"
religion so obviously burlesqued in *Adventures of Huckleberry Finn.*
Writers like Michael Oriard comment effectively on the later novel when
contrasting the characters of Tom to Huck, but at the expense of overlooking the burlesque in the original. Oriard's suggestion that *The
Adventures of Tom Sawyer* "pleases because it validates juvenile play at
the expense of seriousness" is simply not supported by the novel's structure (184). James Cox argues along much the same lines when contending that the novel elevates "play itself" as the theme (147). Saying *The
Adventures of Tom Sawyer* is about "play" is like saying Upton Sinclair's
The Jungle is about sausage; true as far as it goes, the idea ignores what
the novel opposes. "Parody is a road that leads to something else," as
Eichenbaum suggests ("O. Henry" 268). Truly, the association of play
with worship is precisely the point, for that is the most honest "worship" offered by the "creatures here below," acknowledging as it does
our creaturely nature. Twain sets the spirit of play, the "tribute of free,
unscarred, unsmitten *nature*" against grim worship at every point in the
novel.

The juxtaposition of two distinctly opposed modes of worship is
inherently a burlesque on the more formal and traditional mode. A
church service proposes to bring parishioners into worshipful appreciation, as the Doxology says, of God the father, the Son, and the Holy
Ghost. Twain's youthful protagonists, however, find the church service
linked to the quotidian tyranny of time. Within them they carry the
idyll, for the mundane and the hypocritical cannot totally destroy it.
Twain provides very precise descriptions of the order of service in many
works, and it is clear from all of these sources that Twain views the order
of service as both a stolid presence in a sometimes chaotic world and as
a potentially enervating and domineering social force. Even his masquerade as the Reverend Mark Twain embodies the conflict between the
austere iconostasis of adulthood and the natural iconoclasm of childhood. Above the fray is the centuries-old Doxology, at once a formal

creed and a song of praise born anew with each singing. The text proposes a unity, a synthesis of opposing views, just as opposing voices sometimes harmonize in congregational singing. In *The Adventures of Tom Sawyer*, one sees both sides of the equation, but most often Twain depicts the order of service negatively. Huck's memorable complaint in the last chapter of *The Adventures of Tom Sawyer* connects socializing forces with the tyranny of Sabbath time:

> I got to go to church and sweat and sweat—I hate them ornery sermons!
> I can't ketch a fly in there, I can't chaw, I got to wear shoes all Sunday. The
> wider eats by a bell; she goes to bed by a bell; she gits up by a bell—
> everything's so awful reglar a body can't stand it. (234)

It is the "body," both as slang for person and as double-voiced language for the physical aspects of our nature, that can neither sit still nor "stand" the connection between Sabbath and quotidian time. "Which world," asks Rubin, "is real: the daily life of St. Petersburg and of Tom Sawyer, or the natural world of Cardiff Hill? Both are real, and the boy Tom is a part of both" (213). The book contains both, but the narrative structure declares that worship can be free and unfettered. Congregants in moments of honest feeling truly can worship "with one voice and one mouth," as Calvin proposes—and as readers witness at least once in *The Adventures of Tom Sawyer* and *Adventures of Huckleberry Finn* (II: 181). *Parodia sacra* resurrects social practices that are dead, even if ironically celebrating the death and rebirth at a parodic funeral where all praise God, "from whom all blessings flow." Both *The Adventures of Tom Sawyer* and *Adventures of Huckleberry Finn* are "hymns in prose," bringing natural worship immanent in youth into the formal church service, looking toward a resurrection of the dead formalities of worship, just as Twain resurrects the theological genres he burlesques. People worship best, the novel suggests, when they are at play in the fields, forests, and even the churches of the Lord.

MARK TWAIN'S CRUCI-FICTIONS

"The Second Advent" as Twain's Burlesque Life of Christ

[T]he savior is nonetheless a sacred Personage, and a man should have no desire or disposition to refer to him lightly, profanely, or otherwise than with the profoundest reverence.
—MARK TWAIN, Letter to Orion Clemens (Mark Twain's Letters, Paine Edition I: 323)

Good mawnin' Massa Jesus, how'd you leave yo' pa?
—MARK TWAIN, notebook entry[1]

THE DEGREE OF reverence accorded a subject in the nineteenth century was directly proportional to Mark Twain's impulse to burlesque it. While many sober Christians would contend that Christ's advent hardly seems the stuff of burlesque, popular reverent regard for Christianity's foundational narrative demanded that Twain use the form as he had so many other genres of belief. The story of Christ's humble nativity, teaching, crucifixion, and resurrection surpasses even the Adam and Eve mythos as a recognized and revered narrative structure. While Twain adopted and adapted the Adam and Eve story, notably in "The Tournament in 1870 A.D." (1870), "Extracts from Adam's Diary" (1893), "Eve Speaks" (n.d.), "Eve's Diary" (1905), "Adam's Soliloquy" (1905), and "Letters from the Earth" (1909), he worked tentatively and haltingly with the story of Christ, using the narrative in the *Alta California* letters, *The Innocents Abroad* (1869), and in a number of unfinished sketches. The Christ narrative provides structure for many of Twain's major works, but only in "The Second Advent" (1881) does Twain use the Christ story as the central ordering force of his burlesque.[2]

Twain used the Christ story in two seemingly opposed ways throughout his career. On the one hand, he used the central features of the Christ story to establish an allusive structure for such works as *The Prince and the Pauper* (1881), *Adventures of Huckleberry Finn* (1885), *A Connecticut Yankee in King Arthur's Court* (1889), *The American Claimant* (1892), and *Pudd'nhead Wilson* (1894). In these works, the story of Christ's life undergirds the paradigmatic trading of places; just as Christ is incarnated into a lower life for the purposes of rejuvenating souls and society, characters in Twain's cruci-fictions trade places with those lower than themselves for similar purposes, albeit of a less divine nature. Edward Tudor is "incarnated" into the lower classes when forced by circumstances to live as Tom Canty in *The Prince and the Pauper.* In the process, he becomes a worthy leader, and Twain creates a plot and an allusive web drawn directly from Christ's ministry and passion. It is indeed significant that "Edward as King" is chapter 33, for Edward is a type of Christ whose ordeals and degradations result in a ritual crowning. Similarly, Tom Driscoll in *Pudd'nhead Wilson* is traded with the mixed race Chambers and becomes an object lesson of grace when his mother preaches on the text: "dey ain't nobody kin save his own self—can't do it by faith, can't do it by works, can't do it no way at all" (931). Roxy uses the master's son as the Christic "ransom" for her own son, with comical and troubling results. Perhaps the incarnation is most obvious with the character of the Englishman "Lord Berkeley," who suffers comic degradation after being mistaken for an American desperado, "one-armed Pete," in *The American Claimant* (124). Through his experiences this "Lord" becomes truly "a man to worship" (223). Such uses of the Christic paradigm, while comical, are perhaps just high-minded enough to be consonant with Twain's 1878 admonition to his brother Orion, quoted as an epigraph for this chapter, that "the savior is nonetheless a sacred Personage, and a man should have no desire or disposition to refer to him lightly, profanely, or otherwise than with the profoundest reverence" (Mark Twain's Letters, Paine Edition, I: 323).

If Twain occasionally approached burlesque of the Christ story in his novels, in other works he burlesqued it in ways hardly in keeping with his sentiment that the "profoundest reverence" ought to mark our references to him. Most typically, one sees in Twain's works a reverential mien toward Christ simultaneous with a will to burlesque; it is doubtless a mistake to separate Twain's reverential and burlesque treatment of sacred issues as James Wilson does by viewing "the esthetic dimensions of his art" as part of "his resolve to seek a reasonably orthodox faith" (155–56). Such discussion must be largely biographical, but it becomes problematic when Wilson then divorces Twain's "credo" from his "playful irreverence" (156). The result reveals the reason an organic approach unifying attention to both form and content, and intrinsic and extrinsic concerns, is needed. To wrench the sacred from the parody in Twain's practice of *parodia sacra* is impossible. The oscillation is reminiscent of Twain's advice to himself written to Livy in 1871:

> *Any* lecture of mine ought to be a running narrative-plank, with square holes in it, six inches apart, all the length of it; & then in my mental shop I ought to have plugs (half marked "serious" & the others marked "humorous") to select from & jam into these holes according to the temper of the audience. (MTL 4:498)

Overall, any whole work may oscillate between serious and humorous just as one sees the shift between reverence and burlesque. If anything, Twain here understates his case, for it is often impossible to separate the humorous and serious "plugs" in his writing. Frequently Twain writes with such a humorousness of purpose that the two are blended, particularly in *parodia sacra,* where both coexist. In *The Innocents Abroad,* Twain blends the "profoundest reverence" for Christ with burlesque of the Christ story. One sees such traditional moments of reverence as when Twain imagines how "these simple, superstitious, disease-tortured creatures" must have rejoiced when the word went out that "Jesus of Nazareth is come!" (376). Most reverential is Twain's description of his visit to the Church of the Holy Sepulchre. In this lengthy passage, Twain argues that, in contrast to many other "imaginary holy places created by the monks," the place where Christ was crucified is not in doubt (455). He describes the place of Christ's crucifixion effusively and conventionally as "the most sacred locality on earth" (457). Twain contrasts Golgotha to the many sites manufactured for tourists, illustrating his penchant for using the material associated with religion to criticize contemporary society; he also reveals his technique of identifying some place or some thing that is "real" amid so much that is desiccated by virtue of elevation. In his notebooks kept during the *Quaker City* excursion, Twain commented on Bronzino's *Portrait of Prince Don Garzia* and the realism of the baby.

This is a *real* child, with fat face without having an apple in each cheek, has a most silly, winning, chuckleheaded childlike gleeful smile, 2 little teeth just showing in lower jaw—oh, he is perfect! with his well fed body & his uncomfortable little bird grasped in his chubby hand. If he were a Jesus in a Holy Family every woman would want to bite him, & that picture would be the most famous in all the world. Where did they get all those unchildlike infants one finds in the Holy Families? (MTNJ 2: 235)

Twain also labels the usual Christ child in such depictions as "scrawny" and "sick" (MTNJ 2: 235). Artistically, Twain continually grasped at what was *real* in the sacred texts he burlesqued, trying to imagine what the situations described in sacred texts and depicted ad infinitum in all forms of art might really have been like. If the point of the incarnation is to take human form, why then are artistic and literary depictions of Christ so *disincarnated,* spiritualized at the expense of the physical reality? Calvin asserts that the Incarnation demands the "mutual union of his divinity and our nature" (I: 400). Twain seeks just such a real synthesis of physical and spiritual, the promise held forth by the Incarnation.

COWBOY CHRIST

All is not reverential, then, for even the persona of the *Reverend* Mark Twain suggests sacred parody. Twain includes burlesque of the Christ story when discussing the Apocryphal New Testament in *The Innocents Abroad.* He provides extracts based upon his *Alta California* letter of June 2, 1867, in which he describes "a curious book" he had seen at a New York library, William Hone's edition of the Apocryphal New Testament (MTMB 251). Twain selectively includes extracts in his description, as Guy Cardwell suggests, "for comic emphasis" (1012). Working under the guise of simply providing information, Twain carefully places the burden for the burlesque on the "curious book" itself. All the while, Twain creates a comic interplay between the New Testament and the Apocryphal New Testament and between what he says and does not say. Parody is binary, provoking a dialogue between the original and the parodic double, and Twain's lack of commentary only heightens the comic disjuncture between the testament readers know and the version he quotes. Twain accomplishes the burlesque in this instance while labeling the book "frivolous" in both *The Innocents Abroad* (428) and in the

Alta California letters (MTMB 254). In published versions, Twain essentially provided a list of curiosities drawn from the apocryphal work, but in his notebook, he began envisioning the kind of burlesque that would be even less reverential.

> The *home of Joseph & Mary,* where Jesus spent his early life,—walked & talked & taught. *The fountain of the Virgin.* Church of the Annunciation. Naz is built of stone,—upon a hill,—substantial. English Mission school in wh are children whose parents were murdered recently by the Druses. . . . Staircase to *Mary's kitchen—the workshop of Joseph* transformed into a chapel—here Christ worked at his trade.
>
> "J. Christ & Son, Carpenters & Builders."
>
> Recall infant Christ's pranks on his school-mates—striking boys dead—withering their hands—burning the dyer's cloth &c. (471–72)

Indeed, it is primarily through Twain's unpublished journals that one sees his ongoing interest in writing a burlesque of the life of Christ. One can, of course, see some of these elements in such later endeavors as *The Mysterious Stranger Manuscripts,* but "The Second Advent," written in 1881, was his attempt to burlesque the central story, focusing on what would happen if Christ came again in the 1800s. Indeed, within three years after that letter to Orion, Twain had written his burlesque, "The Second Advent," telling the story of Christ's second coming, using it to "make strange" both the Christ story itself and contemporary society. This *risus paschalis,* or "Easter laughter," degrades the elevated story, revealing its roots in gritty folk life, but ultimately, as Bakhtin suggests of such burlesque, invokes "laughter as a joyous regeneration" (RW 78).

The impetus for such a burlesque has many sources. One is imaginative. One might view Twain's frequent use of the Incarnation as a narrative framework for his novels as an attempt to comprehend the Incarnation of Christ, putting it in human terms, incarnating the Incarnation, as it were. In *The Innocents Abroad,* Twain ponders over the difficulty of imagining Christ as a real human being:

> It seems curious enough to us to be standing on ground that was once actually pressed by the feet of the Saviour. The situation is suggestive of a reality and a tangibility that seem at variance with the vagueness and mystery and ghostliness that one naturally attaches to the character of a god. I can not comprehend yet that I am sitting where a god has stood, and looking upon the brook and the mountains which that god looked

upon, and am surrounded by dusky men and women whose ancestors saw him, and even talked with him, face to face, and carelessly, just as they would have done with any other stranger. I can not comprehend this; the gods of my understanding have been always hidden in clouds and very far away. (374)

Through reflective, expressive narrative, Twain does for the Christ story in this passage what he does in "The Second Advent" through burlesque: in Formalist terms, he makes strange the Christ story. Twain focuses here not on the remoteness in time that would be sufficient to inspire a sense of awe on his part, but on the mystery of the Incarnation itself: a god has walked here. Judging by his frequent use of the Incarnation in his narratives, Twain finds both difficult and artistically compelling the very idea that God became man and lived in this place and walked on a particular spot of earth.

In his journal entries, however, Twain envisions much more burlesque ways of fictionalizing Christ's Second Advent. In an 1887 journal entry, he queried, "Who could endure a French Christ?" and in an 1888 journal entry he left the note, "Try to imagine an English Christ" (MTNJ 3: 292, 406). While the former would certainly be more difficult than the latter, Twain mulled over the idea of burlesquing the life of Christ, perhaps having Christ's Second Advent in a location outside of the Holy Land. While Twain presumably wrote "The Second Advent" in 1881, it was never really finished, and all of his notes suggest a burlesque still in a state of evolving.[3] In unpublished notebook entries from the 1890s, Twain imagined Christ in America, speaking with an African American woman who hails him as an old friend, "Good mawnin' Massa Jesus, how'd you leave yo' pa?" (unpublished notebook 31,12). A few years later, Twain wrote that "In [modern] English times, at any period before Anne's time, Christ would have been executed; in these present days, in time of war he might be executed, in time of peace he would be sent to the asylum" (unpublished notebook 37, 45). In each imaginative projection, Twain takes the familiar narrative form and burlesques it with ludicrous details, but always with details that suggest some form of social criticism. Whether it is a Christ from another nationality or a Christ in period clothing, Twain imagines burlesque details that move the Christ story to another time and place. Twain considered the issue in an 1889 journal entry: "Always (of course) Saviors have come in the costume of the time. Pictures of our Second Advent are going to lose something by this, unless clawhammer coats go out, meantime" (MTNJ 3: 540). In "The Second Advent," too, Twain's angel of the Lord "was clothed according to the fashion of our day. He wore a straw hat, a blue jeans roundabout and pants, and cowhide boots" (55). If Twain depicts a gunslinger God in *Roughing It,* he gives readers a cowboy Christ in "The Second Advent."

Twain employs a myriad of details beyond clothing to burlesque the Christ story in "The Second Advent." The story begins as if to say, O little town of Black Jack, Arkansas, how still we see thee lie: "Black Jack is a very small village lying far away back in the western wilds and solitudes of Arkansas" (53). On the one hand, the setting is very like Bethlehem. Twain makes the point that the place is an insignificant province, much like Bethlehem itself, and is "far removed from the busy world and the interests which animate it" (53). Yet, burlesquing details intrude. Instead of whitewashed buildings—log cabins; instead of Romans—Indians; instead of shepherds—ranchers. Twain essentially substitutes contemporary details for biblical details at every turn, following even the form of the scriptures as he creates his parody. Like Matthew, who traces Christ's "fourteen generations" (1:17), Twain begins by providing the genealogy of the new Christ, telling us that "The Hopkinses were old residents; in fact neither they nor their forerunners for two generations had ever known any other place than Black Jack" (53). These names, too, jar us into really seeing what we have already seen a thousand times; this is the purpose of carnival defamiliarization. The Hopkinses! Instead of Joseph and Mary, the parents of Jesus are, in this story, Jackson Barnes and Nancy Hopkins.

Such defamiliarization of the very familiar story brings it alive in a new way. Visiting the Holy Land, Twain had found it difficult to imagine Christ in the world, and one may consider "The Second Advent" as an imaginative incarnational narrative. While the work burlesques the narrative, it refreshes it, offering something very real with elements left out of the traditional biblical account, such as the courtship prior to Christ's conception and how the inhabitants of the village react when it becomes apparent that Nancy Hopkins is expecting a child—before her marriage. The burlesque of the text begins the burlesque of contemporary society.

But by and by a change came; suddenly all tongues were busy again. Busier, too, than they had ever been at any time before, within any one's memory; for never before had they been furnished with anything like so prodigious a topic as now offered itself: Nancy Hopkins, the sweet young-bride elect, was—

The news flew from lip to lip with almost telegraphic swiftness; wives told it to their husbands; husbands to bachelors; servants got hold of it and told it to the young misses; it was gossiped over in every corner; rude gross pioneers coarsely joked about it over their whisky in the village grocery, accompanying their witticisms with profane and obscene words and mighty explosions of horse laughter. (54)

With details of pioneer life and words like "telegraphic," Twain asserts at every point the strangeness of the Christ story in this environment, but he also asserts the strangeness of the Christ story per se. That is, he makes the story strange so that we actually consider it as a literary fact, and further, he develops the material dramatically to suggest what the event might have been like in a real village, all the while burlesquing the theological concept of the Virgin Birth. The inhabitants of Black Jack, Arkansas, clearly have no doubt as to what happened. The Hopkins girl went astray and devised a story to excuse her misbehavior.

Twain's burlesque stylistics inevitably influence thematics, and one effect of the burlesque is to provoke questioning of the ancient story's viability in the modern age. If it is difficult to imagine that Christ could come again in Arkansas, is it not as difficult to imagine the story is at all *true*? "The Second Advent" places Christ's nativity in a place that, for all its strangeness, does bear some generic similarity to Bethlehem as an out-of-the-way place; the strangeness comes primarily from the contrast between the story and the modern setting, not in Arkansas, but in the world at large. The star over Black Jack, Arkansas, is argued over in the story by astronomers who offer conflicting evidence about whether or not it is Venus, about whether one could actually follow a star, about how close a star could be to Earth, and similar issues. The discussions are unimportant in their content, but very important in the way they are framed. The disagreements are *scientific* disagreements involving hypotheses and proofs; these disputes burlesque attempts by some scientists, particularly in the late-nineteenth century, to justify science and theology. In "The Second Advent," whether the arguments reject faith in favor of science is debatable, for the narrative makes both appear ridiculous. Consider just two examples of Twain's parody of verses from Matthew:

Now when Jesus was born in Bethlehem of Judea in the days of Herod the king, behold, there came wise men from the east to Jerusalem, saying, Where is he that is born King of the Jews? For we have seen his star in the east and are come to worship him. (Matthew 2:1-2).	So at last came certain wise men from the far east, to inquire concerning the matter, and to learn for themselves whether the tale was true or false. These were editors from New York and other great cities, and presidents of Yale and Princeton and Andover and other great colleges. They saw a star shining in the east—it was Venus—and this they resolved to follow. ("The Second Advent" 60)

While the language cadences of Twain's parody come right from the sacred text, the whole attitude is not reverential, but rather polemical. In the parody of Matthew 2:1–2, Twain depicts these modern-day wise men as skeptics who, before they worship Christ, must ascertain whether "the tale was true or false" (58). While Twain begins burlesquing these "wise men from the east" here, he burlesques the nativity as well even by referring to it as a "tale." Identifying the star in the east matter-of-factly as Venus also undermines the validity of the story.

And when they were come into the house, they saw the young child with Mary his mother, and fell down, and worshipped him: and when they had opened their treasures, they presented unto him gifts; gold, and frankincense, and myrrh. (Matthew 2:11).	Then the jury and their faction fell upon their knees and worshiped the child, and laid at its feet costly presents: namely, a History of the Church's Dominion During the First Fourteen Centuries; a History of the Presbyterian Dominion in Scotland; a History of Catholic Dominion in England; a History of the Salem Witchcraft; a History of the

> Holy Inquisition; in addition,
> certain toys for the child to
> play with—these being tiny
> models of the Inquisition's
> instruments of torture; and a
> little Holy Bible with the
> decent passages printed in
> red ink. ("The Second
> Advent" 61)

Likewise, the parody of Matthew 2:11 follows the original closely, but burlesques a number of targets, beginning of course with the sacred text itself. In both cases, the wise men fall down and worship the child, but Twain substitutes a library of the abuses perpetrated by Christian churches rather than the traditional gold, frankincense, and myrrh. Twain introduces both lists the same way, but he parodies the original for religious and social commentary.

Among the "wise men" were newspaper editors not convinced by the earlier debates, and the ensuing legal disputes over intercessory prayer, "hearsay evidence," and "special providences" make the matter of Christ's advent look ridiculous by subjecting their discussion to standards of legal proof (61). Twain then essentially inverts the logical argumentation. Rather than argue that there is no such thing as special providence, and having people state that they offered intercessory prayers that were met, he imagines what it would be like if *all* intercessory prayers were answered. Like the "real" baby that Twain wants as part of the Holy Family, one can view this as Twain's attempt to attack a false theology that emanates from false depictions of Christ. One should point out that large portions of "The Second Advent" were originally part of "The Holy Children" (1870s–81), the protagonists of which were "pale and fragile little creatures" much like the emaciated depictions of the baby Jesus Twain criticized (71). Christ's apostles first pray for rain, but when the rain causes massive flooding and hardship, they then pray for it to stop. People react positively to the lesson they have witnessed.

> There was rejoicing in all religious hearts, because the unbelieving had always scoffed at prayer and said the pulpit had claimed that it could accomplish everything, whereas none could prove that it was able to accomplish anything at all. Unbelievers had scoffed when prayers were

offered up for better weather, and for the healing of the sick, and the stay-
ing of epidemics, and the averting of war—prayers which no living man
had ever seen answered, they said. (63)

Disaster results, as one might expect, for "[e]very blessing they brought
down upon an individual was sure to fetch curses in its train for other
people" (66). If one person prays for rain, another person suffers a flood;
if one person prays for relief from the heat, others freeze. Twain even
burlesques Christ's most important miracles involving healing and raising from the dead by imagining the disputes that would arise among
prospective heirs or even enemies of the temporarily deceased. One
lawyer in court cites the resurrection of Lazarus as a form of case law,
arguing that "if Lazarus left any property behind him he most certainly
found himself penniless when he was raised from the dead" (65–66). The
Lazarus text is one that Twain burlesques very specifically, for of all the
miracles, resurrecting the dead is central to Christ's Incarnation. It is in
this context that Christ states, "I am the resurrection, and the life" (John
11:25), and it is also the resurrection of Lazarus that prompts Caiaphas,
the high priest, and the others to take "counsel together for to put him
to death" (John 11:53). In Twain's parodic account, it is the "raising of
the dead and restoring the dying to health" that prompts the citizens to
pass resolutions forbidding Christ and "the holy Twelve" from perform-
ing any miracles; when they do, "they were hunted down, one after the
other, by the maddened populace, and crucified" (68).

"OUR LORD & SAVIOUR JESUS CHRIST
THE FORGOTTEN SON OF GOD" (MTNJ 2: 571)

Burlesque is its own reward; one of the most charming attributes of
Mark Twain as a writer is his inclination to burlesque *any* literary form
that is either sacred, well established, or even momentarily popular. An
existing form thus suggests its own burlesque, but particular situations
in society often motivated burlesque as well. Throughout the 1870s,
Twain used the idea of the Second Advent to make political points. In a
letter to Whitelaw Reid in 1873, Twain wrote about the murderer
William Foster, suggesting he might be "the Second Advent," offering
the further opinion that "Judas Iscariot was nothing but a low, mean,
premature Congressman" (MTL 5: 311–12). In 1872, Twain likewise criticized Mayor Hall, the Tammany politico who had survived numerous

prosecutions but still greeted visiting dignitaries on behalf of the city: "Is there no keeping this piece of animated putridity in the background? If the Second Advent shall transpire in our times, will he step forward, hat in hand, &—. But of course the man is equal to anything" (MTL 5: 245). Most notable is Twain's 1901 parody "Battle Hymn of the Republic (Brought Down to Date)." In this parody, Twain substitutes a "bandit gospel" for the real one, suggesting that the example of Christ is all but forgotten in an age when "Greed is marching on" (474). Twain wrote that parody to criticize the actions of the United States government in the Philippines, labeling the military actions unwarranted adventurism undertaken for business interests. In "The Second Advent," Twain similarly creates a "bandit gospel" in parody that uses the Christ story to satirize his own culture. Many prominent personages appear in the work, including Horace Greeley, the presidents of Princeton and Andover, and the Reverend De Witt Talmadge. Louis J. Budd suggests that Twain was even singling out Arkansas for criticism "because it acted like the other ex-Rebel states while lacking their traditional glamour" (101). The locale for the Nativity certainly suggests gambling and has a backwoods connotation, and Twain may be toying with the idea of the game of blackjack, wherein one card is face up and the other face down; with the first advent already revealed, now we are witnessing the revealing of the second "card," so to speak. Christ was born in "Bethlehem of Judea," and Twain may also have been playing with the names (Matthew 2:1).

In evaluating the import of "The Second Advent," one must consider whom Christ causes trouble for in the burlesque. On the one hand, this Christ does cause trouble for those who embrace the doctrine of special providences, for in answering *all* of their prayers, Christ blesses them with too much of a good thing. Twain's satiric point is obvious. Christ causes trouble for others in the fictional account, too, and here Twain's burlesque of the story more obviously serves the ends of the original. Christ meets with trouble in "The Second Advent" and is crucified, just as he is in the original text, but Christ essentially serves the same social, if not spiritual, function as in the original. That is, the real Christ, son of a carpenter, causes trouble for the scribes and pharisees, just as Christ, son of the blacksmith, causes trouble for the scribes and pharisees of the 1870s and 1880s. For them, Christ was, as Twain wrote in his journal, "Our Lord & Savior Jesus Christ the forgotten Son of God" (MTNJ 2: 571). Among these contemporary scribes are some of Twain's favorite targets.

One of these targets is the Reverend Dr. T. De Witt Talmage, pastor of

Brooklyn's Central Presbyterian Church. Twain was incensed at an article Talmage had written suggesting, seemingly with poorly written satiric purpose, that working men had no place in church if they could not bathe properly before attending. Twain responded with all the satiric power of which he was such an able practitioner. In "About Smells" (1870), Twain imagines Talmage as one of the twelve apostles, but one who would have complained about having to preach to "people of villainous odor every day" (49). Most pointedly, Twain suggests that Talmage "could not have stood the fishy smell of some of his comrades who came from around the Sea of Galilee" (49). "Master," Twain's Talmage informs Christ, "if thou art going to kill the church thus with bad smells, I will have nothing to do with this work of evangelization" (49).

Twain casts Talmage in precisely the same role in "The Second Advent." Notable in the story for his enthusiastic endorsement of Christ, he seems more like one of the raftsmen from *Adventures of Huckleberry Finn* (1885) than a disciple when he first appears.

> Then a young man of the other party, named Talmage, rose in a fury of generous enthusiasm, and denounced the last speaker as a reprobate and infidel, and said he had earned and would receive his right reward in the fullness of time in that everlasting hell created and appointed for his kind by this holy child, the God of the heavens and the earth and all that in them is. Then he sprang high in the air three times, cracking his heels together and praising God. (61)

Talmage has just consigned Horace Greeley to hell, for Twain uses the editor of the *New York Tribune* as an exemplar of the newsman after facts, not faith. Ironically, Talmage turns out to be correct in this fictional account of the second coming of Christ, and Twain criticizes him more for his religious enthusiasm than for his stand on whether this child born in Black Jack is truly the son of God. Twain's Talmage is somewhat startling as a holy roller who "flung himself down, with many contortions, and wallowed in the dirt before the child, singing praises and glorifying God" (62). Attacking Talmage for his overly refined olfactory sense, Twain burlesques him still further by depicting the staid Presbyterian divine as a Bible-pounding holy roller. One thinks of the many works in which Twain satirizes such "wildcat" religious enthusiasm, notably the camp meeting episode in *Adventures of Huckleberry Finn*.

In "The Second Advent," Twain actually refers to his earlier attack on Talmage when the disciple cites as evidence of the child's godhead "the odors of Eternal Land upon his raiment" (62). Twain's point might seem obscure, but throughout the story the "wise men from the far east," that is to say, New England, argue about the question of the Virgin Birth (58). Talmage's assertion in the story connects his enthusiasm for the idea of the Virgin Birth with his desire to banish the odors of workingmen from the church. Thus, Twain's point is that such divines are a bit *too divine,* and that there was a real world with real life and real odors at Christ's nativity just as there was in his own world: weren't there real animals in that stable? Twain's burlesque of the Virgin Birth is simply part of his criticism of organized religion's attempt to deny Christ's human qualities—just as in *The Adventures of Tom Sawyer* he burlesques religion's attempt to deny the human qualities of humans. Twain tries to imagine in this work what the "real Christ" was like, as opposed to the prissy examples offered by the church. The idea of a Christ child so real "every woman would want to bite him" motivates the story (MTNJ 2: 235). Twain's "Second Advent" is a literary incarnation of the Christ story, returning the human side to Christ he saw as edited out by gospels, preachers, and artists.

Twain's criticism of Talmage extended even further, for he identifies him as the Judas figure in "The Second Advent." In the end, when the second Christ and the disciples are all crucified, St. Talmage alone escapes. Clearly, Talmage is for Twain the Judas of contemporary American society who betrays Christ's message. Talmage becomes the second Judas for the Second Advent, betraying Jesus Barnes for "thirty pieces of silver" (68). Religious enthusiasm is always suspect in Twain, for one suspects it must be either hypocritical or a "wildcat" religion, and Talmage's betrayal of Christ shows both Twain's suspicion of emotional religion and his anger at genteel religion. Both are somewhat uncomfortably combined in the character Talmage.

Perhaps Twain's greatest burlesque of his own era in "The Second Advent" is his parody of the second chapter of Luke, in which the angel appears to the shepherds. The wonderful line from the King James Version, "Glory to God in the highest, and on earth peace, good will toward men" (2:14), is lost in Twain's version. Twain preserves the music, having angels join the "choir of drovers who were ranching in the vicinity," but destroys the harmony of the original (59). The angels and drovers sing the same words, but to different tunes, producing an effect not unlike the congregational singing Twain mocks in "A Sunday in Carson" (1863) and *The Adventures of Tom Sawyer* (1876). After the singing, there is no peace, only disagreement, with the various factions of "wise men" arguing about the divinity of the child (59). From the "special providences" that cause so much trouble in Black Jack, Arkansas, to the nascent theological disputes prompted by the Second Advent, people in Twain's story seem incapable of self-government and unworthy of the blessings granted them.

"LORD, THY WILL, NOT MINE, BE DONE"

Clearly, Twain's story burlesques both the Christ story itself and contemporary society. Like such burlesques as "Barnum's First Speech in Congress" (1867), the work mocks a religiously inflected literary form, but fulfills some part of the original's intent. In the case of "The Second Advent," Twain dabbles in the writing of apocrypha to create a text that mocks both the original text, questioning whether it remains applicable in the modern era, even as he uses the text to call the modern era to account. Burlesque has indeed a "double vision," as Cox says (44). The structure of "The Second Advent" resembles in this regard the epochal switch of *A Connecticut Yankee in King Arthur's Court* (1889) that affords Twain the opportunity to criticize the contemporary world and the largely literary world of the Arthurian past. In "The Second Advent," Twain brings the story of the past (with the additional complication that the story told in the past predicts that its central character will return to complete the story) into the present to see whether the ancient narrative has a place in the nineteenth century.

Orthodoxy and burlesque are not necessarily inimical, and Twain concludes with a traditional Christian message—with a Calvinist spin—directed at contemporary readers. This is the lesson of Christ's crucifixion—"Lord, Thy will, not mine, be done."

> *Resolved,* That since no one can improve the Creator's plans by procuring their alteration, there shall be but one form of prayer allowed in Arkansas henceforth, and that form shall begin and end with the words, *"Lord, Thy will, not mine, be done;"* and whosoever shall add to or take from this prayer, shall perish at the stake. (68)

Twain turns the line to parody, for it is now a "resolution" rather than a prayer, but still it does remember its origins. The line is a quotation from Christ's heartfelt address to God while praying in the garden of Gethsemane: "Father, if thou be willing, remove this cup from me: nevertheless not my will, but thine, be done" (Luke 22:42; see also Matthew 26:39 and Mark 14:36).

This *risus paschalis* occurs often in Twain's work. In the attributed piece, "The Stock Broker's Prayer" (1863), Twain parodies "The Lord's Prayer": "Our father Mammon who are in the Comstock, bully is thy name; let thy dividends come, and stocks group, in California as in Washoe" (93). Similarly, in "Our Stock Remarks" (1862), Twain reported that "'[t]here seems to be some depression in this stock. We mentioned yesterday that our Father which are in heaven. Quotations of lost reference, and now I lay me down to sleep,' &c., &c., &c." (176). Such *parodia sacra* has a social function, for Twain obviously targets a culture that has elevated money over God. Twain might also be called the writer who corrupted "The Lord's Prayer" in "The Man That Corrupted Hadleyburg"(1899). Hadleyburg's motto on the official seal had been "LEAD US NOT INTO TEMPTATION," but Twain parodies the Lord's Prayer by having it changed to, "LEAD US INTO TEMPTATION" (438). The parody ironically asserts that to be honest one must recognize the vast gulf separating Christ and Christians.[4] Through these burlesques, Twain focuses less on the grace of Christ, on his salvific power, and more on the extent to which people fail to reach his standard. In this sense alone are Twain's burlesques antiorthodox, for they often focus on man's depravity rather on Christ's power to redeem. Arguably, these parodies that seem to violate Twain's earlier suggestion that one should not refer to Christ "lightly, profanely, or otherwise than with the profoundest reverence" fulfill the text rather than destroy it (Mark Twain's Letters, Paine Edition, I: 323). What is the effect of elevating "Lord, Thy will, not mine, be done" as the essential truth of the Christian faith? With the burlesque, Twain reinstates the Christic mythos. In effect, Twain gives the example of Christ's prayer to God, suggesting that all believers should pray that his will, not ours, be done.

Twain's conclusions in "The Second Advent" resemble his assertions in his parody of "The Apostle's Creed," probably written during the 1880s around the same time as his burlesque of Christ.

I BELIEVE in God the Almighty.

I do not believe He has ever sent a message to man by anybody, or delivered one to him by word of mouth, or made Himself visible to mortal eyes at any time or in any place.

I believe that the Old and New Testaments were imagined and written by man, and that no line in them was authorized by God, much less inspired by Him.

I think the goodness, the justice, and the mercy of God are manifested in His works; I perceive that they are manifested toward me in this life; the logical conclusion is that they will be manifested toward me in the life to come, if there should be one.

I do not believe in special providences. ("Three Statements" 56)

Twain's parody of "The Apostles' Creed" is notable both in what formally remains the same and what is burlesqued. His first line is the only line that remains essentially unchanged from the original, "I believe in God the Father Almighty." Other lines begin with more uncertainty, contrasting to the origin of the word "creed," from the first line "ego credo," I believe: "I do not believe," "I believe," "I think," "I do not believe," "I cannot see how," "There may be," "I believe," and "If I break" (56–57). As one can sense even from the beginnings of the sentences in Twain's creed, after the first line one gets a long list of qualifications. These qualifications refer to Christian doctrine generally, and also to the doctrine embodied in the creed specifically. Twain's parodic version of "The Apostle's Creed" rejects much Christian doctrine, and it is truly antigenre, for the original was spoken by the apostles to voice their belief in Christ's life and ministry as part of God's plan. Twain's creed leaves only the sovereign God intact. His creed praises God, not Christ. Even his slight change to the initial line of the creed by removing the word "Father" from his version strips God of the paternal role asserted by the original, just as, in effect, it removes the son both in form and content. God is defined simply as "God the Almighty."

Similarly, it is ironic that Twain burlesques the story of Christ to reinforce the Sovereignty of God in "The Second Advent." Yet this degradation offers up a text drawn from that story that has all the greater moral force. One of the resolutions made in the story is that "the Supreme Being is able to conduct the affairs of this world without the assistance of any person in Arkansas" (68). Similar sentiments appear in such works as *What Is Man?* in which Twain takes as the text for his dialogue the sovereignty of God and the depravity of humankind. In an 1886 notebook entry Twain fulminated, "Special providence! That phrase nauseates me—with its implied importance of mankind & triviality of God" (MTNJ 3: 246). Twain's burlesque of Christ's life is truly a parodic double of the original, for it follows the form closely only to invert its central point—God's grace visible in the Incarnation of Christ. Instead, Twain's burlesque life of Christ reinstates the importance of God and the relative triviality of man; indeed, one must propose that Twain asserts the relative triviality of Christ. Christ, defined by Calvin as the mediator, provides neither a means of grace in Twain's burlesque nor an *exemplum fidei* in his life and ministry; only in his supreme moment of submission to the sovereign God does Christ provide a lesson for Christians to follow.

{ C H A P T E R   5 }

THE MORPHOLOGY OF MARTYRDOM

Fairy Tale, Epic, and Hagiography in Personal
Recollections *of Joan of Arc*

The author did not invent the content of his work; he only developed that
which was already embedded in tradition.
—MIKHAIL BAKHTIN (MHS 166)

Martyrdom covers a multitude of sins.
—MARK TWAIN (unpublished notebook 46, 16)

DESPITE HIS LATER practice of referring to himself as "Saint Mark," in
a mock canonization, Twain was not inclined to view saints positively.
In *The Innocents Abroad* (1869), for example, Twain summarily dismiss-
es saints and their relics as "Jesuit humbuggery" (45). Relics of the saints
trigger comedy rather than reverence, with Twain chiding, "as for the
bones of St. Denis, I feel certain we have seen enough of them to duplicate him, if necessary" (131). Twain complains less about the idea of
sainthood than about relics and the depictions of them, labeling them
"rude" (103), "coarse" (187, 237), and "grotesque" (164). Twain finds
these visual depictions of the saints unintentionally grotesque, using his
own "grotesque realism" to undermine their reverential seriousness. He
even connects his own use of the term "grotesque" to the origin of the
word when visiting grottoes littered with the bones of dead monks and
saints. A monk who relates the stories of these deceased servants recites
the oral correlatives of the "saints' lives," but Twain finds the tales "as

grotesque a performance, and as ghastly, as any I ever witnessed" (238). Inspecting the "dried-up monks," Twain notices a skull cackling "the jolliest laugh, but yet the most dreadful, that one can imagine" (239). Just as in *Roughing It* (1872), Twain uses "grotesque realism" to undermine the dry seriousness of theology. One sees in *The Innocents Abroad* Protestant chauvinism as well as aesthetic criticism, for Twain questions not solely the theological concept of a saint, but the aesthetic practices of martyrology:

> Here and there, on the fronts of roadside inns, we found huge, coarse frescoes of suffering martyrs like those in the shrines. It could not have diminished their sufferings any to be so uncouthly represented. We were in the heart and home of priestcraft—of a happy, cheerful, contented ignorance, superstition, degradation, poverty, indolence, and everlasting unaspiring worthlessness. (164)

Twain poses here two specific problems of martyrology in *The Innocents Abroad,* problems that would crop up again some twenty-five years later while writing *Personal Recollections of Joan of Arc* (1896). The first is that the uncouth representations of martyrs seem inherently grotesque to Twain but not to devotees of the saint. In *The Innocents Abroad,* the monk who relates the stories of the bones, for example, is oblivious to the grotesque narrative he himself delivers, reciting the facts "quietly" (238). The form is altogether too generic to appeal to Twain, for he always inhabits his genres creatively, sometimes explosively, as he does when making a form that is unintentionally grotesque even more grotesque through his depiction of it. Twain depicts the iconographic form itself as perhaps even more dead than the saints it depicts. Twain details his understanding of the stereotyped forms of martyrology when describing his visit to Italy, for example, confessing that "when I had seen one of these martyrs, I had seen them all. They all have a marked family resemblance to each other" (187). Twain lists the iconographic traits of these "painted monks and martyrs," but he also comments on the "trade-mark" of each saint, the traditional iconography that identities the individual precisely (187–88). Ironically, though the saints themselves are believed to have regenerative powers, the form itself is dead.

The ideology inherent in the martyrological form is likewise alien to Twain, for it expresses the "peculiar devotional spirit of the olden time, which placed a higher confidence in outward forms of worship than in the watchful guarding of the heart against sinful thoughts and the hands against sinful deeds"(197). Identifying, from a Protestant perspective, a fundamental divergence from Catholicism, Twain sounds like Calvin, explicitly rejecting those "forms of worship," just as he recoils from the artistic forms of martyrology. Calvin, who praises the saints and terms them such, still rejects the "fancied intercession" of saints, arguing that those who pray to saints "dishonour Christ, and rob him of his title of sole Mediator" (II: 169). Twain criticizes this practice on the same grounds, saying that Catholicism ranks Christ in the fifth place, after the Virgin Mary, the Deity, Peter, and some "twelve or fifteen canonized Popes and martyrs" (*Innocents Abroad* 242). "No prayer is offered to Christ," Twain hotly asserts in *The Innocents Abroad,* and he "seems to be of little importance any where in Rome" (242). Later, in *A Connecticut Yankee in King Arthur's Court* (1889), Twain returns with vigor to the question of saints and martyrs, and his project is, in some ways, an attempt to create burlesque origination fables for the saints, just as he does for England, thus destroying the foundation of worshipful attention toward both saints and knights in the nineteenth century.

When Twain published his *Personal Recollections of Joan of Arc* in 1896, it struck many with the force of a sea change, for it seemed a ringing endorsement of saints, martyrs, and the Catholic church. The anonymous critic for the *Methodist Review* favorably compared the work to *The Innocents Abroad,* noting that many have "long known that he was capable of better things . . . than a delightful maker of mere horse merriment" (Anonymous 845). Most telling was the response of the Catholic literary community. In 1890, Father Daniel Hudson, writing in the University of Notre Dame's *Ave Maria,* had voiced the opinion of most Catholics when he labeled Twain's *A Connecticut Yankee in King Arthur's Court* "an insult to Catholics" and "an irreverent, vulgar, and stupid volume" (116). Father Hudson's review of *Personal Recollections of Joan of Arc* in *The Ave Maria* was much more favorable, and he believed Twain "portrayed [St. Joan's] beauty of character with a power and sympathy of which no other writer in the English tongue . . . has so far been capable" (729).

Modern critics, too, consider Twain's ideological attitudes toward Catholicism and how such attitudes might have influenced his work. Edward Rosenberger falls just short of identifying Twain's book as another of the saint's miracles, labeling Twain an "agnostic hagiographer" (717). Rosenberger contends that in writing the book, Twain was "doing violence to his theology, contradicting most of his written convictions, completely indulging his one leaning towards faith" (723). Seeking to save the work from perceived irrelevancy in a postbelief era,

Susan K. Harris suggests one should ignore what she believes Twain's intentions were. "Rather than dismissing the novel for its hagiography, however, we should look beyond Mark Twain's intentions to his achievements" ("Narrative" 48). In an era like our own that has extended the canon to include virtually every sort of peripheral genre as worthy of study *on its own terms*, it is notable that hagiography, apparently, is not to be granted that courtesy. Regardless of what critics think of the work today, Twain felt it was his most important work, consistently ranking it above even *Adventures of Huckleberry Finn* (see for example his letter of February 22, 1902 to Helene Picard; Mark Twain's Letters, Paine Edition, II: 719). He claimed to have labored over the project for twelve years, working in a meticulous way indicative of his level of commitment, even belief, in the work. Years later, he wrote to Henry Rogers, "I have never done any work before that cost so much thinking and weighing and measuring and planning and cramming, or so much cautious and painstaking execution" (MTHHR 623). How can one justify ignoring the very work the author felt was his greatest achievement? There must be something in the work that is central to Twain's craft and crucial to understanding him as a writer. Twain referred to *Personal Recollections of Joan of Arc,* after all, when claiming in his *Autobiography* that there exists "only one right form for a story" (267). Form. Twain's *Personal Recollections of Joan of Arc* should not be rejected as hagiography; it ought to be rigorously analyzed *as* hagiography.

Those critics who reject the work because Twain wrote hagiography beg the question in any event, for not a single one of them defines what is meant by the term. Implicitly, hagiography is what happens when one writes about a saint. Would such a work necessarily be a part of Twain's "counter-theology" (Brodwin, "Theology" 235), "anti-orthodoxy" (J. Smith 13), or more generally a retreat from his early Calvinist training? If in fact *Personal Recollections of Joan of Arc* marks a turn toward Rome, it would so qualify, for such a move would be counter to both mainstream Protestant culture of the time and Twain's own upbringing. However, given that Twain's attitudes toward Catholicism remained negative before, during, and after the writing of the work, one must find some other, more reasonable, explanation to make sense of it. *Personal Recollections of Joan of Arc* marks no sea change in Twain's attitudes toward the Roman Catholic Church, or indeed toward religion generally.[1]

At the heart of this ideological question lies genre. Existing proof suggests that Twain remained anti-Catholic throughout his life, so the book strikes some as an "anomaly," but the book is anomalous in *generic* ways that shed light on Twain's achievement. For the discussion in this chapter, Bakhtin's description of hagiography as a genre in which "the form assumes a traditional and conventional character" is exceedingly complex and important (AH 185). Bakhtin envisions the form of a saint's life to be "conventional," "sanctioned by incontestable authority," and "merely receptive" (AH 185). If we understand the hagiographic form to be those stories endorsed by the church, then Bakhtin's definition has some validity. Hagiography has a much longer history than the official history, however, and its origins lie in the oral culture of a folk. Father Delahaye's work with hagiography demonstrates the many elements one sees in the form: "[Hagiography] may assume any literary form suitable to the glorification of the saints, from an official record adapted to the use of the faithful, to a poetical composition of the most exuberant character wholly detached from reality" (2). Father Delahaye records the entire variety of genres washed into hagiography by the "stream of literary activity carrying along with it the debris of the ages": myths, fables, chivalrous tales, legends, and romances (187, 2–3). Such variety of form and content within hagiography leads John Walsh to call it "the most inventive of genres" (1). This generic inventiveness is likewise the hallmark of Twain's work, and for this reason an organic approach discussing the dynamic interplay of form and content is essential. If early reviewers were surprised and in some cases gratified by Twain's seeming turn to Rome, the genre of the book has long been a focal point of disagreement. *The Methodist Review,* for example, questioned "the true nature of the work" but noted its "canonical form," calling it tentatively a "biography" while at the same time identifying it as both a "romance" and a "history" (845). Contemporary critics have labeled the book hagiography (Rosenberger, Harris), "Twain's tedious hagiography" (Stahl "Myth" 215), "divine realism" (Paine II: 1031), a "dramatic monologue" (Bradley 3), a "fictionalized biography" (Maik 10), a "meta-romance" (Zwarg 61), and—most piquantly—"Twain's historical transvestite novel" (Skandera-Trombley 90). Such critical disagreement, not to say confusion, leads Victoria Thorpe Miller to query, "Is this work biography? History? Romance? Some combination of these?" (59). Although she leaves the questions unanswered, these are precisely the questions to ask, for comprehending the genre is crucial to understanding Twain's work. Genre and ideology interrelate in any work, but so much more so in hagiography, rendering the work an anomaly, a "riddle" like Joan herself, until one deciphers the generic structures. Jason Horn's comment is correct: "Twain was to find no literary blueprint for constructing Joan of Arc" (70). That is, Twain rejected many of the stereotyped traits of "official" hagiography as he constructed his work, excluding many of the registered trademarks of the genre, so to speak; instead, he drew on other forms even as he created his own literary work, creating a nearly burlesque hagiography that undermines in many respects the church most associated with hagiography. In so doing, Twain avoided the coarse depictions he had criticized in *The Innocents Abroad,* at the same time reconnecting hagiography to its folk roots, the "popular literature" that Father Delahaye identified as playing an important part in the genre's evolution (222). Writing about the composition of *Personal Recollections of Joan of Arc* in his autobiography, Twain famously stated, "There is only one right form for a story and if you fail to find that form the story will not tell itself" (267). Twain had no single blueprint for his work, nor did he really have a single form; what he had were *three right forms* for *Personal Recollections of Joan of Arc,* each of them allied with the popular folk literature that initially created hagiographic form.

Twain embraces three subgenres of Romance to construct his book, each corresponding to a separate section, though they intertwine throughout. The three strands are the Fairy Tale, Epic, and Hagiography. Twain introduces all three in the first chapters of his book, but then relies on each to provide much of the architectonic structure for books I–III. Thus, Twain relies on the fairy tale to provide the structure for book I, "In Domremy." In book II, "In Court and Camp," the Medieval Epic exerts the primary structural influence, in particular the Chanson de Geste, "The Song of Roland." For book III, "Trial and Martyrdom," Twain relies on the hagiographic form primarily. In the end, these three strands, intertwined throughout and related generically through romance, culminate in one point, Joan of Arc's death. Each of the three operate by a different set of imperatives, for as Bakhtin argues, "every genre has its methods and means of seeing and conceptualizing reality, which are accessible to it alone" (Bakhtin and Medvedev, *Formal* 133). Joan of Arc functions in strand 1 as a fairy tale hero whose defeat at the hands of a wizard or man-pig (Cauchon) results in her death. Strand 2 tells the story of a victorious military leader who, like Roland, saves France at a tremendous personal sacrifice. Strand 3 tells of the confessor of the faith who achieves a martyr's death at the stake. While each of the three genres takes primary responsibility for governing their individual books, their generic imperatives are influenced and at times warped by the competing genres. This is particularly so since all three genres emerged, historically, from the folk culture of magical tricksters, military heroes, and spiritual leaders. The influence of the three genres is immense, for, as Bakhtin argues, literary genres express "the most stable, 'eternal' tendencies" in literature (PDP 106). "A genre lives in the present," he argues, "but always *remembers* its past, its beginning" (PDP 106). In Twain's romance, all three strands remember their past and blend to craft a story of witch-warrior-saint. We see all aspects in Joan of Arc, who first hears her "Voices" at the "Fairy Tree," who wins military renown as the head of a great army, and whose prophecies lead finally to the stake.[2]

The fairy tale element of *Personal Recollections of Joan of Arc* includes both the surface elements of content, such as the inclusion of certain fairy tale character types, and the underlying structural element. As such, the fairy tail genre operates in the work as a structural *primus inter pares.* By applying Vladimir Propp's system of analysis described in *Morphology of the Folktale,* one can see the bones of the narrative plainly, and they are the ancient, bleached bones of the fairy tale as well as the holy relics of a saint. A major assumption made by Propp is that fairy tales can be studied the way a scientist studies a biological specimen. "The result will be," explains Propp, "a morphology (i.e., a description of the tale according to its component parts and the relationship of these components to each other and to the whole)" (19). Propp begins with a set of principles, assuming that fairy tales can be analyzed by the "functions of characters" as opposed to themes, and further asserts that the "sequence of functions is always identical" (21–22). Commenting on Propp's morphology, Roman Jakobson suggests that the "rigid structural laws" governing fairy tales exist because "both language and folklore demand a collective consensus and obey a subliminal communal censorship" (*Main Trends* 48). One can apply Propp's morphology to many literary forms, but it is particularly appropriate for hagiographic analysis, given the genre's folkloric roots. Moreover, as Father Delahaye maintains, hagiography is both remarkably inventive and yet quite wedded to its traditions, accounting for the "family resemblance" Twain had noted. "This is the result," Father Delahaye suggests, "of eliminating as far as possible the individual element, in order to retain only the abstract form" (24).

Many critics have taken Propp's morphology to task for precisely this abstraction, which is, in fact, its primary virtue. In their critiques of Propp, structuralists such as Claude Lévi-Strauss and A. J. Greimas seek, in essence, to rethematize formal analysis, subsuming form into content,

often for specific ideological agendas; both have been said to have updat-
ed or revised Propp, when in reality they distort his distinctive contribution. Greimas, while identifying Propp as an important "precursor"
(205), pursues "a more general actantial model" that in reality differs
from Propp nearly as much as his Marxist critics had in 1928 (223).
Propp had set his functional analysis in opposition to the Arne-Thomp-
son thematic catalogue, but Greimas uses this as a "point of departure
for a description of the relationship between functions," which in practice dissolves formal considerations into discussions of content (223). So,
too, does Lévi-Strauss submerge form into the content of myth, criticizing Propp's morphology for its "high level of abstraction" (180). These
criticisms reveal the strength of Propp's morphology, which preserves
the integrity of form in its dialogic relationship to content, providing an
x-ray of the objects it studies. More recently, Paul Ricoeur seriously mis-
reads Propp's achievement when he suggests it imprisons readers and
presumably critics, too (2: 39). "The form is that of the single story
underlying all the variants," Ricoeur argues, further suggesting that
"every Russian fairy tale in the collection Propp works with is only a
variant of a single fairy tale" (2: 34). Propp simply seeks to uncover the
deep structures that govern the fairy tale genre, not limit the kinds of
stories one *may* tell or the interpretations one tale may provoke; such
numbers are limitless. One should not deduce from one hundred stops
on a subway the lesson that all journeys are the same, or that the stories
told about those journeys would be the same. Moreover, Propp does not
state that his morphology is all; rather, quite the opposite, he states that
it is a useful starting point in literary analysis, albeit one that many leap
over in ways more saltatory than salutary. In *Theory and History of Folklore,* Propp responds to his critics, also reiterating his earlier point that
"formal analysis, that is, a careful systematic description of the material,
is the first condition, prerequisite, and the first step of historical
research" (71–72). Indeed, for a study such as the present one, which
unites an attention to form and content, Propp's morphology reveals precisely those *ideological* issues that have stultified generations of critics.
The surface elements in Twain's work suggesting the fairy tale origins of
the plot are many: the fairy tree, the fairies themselves, an ogre, a talking
pig, a princess in a dungeon, and an accused witch who is killed at story's
end. More significant than these *trace* elements of the fairy tale genre,
however, which might be ascribed to mere "mood" or "atmosphere," are
the underlying structural elements that generate them, the "abstract
form" analyzed so well by Father Delahaye and Vladimir Propp.

$$\alpha \left\{ \begin{matrix} \gamma^2\delta^2 \\ \gamma^1\delta^1 \end{matrix} \right\} A^{19}\uparrow D^2 :[E^9F^9G^2 \left\{ \begin{matrix} H^1H^3 \\ I^1I^3 \end{matrix} \right\}]^3 K^8K^9[Pr^3Pr^6]^3=Rs^{10}T^3:UW$$

Figure 5.1 Twain's work expressed in Propp's morphology

Propp's morphology allows for a detailed analysis of a tale's structure and a description of it using a system of functional notations. By applying the morphology to *Personal Recollections of Joan of Arc,* one can see that Twain's work follows the pattern of a fairy tale. One can express Twain's work in the form of an equation (Figure 5.1).

Twain considered the work one of his best written tales and, along with *The Prince and the Pauper* (1874), it is generally thought one of his most carefully crafted tales, even by those who dislike the result. Twain spent a great deal of time searching for the "one right form" for his story; whether he made a systematic study of fairy tale form is impossible to say, but given what we know of the kind of research the writer engaged in for his work, it is a possibility that cannot be discounted. Certainly, as Victor Royce West proves in his early and important study *Folklore in the Works of Mark Twain,* the writer had a wide knowledge of folklore gained from both "book-derived traditions" and the oral traditions of African American slaves and other inhabitants of the Mississippi Valley (77–78). Regardless of the source, what emerges from the morphological analysis bears out Twain's claims about careful execution, explaining many of the ideological questions involving his attitudes toward Catholicism and the supposed sea change of *Personal Recollections of Joan of Arc.* Twain structures this tale according to the dictates of some of the most ancient forms of folk narrative, employing the three narrative strands in highly complex ways that reveal his great artistry even while clarifying some points of ideology suggested by his writing the life of a saint. "Form and content in discourse are one," Bakhtin reminds us, and analyzing one will always reveal the other; a scholar's ideological biases are easily discerned in criticism, but one can gain a full awareness of the *writer's* ideological preoccupations only through an organic analysis. In *Personal Recollections of Joan of Arc,* Twain's ideological biases can be revealed only by conducting an analysis of the morphology of martyrdom in the work.

BOOK I: THE FAIRY LAND

The initial situation in book I, denoted α in the morphology, is that a young girl, who later becomes the famed Joan of Arc, grows up in a rural French province. As in so many fairy tales, little is expected of the child. Yet the rural locale is important and is set in contrast to the king and court. As with the stories of the boy who becomes King David and the infant who becomes Christ, both of whom the girl is compared to in the text, Joan of Arc's modest origins are marks of distinction rather than the opposite. In the fairy tale genre, one thinks of Hans Clodhopper, Jack the Giant Killer, or Hans My Hedgehog, whose rural naïvete masks a native insight and wisdom that later become apparent. Moreover, the setting in Twain's work is a magical one, and the Church's sway over pagan beliefs is incomplete. The narrator, Sieur Louis de Conte, lavishes much attention, particularly in the work's early chapters, on details belonging to fairy tale: "prodigious dragons that spouted fire and poisonous vapors from their nostrils"; Joan of Arc's "voices"; the fairies; and the fairy tree they dance around, *"l'Arbre Fée de Bourlemont"* (558, 564). Twain, argues Jason Horn, "was not willing to allow the Church to absorb the lore of the fairy tree, along with the supernatural powers associated with it, into its own. Rather, he set the Church in conflict with the power of the tree, and thus against, Joan, who plays within its shadow" (87). This is a significant point, for even when the genres of fairy tale, epic, and hagiography intertwine in medieval romance, it is most typical of that genre and time that "both the supernatural forces and the world order in which they function explicitly emanate from God," as Ojars Kratins observes (354). This is certainly not the case with Twain's romance, in which the fairy tale elements serve to blunt the "official" hagiographic elements.

The fairy tale proceeds with the usual pattern of conflicting orders. On the one hand, Joan of Arc's voices order her to travel to the governor and request from him an army to liberate France. This charge is noted as γ^2 and is opposed by her father's interdiction γ^1. Joan of Arc's simultaneous adherence to the angelic voices and the violation of her father's interdiction are denoted δ^2 and δ^1 respectively. The scene where Joan receives her charge is at once pagan and biblical, and de Conte describes it as

> a most strange thing, for I saw a white shadow come slowly gliding along the grass toward the Tree. It was of grand proportions—a robed form, with wings—and the whiteness of this shadow was not like any other

whiteness that we know of, except it be the whiteness of the lightnings, but even the lightnings are not so intense as it was, for one can look at them without hurt, whereas this brilliancy was so blinding that it pained my eyes and brought the water into them. I uncovered my head, perceiving that I was in the presence of something not of this world. My breath grew faint and difficult, because of the terror and the awe that possessed me. (599–600)

The passage contains biblical cadences that clearly associate the scene with many cognate passages in scripture, the transfiguration not the least among them (See Matthew 17:2, Mark 9:3; and Luke 9:29). One also thinks also of Job's "Fear came upon me, and trembling" (4:14). At the same time, although Joan of Arc knows that the figure is the archangel Michael, readers are kept in ignorance until the next chapter. In the description above, the experience is uncanny, magical, and pagan, for the figure is not necessarily angelic, but simply "something not of this world" (600). Only later is the passage brought into the Judeo-Christian fold.

Revealed as the Archangel Michael, however, this figure has the authority to command Joan to approach the governor. Any angel's voice would count, presumably, but Michael's is of such antiquity and tradition that it is practically unassailable. Yet, his charge is opposed by a charge itself bearing great authority. After Joan of Arc's initial approach fails, her father learns of her plan and forbids her from approaching the governor again, saying "rather than see her unsex herself and go away with the armies, he would require her brothers to drown her; and that if they should refuse, he would do it with his own hands" (610). Her father's threat presages the later conflict with church authorities; both her father and the Church renounce their positions as antagonists later, the church doing so only after killing Joan of Arc.

The conflict over the voices, and between Joan of Arc, her father, and the church government, is essentially a conflict between hierarchies of authority. On another occasion, Joan of Arc and her father spar over the feeding of a vagrant soldier. Defying her father's orders, Joan welcomes the soldier, who later recites "The Song of Roland," a major epic strand in the work. She similarly spars with the church authorities who conflict with the dictates of her inner voices. The introduction of the epic strand at this juncture is significant, for it elevates the argument with her father and the Church to an epic and theological plane. In "The Song of Roland," the French are engaged in a religious conflict—fighting against the Moors. Twain had good reason to invoke the French national epic, for the epic theme of battle is one of the narrative strands, but the thematic similarity between Joan of Arc's battle and Roland's is unmistakable. Just as Roland fought against a dangerous religious foe, so too does Joan of Arc engage in a battle to purge French soil of a foreign adversary, the English. Just as Roland fought against the Moors, Joan of Arc battles an infidelous French Catholic hierarchy. Twain roundly criticizes the French, first for forgetting the example of the great leader Roland, and later for forgetting the example of the great Joan of Arc.

Over her father's objections, Joan of Arc is determined to fight the English. Figure A[19] refers to a declaration of war in Propp's morphology. In Twain's adaptation of the fairy tale form, the setting renders this idea somewhat equivocal. Joan of Arc's activities occur during the Hundred Years' War and could only with qualification be called a *beginning* of a war, for we are told that "ninety-one years" of the conflict had gone by (783). It is true that, with Joan of Arc following the dictates of her voices, the battle has finally been joined, and one might aptly term it the beginning of the end of the war. As she declares, "God has chosen the meanest of His creatures for this work. . . . I am to lead His armies, and win back France, and set the crown upon the head of His servant that is Dauphin and shall be King" (604). After this declaration, Joan of Arc's behavior changes from one of quietude to one of command and, as the narrator says, "None who met Joan that day failed to notice the change that had come over her" (605). It is somewhat unexpected that such a change occurs in Joan of Arc before her final and successful meeting with the governor, but the fairy tale form, as Propp notes, has the declaration of war occurring before departure and before the meeting or interrogation, and Twain follows that form precisely with his work.

So it is that Joan of Arc departs her childhood home, an action denoted by the figure ↑, and engages in important meetings with the governor, the greeting and interrogating denoted D^2. The figure D^2 is immediately followed by the sign :, indicating trebling. Propp notes the importance of trebling, and its variety:

> We have similar connective elements in various instances of trebling. . . .
> We shall only mention that trebling may occur among individual details
> of an attributive nature (the three heads of a dragon), as well as among
> individual functions, pairs of functions (pursuit-rescue), groups of functions, and entire moves. Repetition may appear as a uniform distribution

(three tasks, three years' serviced), as an accumulation (the third task is the most difficult, the third battle the worst), or may twice produce negative results before the third, successful outcome. (74)

The structural dominant of Twain's work is trebling. Twain builds *Personal Recollections of Joan of Arc* by trebling the generic strands of fairy tale, epic, and hagiography, embodying them in three separate books, but twisting those strands with many other trebled elements. Lévi-Strauss sounds like the formalist Shklovsky talking about "laying bare the device" when he states that trebling "has as its function to make the structure of the myth apparent" ("Structural Study of Myth" 443). In the case of Twain's design, this is ironically true, for fostering a fairy tale milieu is central to how Twain constructs a believable example of hagiography. Readers dispute every detail of theology, but everyone knows that a genie grants three wishes. Twain's insistent trebling makes absolute the folkloric nature of the world he describes. As the Brothers Grimm tell us in "The Cat and the Mouse Set Up Housekeeping," "All good things come in threes," and virtually every action, good or bad, is trebled in Twain's work (7). Joan of Arc's first of three meetings is most telling, for Twain emphasizes the previous conflict between the heavenly commands and the earthly interdicts. When Governor Robert de Baudricourt queries, "Who has sent you with these extravagant messages?" the following exchange occurs:

"My Lord."
"What Lord?"
"The King of Heaven." (608)

Twain's use of the "double-voiced" word "Lord" is highly significant here, for the future saint and the present governor speak different languages and owe fealty to different realms. Governor de Baudricourt interprets the term "Lord" as denoting a particular temporal authority. Joan of Arc, of course, refers to the Lord of the spiritual realm. Both uses would justify capitalization of the term; both demand authority. The collision of their languages increases the drama of the scene, but also asserts the grounds for Joan of Arc's disagreement with all earthly authorities. The trebling increases the drama as well, for Joan of Arc "went and confronted the governor again," but to no avail (616). Following her second trip to the governor, Joan acquires several allies, just as before the second meeting she had acquired wide popular support. The Sieur de Metz swears fealty to Joan of Arc, and then "the very governor himself was going to visit the young girl in her humble lodgings" (617). Twain uses the trebling as an "accumulation" to prepare for Joan of Arc's third visit to the governor, where she adjures him: "In God's name, Robert de Beaudricourt, you are too slow about sending me" (618). She asserts the supremacy of her voices over his one voice, despite the fact that she needs his assent to proceed. All temporal authorities are inferior to the authority of the voices she hears in her head. Just as Twain introduces the epic theme by having the soldier recite portions of "The Song of Roland," he introduces a sublimated discussion of antinomianism through Joan of Arc's consistent adherence to the interior voices as opposed to the exterior ones. Like Twain himself writing in *The Innocents Abroad,* Joan of Arc rejects the outward forms of religion. "If [Joan] was to be a heroine," suggests Louis J. Budd, "her visits from angels and even her prophecies had to be treated with respect" (163). Twain, concludes Budd, "had to let up on Joan's religion" (163). Joan's religion and her prophecies and angels are not one and the same, however, for Twain is no official hagiographer, but a storyteller returning the form to its folk roots. By doing so, particularly in book I, he sublimates Joan's visions in fairy tale. Twain can thus treat *her* with deference, while deferring his discussion about the authenticity of her visions, which can be viewed as part of the magical fairy tale milieu. Generally, Twain disparages prophecies as inexact and misleading, as discussed in chapter 7 of this study. Twain is most critical, however, of Joan's religion. Twain's Joan is hardly a *Catholic* saint at all. This is all the more important given that our narrator finds occasion to mention John Huss, a Protestant martyr who, like Joan of Arc, was burned for valorizing individual authority over authority of the Church; both martyrs champion direct revelation rather than recognized temporal authorities. Twain thus establishes the conflict of *Personal Recollections of Joan of Arc* very quickly, expressing the work's central theme as a mythic opposition between temporal and spiritual authority, but also between the Catholic Church and an important figure in the Protestant Reformation.

The exchange between Joan of Arc and Robert de Baudricourt has something of a carnival element to it as well. In Bakhtin's definition, Carnival involves overturning the usual and ordinary to "degrade an object" and so "hurl it down to the reproductive lower stratum" (RW 21). Joan of Arc's response "My Lord" is a carnival reversal of the expected, and turns the world of the court on its head. This is a central element of hagiography, as Stanley Brodwin suggests, for "the martyrological tragedy gains its emotional force by dramatizing the martyr's act of smashing through or transcending the irreconcilable confrontation between opposing groups, each of which can claim God or the goal of history on its side" ("History" 74). Joan of Arc may not intend her response, "My Lord," to mock, but it is insolent and confrontative. The governor responds in confusion, "What Lord?" Her answer is not, "The Lord, my God," but rather "The King of Heaven." The king, to be sure, but not the pathetic King Henry. Twain creates a carnival "decrowning" of temporal authority—theological and aristocratic—by having Joan of Arc use such language. The King of Heaven has sent her on this errand, and if her mission is, in part, to crown a king of France, it is at the Almighty's behest and not at Henry's command.

BOOK II: PETRIFIED FORMS

The epic form governs "In Court and Camp," the second book. Twain constructs his three-stranded narrative with elements of fairy tale, epic, and hagiography, but once de Beaudricourt gives his support to Joan of Arc, the epic elements are given full sway. In book I, Joan of Arc is "on the verge of a revelation of some sort," a revelation that occurs in book II. Indeed, book II begins both with Joan of Arc's announcement that her voices "are not vague, now, but clear" and with her issuing specific commands (613). Twain depicts Joan of Arc as a leader in this section, in contrast to his treatment of her in most of book I, where he emphasizes her fey qualities. She becomes less of a pagan seer and protomartyr in book II, which finds her becoming an epic hero, one who "hears the roll of the drums and the tramp of marching men" (613). Her bearing, we are told, is "martial" (613). Summing up Joan of Arc's achievements, the narrator makes this statement:

The great deeds of Joan of Arc are five:
- The Raising of the Siege.
- The Victory at Patay.
- The Reconciliation at Sully-sur-Loire.
- The Coronation of the King.
- The Bloodless March (788).

The diction and syntax are those of epic, and the passive voiced "The great deeds of Joan of Arc are five" has cognates in epics from "The Song of Roland" and "El Cid" to "The Lay of Igor's Campaign." The use of the word "deed" itself has an archaic, epic ring about it.

At the same time, the fairy tale elements are still very much in play, and Twain's narrator describes the war in fairy tale terms:

> It was an ogre, that war; an ogre that went about for near a hundred years, crunching men and dripping blood from his jaws. And with her little hand that child of seventeen struck him down; and yonder he lies stretched on the field of Patay, and will not get up any more while this old world lasts. (785)

With its "crunching men and dripping blood" description, the ogre certainly resembles the many monsters common to epic, such as the Cyclops that consumes Odysseus's men or Grendel and the Lady Monster that feed on the Danes in *Beowulf*. The ogre's presence in Twain's narrative indicates the shared familial origins of Fairy Tale and Epic, but also suggests that the narrator lives in a world that still thinks in terms of fairy tale. More to the point, the metaphor re-creates that fairy tale Weltanschauung for the reader through the descriptive medium. The description "makes strange" the field of battle, re-creating it as a fairy tale passage of arms between a heroine and a *real* ogre. The comparison to the ogre is not just a passing one, but is rather an extended metaphor that depicts very vividly the ogre of war, contrasting the large, ravenous creature with the "little hand" that strikes him down. The shift into the present tense, "yonder he lies stretched on the field of Patay," brings the fairy tale world into the present. Like the giant in "Jack and the Beanstalk," the ogre, slain by a much smaller opponent, lies dead. The fairy tale expresses the *reality* of the time, for the time during the Hundred Years' War is inherently *unreal:*

> Children were born, grew up, married, died—the war raged on; *their* children in turn grew up, married, died—the war raged on; *their* children, growing, saw France struck down again; this time under the incredible disaster of Agincourt—and still the war raged on, year after year, and in time *these* children married in their turn. (784)

The narrator brings history into the present, conjures it, one might say, through trebling the magical three: "children," "*their* children," and "*these* children." When the narrator describes music as that "magician of magicians; who lifts his wand and says his mysterious word and all things real pass away and the phantoms of your mind walk before you clothed in flesh," one comprehends that his statement precisely express-es the fairy tale world milieu with which the work is concerned (808). Lawrence Shanahan argues that "whatever reaction Twain expected from his audience when he introduced Joan's visions, he must have anticipated incredulity at de Conte's tales of dragons and fairies" (137–38). Quite the opposite is true; indeed, fairy tale expresses the mythic battles of good and evil and makes the unbelievable believable. In order to make Joan of Arc's visions believable as a story, Twain builds his narrative as a fairy tale, which operates with different standards of believability than other narrative forms. In his admirable study of folk-lore in Twain's work, Victor Royce West rightly suggests that the folk-lore in *Personal Recollections of Joan of Arc* "served as a preparation for the reader's acceptance of Joan's Voices" (9). Reconnecting hagiography with its folk roots, Twain employs the elements of fairy tale to create a believable *fiction*—as fiction. In this, Twain resembles the ultimate author of all hagiography: the folk. The difference between fairy tale and hagiography is between the suspension of disbelief on the one hand and the imposition of belief on the other.

More significant than the fairy tale allusions are the underlying fairy tale structures Twain employs. Twain creates a structure for book II that is very much a fairy tale, featuring the trebling so common in epic and fairy tale battles (Figure 5.2). The outer, square brackets with the super-script three indicate the entire enclosed action occurs three times in suc-cession. Within the brackets, one notes that Joan experiences victory in combat, E^9, occurring with a magical agent appearing of its own accord in time of need, F^9, and that the hero rides into battle G^2. The inner brackets indicate that the hero struggles with the villain in battle, H^1, achieving victory in open battle, I^1. At the same time, the hero engages in a game, a common element in fairy tale battles, H^3, and wins the game, I^3. The game in Twain's work is a metaphorical contest, the coordination

$$[E^9F^9G^2 \left\{ \begin{array}{c} H^1H^3 \\ \\ I^1I^3 \end{array} \right\} I^3$$

Figure 5.2. Trebling in Book II

of the military and political objectives amid many obstacles, not the least among them being the duplicities of the court and king. Specifically, the Sieur Louis de Conte likens Joan's "great acts" to a chess game. "Each move was made in its proper order, and it *was* great and effective because it was made in its proper order and not out of it" (791). One might make similar claims for Twain's *Personal Recollections of Joan of Arc,* for the fairy tale structure underlies every aspect of the work, all in the proper order, and so works its magic even—perhaps especially—when the structural tricks pass unnoticed by readers.

Of Joan of Arc's five achievements, then, three are great military successes: the raising of the Siege of Orleans, the Victory at Patay, and the Bloodless March. In each case, Joan succeeds in battle, and in each case her magical gift of voices appears unbidden in time of need. Shklovsky notes the trebling in "The Song of Roland," such as Roland striking his sword against a rock on three separate occasions, and connects the structure of the epic to that of the folk tale, where such repetitions are common (28). There are many such trebled elements in *Personal Recollections of Joan of Arc,* such as Joan declaring, "The English shall go in three days" (727); announcing, "In three days' time the place is ours" (793); and asserting, "If I had had my freedom three years, I would have delivered him [the duke of Orleans]" (901). In addition to trebling associated with such verbal iterations and repetitions, Twain uses a trebled structure. Joan, as discussed earlier, approaches the governor three times, but is heeded only on the third visit. Likewise, on three separate occasions, she is cross-examined by Catholic authorities. Each example of structural trebling is dramatically attached to a particular book: the visits to the governor belong to book I; the triad of battle belongs to book II; and the triad of Inquisition belongs to book III, though one trial occurs in each book, a significant structural deviation that will be discussed later in this chapter. The trebling of battle is a crucial device for Twain, for it is by far the most dynamic of the three structural features. The three battles, while following the same generic pattern, are quite different in their development, and each victory serves the development of character and plot in distinct ways. These battles do not follow the usual pattern of accumulation noted by Propp, and this is very significant, for the unusual structure reveals much about the ideological questions provoked by Twain's hagiography.

Joan of Arc's first great battle is the lifting of the siege of Orleans and the related attack on Jargau. As with all elements of the work, this battle scene contains elements of the fairy tale, hagiography, and epic. In addition to her voices, Joan's magical agent is the "seeing eye," a gift that "pierces through and reads the heart and the soul, finding there capacities which the outside didn't indicate or promise, and which the other kind of eye couldn't detect" (678–79). The idea of vision dominates this section, for Joan's "visions" occur throughout the book in a quickening of the plot. Her angels grant her insight into the future as it pertains to the military project, and the narrator informs the readers that "*she had seen the vision of the Tree,*" a portent of her death and obvious symbol of crucifixion and martyrdom at the stake (773; original italics). Throughout this section, the fairy tale elements likewise begin to occur in greater force. Joan uses "enchantments" and casts a "spell" on others (665). As Joan approaches Orleans, her staff are transported to a "fairy-land" (698); the Paladin becomes alternately a "windy giant" and "a dwarfed Paladin" (700, 703); and a new soldier is introduced who, at over seven feet tall, is called "the Dwarf" (710). One person in this section concludes that "Joan was either a witch or a saint" (618).

If Joan is a saint in this military section, one must still question what kind of saint she is. In Twain's presentation, Joan is really more of a Protestant, even Calvinist, military leader than a Catholic one. Her army is described as a "reformed army," and the double-voiced quality of the term "reformed" complicates notions that Twain's work suspends literary hostilities with Catholicism. Joan certainly does "reform" the army and make of it an efficient fighting unit, but it is also a Reformed, or Calvinist, army and part of the Reform-ation in many respects. Consider what it means that the army is "reformed." The character that serves as the prime example of this reformation is La Hire, the profane soldier whose soul Joan of Arc "worked earnestly and tirelessly" to save (686). She does reform him in the sense that he eschews profanity and alcohol, but the real reformation targets the forms of religious practice in ways that would justify calling *Personal Recollections of Joan of Arc* a burlesque hagiography. Told to pray, the man simply does not know what to do. La Hire is "ignorant of how to frame a prayer, he had no words to put it in" (686). The idea of "framing" a prayer and having no words "to put it in" suggests that Twain, who relies so heavily on established religious literary forms in this and other works, rejects the traditional Catholic forms of prayer, the "peculiar devotional spirit of the olden time, which placed a higher confidence in outward forms of worship," as he called it in *The Innocents Abroad* (197). One sees here the truth of Susan K. Harris's statement that Twain used "a Catholic narrator to communicate an essentially anti-Catholic theme" ("Narrative" 48). Indeed, the narrator revels in the fact that La Hire "stood there before her and put up his mailed hands and made a prayer. And it was not borrowed, but was his very own; he had none to help him frame it, he made it out of his own head" (686). Like his leader, La Hire relies on "inner," even antinomian voices, rather than dictated forms of worship. Joan of Arc has indeed "reformed" her army; she has made La Hire into a Protestant.

The epic motif is most pronounced in book II during the Orleans campaign. With the cry "For France!" Joan of Arc's army marches on the English occupiers (739). Twain's description of the attack on Jargau, part of the Orleans campaign, is without a doubt, the most masterful scene in the work. "At eight o'clock," the narrator informs the reader, "all movement ceased, and with it all sounds, all noise" (766). It is extraordinary that in a paragraph where Twain suspends the tyranny of time, even in the midst of the Hundred Years War, he begins by noting the time at which everything *stops*. Twain crafts a sense of fairy tale enchantment, as if Joan of Arc, the witch, has cast a spell on the town. One thinks of the many folk tales involving enchanted castles and individuals, tales such as the Brothers Grimm version of "Brier Rose," where in the first half of a notable paragraph, everything is frozen in time, and even "the cook in the kitchen was still holding out his hand as though to grab the kitchen boy" (177). At the Prince's kiss, everything comes alive and "the cook boxed the kitchen boy's ear so hard that he howled" (178). Likewise, in Twain's depiction, the castles of Jargau are enchanted and even the "flags on the towers and ramparts hung straight down like tassels," for the air itself has stopped moving (766). The people are enchanted, too, and are all frozen in time. A man with a hammer has stopped in mid-action, children have stopped playing, and above it all is "a young girl prettily framed in an open window, a watering-pot in her hand and window-boxes of red flowers under its spout—but the water had ceased to flow" (766). The description is really a picture, for the girl is "framed," and nothing moves. Twain weaves a tapestry depicting a medieval walled city engaged in peaceful pursuits, but on the verge of destruction.

As the narrator says, "Everywhere were these impressive petrified forms; and everywhere was suspended movement and that awful stillness" (766). If one sees this formal contrast in fairy tales, the "petrified form" is often seen in epic, too. One thinks of the Shield of Achilles in *The Iliad* that depicts two towns, the town at peace and the town at war. Twain himself uses the contrasting form on numerous occasions, most notably in the "S-t-e-a-m-boat a'comin'!" passage in *Life on the Missis-*

sippi (1883), where one minute Hannibal is a "white town drowsing" and the next minute "the dead town is alive and moving" (254). In *Personal Recollections of Joan of Arc,* too, Twain uses peripety, a major shift in the action, to move from one emotional mood to the next and to move from one time period to the next. For the "still life" picture, which is "framed" and transmuted into an aesthetic object is an *old* picture, a tapestry of an *old world* scene in a medieval walled city. Just as one sees the historical movement from village life to larger commercial connections, and the consequent waking up of the city in *Life on the Mississippi,* in *Personal Recollections of Joan of Arc,* one sees the birth of a new world on the rubble of the old. In the paragraph that follows, the peace is shattered, and Twain uses the striking visual image of the girl watering the window-boxes to convey his point: "The startled girl dropped her watering-pot and clasped her hands together, and at that moment a stone cannon-ball crashed through her fair body" (767). Like the kitchen boy in "Brier Rose" who gets his delayed blow as soon as the spell is broken, the maiden is awakened from her enchantment into a world of pain, and as the victorious commander strides through Jargau, "the new recruits squeezed their way to her side to touch the sword of Joan of Arc and draw from it somewhat of that mysterious quality which made it invincible" (769).

The second battle in the triad is the battle of Patay, which also ranks as one of Joan's great achievements. Like the other battles, it is associated with the three strands of fairy tale, epic, and hagiography, but in this battle her qualities as a tactician are more pronounced. While she does use her prophetic powers, and notes after winning the battle that "[i]n a thousand years—a thousand years—the English power in France will not rise up from this blow" (781), it is her decisiveness as a warrior that stands out at Patay along with the role played by God. In this book so consistently constructed on threes, Joan of Arc's orders are themselves trebled, and she restrains her soldiers, saying, "Not yet—wait," then "Wait—not yet," and finally "Follow me!" (780–81). The trebling increases the dynamic quality of the scene, but culminates with the biblical language of "follow me," suggesting she is a Christian warrior. In contrast, the descriptions of her army are elemental and more typical of epic traditions. Twain uses language of natural forces, comparing the army to a "stormwind," a "thundering," and an "avalanche" (780–81). Even so, Joan's take on the Battle of Patay is telling: "The praise is to God. He has smitten with a heavy hand this day" (781). Her statement is a surprisingly mundane comment on the great victory. Moving from the

Orleans campaign to the descriptions of the Battle of Patay marks a diminution in Joan of Arc's role as warrior. Her comments on the battle do associate her victory with biblical origins, and the language also suggests epic battles in which anthropomorphic gods take a direct role in human battles. In both cases, Twain subordinates the role of the warrior to the deity in charge of all human affairs.

The third battle, the Bloodless March, is perhaps the strangest of the battles, for it is really not a battle at all, but the wholesale surrender of the English strongholds. Shklovsky describes trebling elements as a staircase, but in this case it might be a staircase to heaven, so to speak, for the movement actually marks a decrease in *military* heroism with each battle, as the individual prowess of Joan or her soldiers is not displayed. In terms of the hagiographic thread, such a movement makes sense, for the honor is placed outside of the individual hero. A saint *is* a hero, but a hero who relies on God. In epic, too, while we might expect an increasing order of heroism in the three battles, such is not always the case. Beowulf, for example, performs three major feats in his epic, but the last one against the dragon is one in which his mortality is ever present and his strength, though still great, is not what it once was. In "The Song of Roland," the hero experiences a lessening of heroism in the military sphere, but an increase in terms of character or fighting against great odds. Yet Twain's work differs, for in the epics, great battle scenes still confront the audience or reader. In Joan of Arc's last great battle, *there simply is no fighting*. Dramatically, each of the battles is less significant as battle and hence as epic, displacing the dramatic conflict to the theological battle of book III. The hagiographic form asserts itself in harnessing Joan's great campaigns into the spiritual realm in which her role as a saint increases even as the specific military success of her work is deemphasized. Her first battles, the associated battles of the Orleans campaign, are the most epic and most detailed. Description of the Battle of Patay is less detailed and less heroic, with God's role in the victory emphasized. The third battle is the bloodless march and features no actual fighting. "It was not a campaign," as the Sieur Louis de Conte observes, "it was only another holiday excursion. English strongholds lined our route; they surrendered without a blow" (828). One recalls the Battle of Jericho, with Joshua's army marching three times around the walls and blowing the trumpets. The walls fall down. The greatness in that battle is to God, just as Joan's decreasingly militaristic epic trebling prepares for the final battle, a verbal battle fought against the Catholic Church.

Twain's use of epic form in book II is thus a brilliant inversion of the typical "accumulation" associated with trebling. In "Two Little Tales" (1901), Twain relies on a similar structure, embedding his fairy tale "How the Chimney-Sweep Got the Ear of the Emperor" within the larger narrative "The Man with a Message for the Director General." Twain divides the overall narrative into three parts, the second section being "How the Chimney-Sweep Got the Ear of the Emperor," and that second section is itself formally divided into three parts, so that the entire structure of the narrative is constructed on accumulating triads. The first tells of the emperor's sickness during wartime; the second tells of the chimney-sweep's idea for a cure by having the emperor eat a slice of watermelon; the third tells of the remarkable cure. How the sweep conveys the message is the crucial point, for it is passed from one friend to the next, "link after link, like a chain" (504). This solution is "easy as a-b-c," and the same is true of the tale's structure, for it follows the typical fairy tale structure in its adherence to the rule of three (504). Twain employs precisely this structure in *Personal Recollections of Joan of Arc*, with the notable difference that the triad in book II is a decrescendo rather than a crescendo. Structurally, both *Personal Recollections of Joan of Arc* and "Two Tales" adhere to the fairy tale form typified by Andersen's "How to Cook Soup upon a Sausage Pin," with the first and concluding sections of the tale providing the bookends for the triad in the center, so that one has, in essence, book I, book II, and book III, with the middle itself consisting of three separate parts. Not only does this structure draw attention to the fact that one is reading a fairy tale, it also decenters and decelerates the story. Joan of Arc's *military* accomplishments decrease in their military aspect, even as her *spiritual* victories over the enemy increase. It is not that the epic elements are no longer important, but rather that the hagiographic form absorbs its dramatic force. The epic strand is significant precisely in its dynamic diminution. Situated in the center of the work, the epic elements follow this pattern of trebling (Figure 5.3):

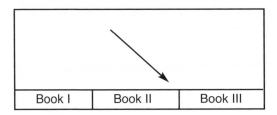

| Book I | Book II | Book III |

Figure 5.3. Epic strand descending

This diminution occurs wholly within book II, while the trebling of investigations is evenly spread out, with an investigation in each book. Moreover, the investigations increase in intensity, so that together, due to the trebling of investigation that spans the composition, the two patterns look like this (Figure 5.4):

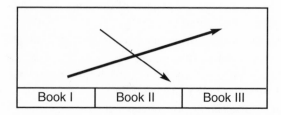

Figure 5.4. Hagiographic strand ascending

The thematic conclusion one must draw from this structure is that, as the work unfolds, the spiritual or hagiographic form dominates the epic form. Even as Joan of Arc's battles decrease in their epic qualities, the third spiritual battle of the *proces verbal* remains to be fought, and the hagiographic element is therefore ascendant. The increasing hagiographic strand and the decreasing epic strand need to be considered in the context of Nadeau's perceptive genetic study of Twain's *Personal Recollections of Joan of Arc*. Nadeau argues that the oral elements in the tale come from the Chansons de Geste, in particularly the traditional bragging called "gabs" (319). Nadeau suggests that Twain uses the Chanson form "in a series of three basic enlargements," quoting Paladin's three recitations of his own prowess in battle in which the soldier is more and more the epic hero (322). Zlatic, too, notes that Paladin's stories are "amplified" with each telling and views this as part of the oral heroic culture (295). Paladin, for example, "spoke of the governor of Vaucouleurs, the first night, simply as the governor of Vaucouleurs; he spoke of him the second night as his uncle the governor of Vaucouleurs; the third night he was his father" (658–59). In the same scene, Twain stresses how the *details* of the story "grew, in the same way" (659). "First the four silver trumpets were twelve, then thirty-five, finally ninety-six" (659). This is the same trebling structure Twain uses throughout, but in each case one sees the "accumulation" that Propp identifies as part of trebling. These elements form a counterpoint to the narrative structure of book II, for Twain inverts the usual epic accumulation, relegating it to a burlesque counterpoint in the character of Paladin. Adding this counterpoint (in the broken gray line) to the diagram generates this schematic (Figure 5.5):

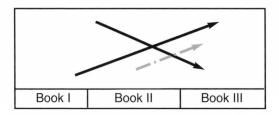

Figure 5.5. Burlesque epic ascending

With hagiography ascendant in the black line, and the epic strand decreasing in intensity, the burlesque epic follows traditional accumulation through trebling. Twain's complex structure of book II and its relationship to the entire structure initiates a dialogue of conflicting, though related, generic forms. Thematically, the complex structure intimates that just as Joan of Arc is no common saint, she is an atypical warrior as well.

The battles in book II allow Joan to break the spell, K^8 in Propp's morphology, and resuscitates the dead corpse, K^9, of France, bringing it back to life, a turn of phrase used many times in the work (e.g., 546, 689, 783, 842). On one occasion, the metaphor is made more personal, when "the Dwarf" proclaims, "I will give all my heart to *you*—and all my soul, if I have one—and all my strength, which is great—for I was dead and am alive again; I had nothing to live for, but now I have!" (710). The repeated elements (heart, soul, and strength) recall several related biblical injunctions, most obviously Deuteronomy 6:5, "And thou shalt love the Lord thy God with all thine heart, and with all thy soul, and with all thy might." The New Testament iterations of the injunction include "mind" with the other three elements, as in Matthew 22:37 and Luke 10:27. It is notable that Twain opted to use the Old Testament text, with its trebled elements more in keeping with the structure of his own narrative. Twain conflates this verse with "for I was dead and am alive again," possibly referring to Luke 15:32, a line from the parable of the prodigal son: "It was meet that we should make merry, and be glad: for this thy brother was dead, and is alive again; and was lost, and is found." Another likely source is Revelation 18, "I am he that liveth, and was dead." Twain reread the prophetic works during this period, and one sees the influence on many of the later writings, as will be discussed in the chapter on the *Mysterious Stranger Manuscripts*. Book II concludes with the end of Joan's military career even as she has magically achieved her greatest success, the saintly miracle of raising the dead. Ironically, the book concludes with the deaths of the Dwarf and "the windy giant" Paladin, but it owes much to "The Song of Roland" and resembles, too, such epic defeats as "The Battle of Maldon." Certainly, one sees the epic heroism of the comitatus, but these are elements Twain carefully reins in, harnessing them to the service of hagiographic form.

BOOK III: THE *PROCES VERBAL*

Yet another trebled element in the construction is the *Proces Verbal,* as Twain defines it a "Bill of Particulars" and a "detailed list of the charges against [Joan of Arc]" (850). As Twain notes of the *proces verbal,* it "formed the basis of the trial" (850). The *proces verbal* is one special type of hagiographic text, a record, as Father Delahaye defines it, "of the interrogatories of martyrs," their cross-examinations before offical authorities (111). Such *"official reports,"* Father Delahaye argues, "are entitled in theory to the first place in importance" (111). While he notes how hagiographers dramatize these transcriptions, Father Delahaye recognizes that such court scenes or tribunals often seem synonymous with the genre itself, rather than one of its many types. Twain elevates the three examples of this type in the structure of his narrative, giving them if not the "first place in importance," something close to it; the three examples of *proces verbal* provide the official hagiographic structure, and however much Twain employs folk elements of epic and fairy tale to render his account "unofficial," it establishes a narrative legitimacy his hagiography would not otherwise enjoy. This trial in the third book mirrors the two preceding trials, in books I and II. Thus, the *proces verbal* contrasts with the epic trebling, all of which occurs in book II, in that it spans the entire work, as discussed previously. Likewise, the *proces verbal* contrasts with epic trebling in that it truly is an "accumulating" triad, with each successive trial growing in significance, length, and drama. The *proces verbal* in the last book is essentially the same as what is charged against Joan of Arc in the first two books, amplified by an order of magnitude: "heresies, witchcraft, and other such offences against religion" (850). The first two occasions are relatively benign, as we shall see, but the last one governs much of book III and is a concerted effort to kill the hero. The morphological denotations Pr^3Pr^6 are used to signal these events, for the villain attempts to destroy the hero, Pr^3, and the hero is pursued by a villain transformed into an animal, Pr^6. Twain makes much of the fact that the villain opposing our hero in book III is a talking pig, Bishop Cauchon. This is a progression of sorts from book II, where the opponent had been a sly fox, the Reynard of the folk tale, and from book I, where her opponent had been the good, but feline, Père Fronte.

The first of the triad occurs in book I, after Père Fronte conducts a formal ceremony to banish the fairies from the fairy tree. Joan has been sick and so was unable to argue for the fairies, but after her recuperation, she learns what has happened and confronts the priest. The verbal sparring that occurs is a clear preparation for the later examples where Joan's very life is in jeopardy, for Twain includes in this first interrogatory both the dynamic cross-examination and a suggestion of martyrdom. Père Fronte humors the child and offers to "put on sackcloth and ashes" as penance (566). Joan ultimately takes the punishment herself, and the priest calls it "a humble martyrdom, and not of a sort presentable in a picture" (567). The priest then engages in a game, beginning in an offhand way to question Joan. "That was the way he always started out when he was going to corner me up and catch me in something," the narrator asserts, and proceeds to compare the priest's verbal game to a "trap" (567). The Sieur Lous de Conte "knew he was going to drop corn along in front of Joan now," metaphorically referring to the Socratic method of leading a person toward certain conclusions as a method of catching an animal. The "Old Man" in Twain's *What Is Man?* employs this technique, too, with about as much success, a topic discussed in the next chapter. Joan in this example of the *proces verbal* is cast as the animal being hunted, while the priest is the hunter or perhaps a cat, for he would "corner" his prey and he takes delight in his work (567). Ultimately, he loses the cross-examination and finds "that he had set a trap for himself," just as other, less benign inquisitors discover in later inquiries.

While the epic battles exhibit a decreasing dramatic value, each cross-examination is longer, more serious, and threatens more dreadful consequences. These contrary movements create a gradual replacement of the epic form with the hagiographic form, substituting a different definition of heroism in the conclusion of the work. In her first cross-examination, Joan pleads with Père Fronte for the rights of the fairies, suggesting the priest was wrong to banish them. In the second book, the fairy tale elements of the narrative are likewise central to the cross-examination, but Joan has changed in the depiction. True, the priests again try their verbal hunting, but "the traps caught nothing" (663); Joan of Arc is no longer just the prey of Catholic authority, she is also a hunter in her own right. "The rats were devouring the house," de Conte laments, "but instead of examining the cat's teeth and claws, they only concerned themselves to find out if it was a holy cat" (664). Joan of Arc is the cat in this comparison, but the *proces verbal* in book II lasts for three weeks and Joan is "daily questioned and badgered" before the Church's eminent theologians (664). The metaphor intimates that vicious animals surround and bite at her. In her responses, which are ultimately successful, Joan rejects "every ancient and illustrious authority of the Roman Church" (668). She uses "enchantments" and "cast[s] that spell upon them" and the animal metaphors suggest she is a magical shapeshifter, able to take animal form when necessary (665). Finally, she makes the following announcement:

> Listen! The Book of God is worth more than all these things ye cite, and I stand upon it. And I tell ye there are things in that Book that not one among ye can read, with all your learning! (668)

She begins with the epic invocation Hwæt! from *Beowulf* but then begins to sound more like John Huss defending himself for disseminating the Bible than a future Catholic saint defending the faith. Like Huss, Joan of Arc declares the supremacy of the Bible over doctrine, champions individual liberty of conscience, and becomes, after martyrdom, a *national hero,* just as the martyrdom of Huss precipitated the Czech revolt against papal authority. Similarly, like "the holy fox of Rheims," those who participate in the *proces verbal* of book II are throughout the three weeks of the interrogation described in vulpine ways (662). The "sly Dominican," for example, begins his cross-examination just as Père Fronte had, "in a sort of indolent fashion, as if the thing he was about was a matter of no moment," making everyone in the audience "cock up his ears with interest" (665). The entire scene suggests the familiar fables of Reynard the Fox, but in this case the witch tricks the fox, for the question of whether Joan is a witch (618, 630) or sent by God is finally answered by everyone in attendance: "This child is sent of God" (668).

In book II, the church is depicted as hierarchical and domineering, and—through association at least—as a "sly fox," but ultimately it reaches a humane decision. The hagiographic and epic strands inter-twine with the fairy tale strand as Joan of Arc leads a march toward Orleans accompanied by her soldiers and a "body of priests singing the *Veni Creator,* the banner of the Cross rising out of their midst; after these the glinting forest of spears" (688). Still, the narrator compares the long column to a "mighty serpent," introducing a satanic folk symbol into an otherwise buoyant moment when the three strands of the narrative are structurally and thematically allied. In book III, however, the strands unravel. Joan of Arc as an epic figure is sublimated—the natural progression of the structural diminution of the *epic* trebling—and she is abandoned on the field; Joan, as the heroine of the fairy tale, is pursued by a villain intent on her murder; Joan, as the witch of the fairy tale, is killed; and Joan of Arc, the martyr, is burned at the stake. The *proces verbal* of book III is a fight to the death between Joan of Arc and her enemies.

In essence, Twain constructs the third book as a longer and more dramatic version of the two previous cross-examinations by Catholic authorities, so the theological form of the *proces verbal* and the theological content are certainly present. At the same time, even as the hagiographic narrative strand reaches its apex in book III, and legitimates Twain's story, the folk roots of hagiography undermine to some degree the force of the official hagiography, delegitimizing precisely the institution that later uses the *proces verbal* as the basis for Joan's canonization. Twain depicts Joan of Arc's patriotism throughout the book, emphasizing her military bearing at many points in the narrative. Even as some of the English soldiers refer to her as "a vile witch," others "feared Joan, but they admired her for her great deeds and her unconquerable spirit" (852). Indeed, in the end, Twain's narrator refers to her singularity in "profane history," a deviation from the sacred history of hagiography (970). Phipps's declaration that the book is told "without skepticism" is only partly true (3). Skepticism is suspended by the formal choices Twain made, but skepticism is both suspended by, and immanent in, the fairy tale form. In considering this "profane history," one should consider that the word "profane" comes from the Latin *pro fano,* meaning before or outside of the temple. *This* Saint's Life is written outside of the temple, or perhaps from a competing temple next door, by one who may or may not be a Christian but is certainly not in communion with Catholicism. Reconnecting hagiography to the folk outside of the temple creates a folk hagiography that is, in fact, more traditional and ancient than the church itself. Joan, in the end, is "the

Genius of Patriotism—she was Patriotism embodied, concreted, made flesh, and palpable to the touch and visible to the eye" (970). Her incarnation, then, is only partly as an avatar of Christ, but primarily as an incarnation of patriotism, with a capital "P." In this sense, Twain depicts Joan of Arc as a *nationalist* martyr, just as he used such language in 1902, when writing his burlesque "Concerning 'Martyrs' Day'" and outlined his plan to honor national martyrs in a "holy" way, all the while conflating spiritual and nationalist language (307).

The fairy tale elements emerge, too. Twain fuses the epic and fairytale qualities when Joan is said to have "the gift of turning hares into heroes," for example (930). More significantly, her opponents, often described in martial terms, are the animal villains of fairy tale. Twain stresses the porcine qualities of Cauchon, obviously punning that his name sounds like *cochon*, French for "pig." Cauchon is not just stout, but is the very incarnation of a pig:

> When I looked again at that obese president, puffing and wheezing there, his great belly distending and receding with each breath, and noted his three chins, fold above fold, and his knobby and knotty face, and his purple and splotchy complexion, and his repulsive cauliflower nose, and his cold and malignant eyes—a brute, every detail of him—my heart sank lower still. (853)

The narrator describes Cauchon as a fairy tale monster, a man-pig who combines the worst traits of both species. The Sieur Louis de Conte also repeats jokes told by the townspeople, such as "every time Cauchon started a new trial the folk said 'The sow has littered again'; and every time the trial failed they said it over again, with its other meaning, 'The hog has made a mess of it'" (924). Each night, English soldiers paint the side of the bishop's residence with "pictures of hogs in all attitudes except flattering ones; hogs clothed in a Bishop's vestments and wearing a Bishop's mitre irreverently cocked on the side of their heads" (925). The carnival underside of the trial serves to lighten the somber tone of the narrative and creates, in Bakhtin's terms, a "carnivalized Catholicism" that undermines the hierarchy amid the "liberating and renewing principle of laughter" (RW 57). The popular "folk" reaction, as Twain calls it, is part of his project of reuniting hagiography with the folk, a project visible both in superficial elements and in the deep structure of the narrative revealed by morphological analysis. Irreverence cannot always trump theology, however, and if Cauchon is a hog, he chooses for his fellow judges "tigers," rejecting any "lambs" that might try to slip in (895). Still later, the judges are "those wolves in the black gowns who were plotting her death and the blackening of her good name" (920). Maik incorrectly claims that criticism of Catholicism is "quite explicit" only in book III and even then is directed "at one character: Bishop Cauchon" (135). On the contrary, not only does the anti-Catholic element pervade the work, Twain directs his ire at other figures in the hierarchy of the Church, many of whom are characterized as dangerous animals in their own right, some more dangerous than swine (135). The animal metaphors become increasingly carnivorous; the bishop is not just a "fox" any more, which does have some positive connotations, but the bishops are a pack of "wolves" intent on killing her. The emphasis on blackness and darkness, suggesting satanic forces, supports the impending denouement at the stake.

Still, hagiographic elements do dominate this section, and the hagiographic trebling ascends toward its tragic conclusion against the background of a dynamic diminution of the epic elements and the static, though pervasive, fairy tale elements. The narrative situation is, therefore, inherently one of tremendous tension, for even the triadic structure that in this story elevates hagiography is taken from the stock in trade of fairy tale. So marked is the triadic structure by its fairy tale origins and associations, hagiography, even as it subsumes epic, cannot subsume fairy tale. As Propp rightly argues, "The wondertale possesses such resistance that other genres shatter against it; they refuse to merge. If a clash tales place, the wondertale wins" (*Theory* 93). In such a contest, even Joan's miracles are not wholly the stuff of hagiography.

Because the inquisitors in book III pore over Joan of Arc's life, searching for any evidence against her, the book tends to be summative and recounts her many actions. One of these is her miraculous resurrection of an infant that "had been dead three days" (893). Immediately after she "prayed it back to life," she baptized the infant before it died. Joan's action is the sort of miracle so crucial for hagiographic writing and correlates to her resurrecting the dead body, France, so that one sees the triad of fairy tale and is at least reminded of the epic elements of battle. The resurrection of the child also recalls Twain's repeated use of material involving beliefs about infant baptism to question a dogmatic, legalistic religion.

Joan of Arc's heroism in this section remains largely a theological heroism, and she becomes, as Bertram Mott suggests, "a Calvinist Christfigure" (253). Numerous times in the courtroom, Joan of Arc declines to answer, citing a higher authority than the church. In Twain's presentation, the church insists that all acknowledge it is as the highest authority on earth and as a necessary channel for Joan, or anyone else, to go through. Joan, so great a military leader and political strategist, refuses to follow the temporal chain of command when it comes to theology, recognizing only the empyrean chain of command. At one point, Cauchon seeks information about her revelations and "brought down his fat hand with a crash upon his official table," but still Joan of Arc asserts, "my Voices have forbidden me to confide them to any save my King" (857). The "official" table stresses Cauchon's position in the hierarchy, but his is an insufficient authority to supersede the voices. When questioned about the "species of form" taken by the angels, Joan again refuses to answer (863). Later, she asserts when it is suggested that she cannot attend Mass in male attire: "I would rather die than be untrue to my oath to God" (910). Throughout book III, Joan of Arc is offered the choice of tendering allegiance to the Church's authority or to the authority of her own direct revelations from God. The conflict is the same conflict she experienced with the churchmen at Poitiers in Book II and with Père Fronte in book I. Likewise, the conflict originated with the fundamental conflict established quite early in the story, the conflict initiated when Joan of Arc's voices ordered her to become a military leader, γ^2, a charge opposed by her father's interdiction γ^1. Just as she chose to adhere to the angelic voices rather than her father's, Joan of Arc consistently adheres to the dictates of her inner voices rather than the Church's orders. Little surprise, then, that she chooses the stake when she is told categorically, "If you do not submit to the Church you will be pronounced a heretic by these judges here present and burned at the stake!" (922).

Although a rescue is considered by some of her friends, it proves impossible, but the ending is hardly a victory of evil over good as it might seem; such a conclusion would be antithetical to *any* of the three genres Twain employs. In fairy tale, good triumphs over evil; in epic, even defeats like the "Battle of Maldon" are linked Alamo-like to ultimate success; and in hagiography, of course, death is a necessary precursor to martyrdom. The remainder of *Personal Recollections of Joan of Arc* can be denoted in Propp's morphology thus: $Rs^{10}T^3$:UW. The rescue, Rs^{10}, is equivocal, for the "Rescue by leaping to a tree" is a common fairy tale device. Joan of Arc's "leap to a tree" is her choosing of the stake—as the symbolic cross—over submission to the church. The rescue is thus one that kills her, but saves her soul, and when an English soldier "broke a stick in two" to make a cross for her, the act unites in symbolic trinity the fairy tree, the cross, and the stake. The denotation T^3 is the "transfiguration through new garments," with the sign : denoting trebling. Throughout her trial, Joan of Arc's wearing of male attire has been at issue. A completing triad is Joan's changing of garments from her ordinary clothing in book I to male attire in book II, to her "long white robe" as she is burned in book III (962). Joan is literally transfigured through these clothes, and the garment suggests Christ's transfiguration, but also completes the trebling of clothes, recalling Joan's initial meeting with the "white shadow," her adopting of white armor, and finally wearing the "long white robe" of the saint. Joan of Arc is a Protestant martyr killed by the Catholic hierarchy for listening to an inner voice, and her defeat as a hero from fairy tale or epic comes at precisely the same moment as her martyrdom. The terms used to describe Joan of Arc's martyrdom are, in Bakhtin's terms, "double-voiced," and reinvoke the Weltanschauung of epic: "But what my Voices have said clearest is, that I shall be delivered *by a great victory*" (902; emphasis in original). Similarly, her voices tell her, "Submit to whatever comes; *do not grieve for your martyrdom;* from it you will ascend into the Kingdom of Paradise" (902; emphasis in original). The language combines the idea of Christian submission, but uses heroic and fairy tale elements to convey just what the nature of the victory will be. She must "submit," which as a warrior is precisely what she would not do, either in battle or to the Church. Further, the *"great victory"* that is promised is couched in the language of warfare, but is linked to the hagiographic ethos. The fairy tale, epic, and hagiographic strands merge in the idea of "Kingdom" as well; the expression "Kingdom of Paradise" is less stereotyped than "Kingdom of Heaven," and so is less determined as belonging to the genre of hagiography. Rather, the term "Kingdom of Paradise" suggests all three narrative strands. The villain, Cauchon, is in the end defeated, denoted U, even as Joan continues her "accession to the throne," denoted W. The defeat of Cauchon consists of the "Trial of Rehabilitation" conducted twenty-three years after Joan of Arc's death, a trial that condemned Cauchon and endorsed Joan of Arc as "spotless and perfect" (969). The ultimate "accession to the throne" of sainthood was, as Twain mentions in a note, "impending" even as he wrote his hagiography (805). In the end, like any good fairy tale princess, Joan of Arc is carried off by her prince to his kingdom; hagiography identifies the prince as Christ and the kingdom his paradise. The "ever after" they happily live in is the Christian's eternity.

EPILOGUE: "THE FABULOUS HISTORIES OF THE SAINTS"

In December 1904, ten years after *Personal Recollections of Joan of Arc* appeared, Twain published an essay, "Saint Joan of Arc," canonizing her years before the Church accomplished the task in 1920. In this piece, Twain still views his protagonist as something of an enigma, labeling her "the *Riddle* of the Ages" (591).Twain writes that the court transcripts of Joan of Arc's prosecution and subsequent rehabilitation provide "a vivid picture of a career and a personality of so extraordinary a character that we are helped to accept them as actualities by the very fact that both are beyond the inventive reach of fiction" (584). Her hagiography, that is, is too unbelievable not to believe. Twain further notes in his essay that Joan of Arc grew up reading "the fabulous histories of the saints," and one assumes the term "fabulous" is used to refer to fables and folk tales; Twain's comment is a generic identification and not a literary appreciation. From the beginning, Twain writes *Personal Recollections of Joan of Arc* with this central assumption: a "vivid picture" of Joan of Arc's life can only be believable if it is truly "fabulous," a fairy tale. A proper conception of genre, Bakhtin assures us, considers "form as stereotyped, congealed, old (familiar) content" (MHS 165), and Twain builds his work using the morphology of a fairy tale to restore hagiography's ancient folk roots. Commenting in *The Innocents Abroad* on St. Joseph Calasanctius, whose hagiography, Twain said, "puts my credulity on its mettle," the writer confesses that reading of miracles

> in a book written by a monk far back in the Middle Ages, would surprise
> no one; it would sound natural and proper; but when it is seriously stated
> in the middle of the nineteenth century, by a man of finished education,
> and LL.D., M.A., and an Archælogical magnate, it sounds strangely
> enough. (234)

That, in a nutshell, has been Twain's artistic dilemma decades later. How can one write hagiography that is "seriously stated" in the nineteenth century, particularly if one is a Protestant and something of an anti-Catholic?

The three-stranded structure of *Personal Recollections of Joan of Arc* is Twain's answer to that question. Returning to the folk roots of fairy tale, epic, and hagiography allows Twain to remove hagiography from the purview of the Catholic hierarchy that he rejected throughout his career. The book is hardly evidence of a "counter-theology" or an "anti-orthodoxy"; on the contrary, these elements place it firmly within the domain of Protestant orthodoxy. Twain's hagiography, then, is not a retreat from his early training but a deeper involvement in it, for his rejection of ecclesiastical authority is very much a part of his Calvinist inheritance.[2]

Twain was able to oppose the institution of the Catholic church and create an aesthetic work in the category of folk belief that is less a matter of faith than of respect—and aesthetic enjoyment. Embracing a hybrid form, Twain crafts a work with three "right forms": a fairy tale replete with dwarves, fairies, ogres, a talking pig, and a witch; a national epic with several worthy adversaries; and a hagiography where the saint achieves martyrdom at the hands of the church Twain loved to hate, Roman Catholicism. The Sieur Louis de Conte assures us that "soldiering makes few saints" (796). The "Translator's Preface" asserts that "She was perhaps the only entirely unselfish person whose name has a place in profane history" (546). The ending of the book likewise asserts that no one like Joan of Arc exists "whose name appears in profane history" (970). These claims are bookends placing this hagiography on the shelf holding volumes of profane, not sacred, history. Just as the burlesque persona the Reverend Mark Twain has one foot in the church and the other *pro fano,* the Sieur Louis de Conte draws upon, and deviates from, official hagiography. Roman Jakobson argues that one reading a poem, "has a vivid awareness of two orders: the traditional canon and the artistic novelty as a deviation from that canon" ("Dominant" 46). Crafting his saint's life with three genres, adhering to none of them slavishly, Twain creates a constant awareness of form. In so doing, he renews the hagiographic form that had veered too far from its clandestine traditions. *Personal Recollections of Joan of Arc* is hagiography, but it is hagiography reattached to its folk roots by a writer aware of the difficulties facing modern hagiographers. Through his use of the triad of fairy tale, epic, and hagiography, and in particular by employing the morphology of a fairy tale, Twain at once makes Joan of Arc's story believable, without making of it a matter of belief. By blending the genres, Twain creates a believable *story,* but not something one would feel compelled to accept as *gospel.*

Q: WHAT DO SOCRATES AND THE *SHORTER CATECHISM* HAVE IN COMMON?

A: Dialogic Influences on Mark Twain's What Is Man?

Shakespeare, like any artist, constructed his works not out of inanimate elements, not out of bricks, but out of forms that were already heavily laden with meaning, filled with it. We may note in passing that even bricks have a certain spatial form and, consequently, in the hands of the builder they express something.
—MIKHAIL BAKHTIN, "Response to a Question from *Novy Mir*" (5)

No, you mean Shakspeare's imitations. Shakspeare created nothing.
—MARK TWAIN, *What Is Man?* (130)

ON MAY 9, 1875, Olivia Clemens, wife of writer Mark Twain, sat writing a letter to her mother. "Mr. Clemens is reading aloud in 'Plato's Dialogues,'" she began, "so if I write incoherently you must excuse it" (Gribbon, *Mark Twain's Library* 2: 549). This "polyphony in the parlor" is emblematic of the sometimes unexpected influences on Twain's work; far from causing Twain to "write incoherently," as it may have for Mrs. Clemens, the writer thrived on a plurality of voices and influences. In the last decade, scholars have increasingly examined minority and female voices in Twain's writing, analyzing the extent to which these voices contribute to a dialogic form. Scholars have been far more reluctant to analyze the *literary* influences on Twain's writing, however, even

140

though his reading was one of his greatest sources of "voices" and dialogic writing. The culprit may be, as scholar Alan Gribben contends in *Mark Twain's Library: A Reconstruction,* the "widely accepted representation of him as an unread man" (xvii). After Gribben's work, however, and the work of those who have followed, it is impossible to view Twain as an unread, uneducated, literary idiot savant; still, many critics persist.[1] Doubtless, too, the tendency of critics to analyze content as distinct from form is partly to blame as well. Like the other chapters in this study, this analysis is not an exercise in neoformalism, though such an approach has much to recommend it as a corrective to strictly social, political, and ethical approaches, but is rather along the lines of a Bakhtinian and New Critical organic approach that attends to form and content at the same time. Like any reasonable being, and any successful writer, Twain concerned himself with questions of content *and* form.

Indeed, one of the most influential sources of dialogic writing in Twain was the dialogue itself, a genre that highlights both form and content. From the very earliest stages of his writing career, Twain found the dialogue form compelling. His early notebooks, written when he was piloting a riverboat on the Mississippi, contain transcriptions of Voltaire's dialogues. Reading Voltaire to learn French, Twain found he enjoyed studying the dialogues, sometimes using them as a starting point for his own literary creativity (see especially MTNJ 1: 59). All in all, Twain copied portions of three of Voltaire's dialogues into his notebook: "Dialogue entre un Plaideur et un Avocat," "Dialogue entre un Philosophe et un Contrôleur Général des Finances," and "L'A, B, C, ou Dialogues entre A, B, C" (MTNJ 1:51–53, 56–57, 59–60). Throughout his career, Twain himself selected the dialogue form frequently, employing it in such diverse works as "The Winner of the Medal" (1867), "The Revised Catechism" (1871), "An Encounter with an Interviewer" (1874), "Colloquy between a Slum Child and a Moral Mentor" (circa 1860s/1880s), "The Dervish and the Offensive Stranger" (1902), "Dialogue on the Philippines" (1902–3), "The Recurrent Major and Minor Compliment" (circa 1903), "Concerning Copyright" (1905), "A Helpless Situation" (1905), large portions of "3,000 Years among the Microbes" (1905), and of course the infamous "Little Bessie" dialogues (1908–9).[2]

Albert Bigelow Paine notes that Twain favored the dialogue "for polemic writing," and there is a good bit of truth to this statement, particularly when one considers his dialogues on copyright reform (III:1158). Twain's comments about the "Socratic catch," by which one might lead others into adopting one's point of view, demonstrate that he did see the polemical value of dialogue as a form that transfers content (MTNJ 2:274). One can "catch" an opponent, but one can also play "Socratic catch," tossing words and ideas back and forth like players on a baseball field. More than polemic, the dialogue form fascinated Twain because above all it is philosophical theater and announces itself as philosophy by its very form. Deciding to write "a dialogue" virtually ensures that what one writes will be recognized as philosophy of one sort or another. Dialogue, too, is essentially plotless narrative, and imitates the realistic dialogue at which Twain excelled. One suspects that Twain's interest in the Socratic dialogues had at least as much to do with the interplay between characters in a formal dialogue setting as it did with the development of the philosophical ideas. What happens when two people bump into each other and start talking is, for Twain, the stuff of life and hence the stuff of art.

What Is Man? expresses Twain's attraction to the dialogue form more obviously than any other work. In this work, Twain creates a dialogue between an "Old Man" and a "Young Man" discussing such heady topics as "God," "Free Will," and "Man the Machine." Historically, critics have tended to understate the influence of literary genres and forms on the writer's works, and criticism of *What Is Man?* is no exception.[3] Lewis Simpson, for example, criticizes the "tendency to discover in [Twain's works] more structure or pattern than is truly present in the thought of the author who wrote *What Is Man?*" (617). More positively, Linda Wagner-Martin identifies the "implicit models" for Twain's dialogue as the "popular 'conversations' so important in the intellectual circles comprised of his peers" (6). Doubtless, this environment of dialogue was important, but the informal conversations were hardly the real "models" for Twain's dialogue. Symptomatic of the critical misunderstanding of *What Is Man?* is that many critics ignore its form completely. So convinced is she that Twain's influences were extraliterary, Wagner-Martin refers to Twain's dialogue as an "essay" (2). Nor is she alone in this. Intentionally or otherwise, many critics call *What Is Man?* an "essay." William Spengemann, without any explanation, dubs *What Is Man?* an "essay" (129). Sherwood Cummings in *Mark Twain and Science* labels it a "philosophical essay" (45). Eberhard Alsen tags the dialogue a "long essay" (12). While *What Is Man?* is "a singular essay" for Carl Dolmetsch (232), Hyatt Howe Waggoner deems it "that much derided essay" (364). Most recently, Chad Rohman has stated that the "essay's key aspect is uncertainty," employing the term at other points in his own essay as well ("What" 60).

What Is Man? was at one time an essay. When Twain read his piece "What Is Happiness?" to the Monday Evening Club in 1883, it was in essay form, but Twain reports that in 1898, "I wrote out and completed one chapter, using the dialogue form in place of the essay form" (MTE 241). Possibly that explains why even Twain's daughter Clara referred to *What Is Man?* as an "article" and not as a dialogue (208). First published anonymously in 1906, when the dialogue was finally collected and published with Twain's other work, it appeared under the title *What Is Man? and Other Essays,* perhaps leading some to count it as an essay itself.

Legitimately, one may think of Twain's dialogue in the literary context of an "essay" akin to Pope's "Essay on Man." Twain, after all, quotes Pope's line, "An honest man's the noblest work of God" (quoted in *WIM?* 164). Calling Pope's poem an essay, however, does not make it prose, anymore than calling Twain's dialogue an essay renders it an article. In the absence of any discussion connecting Pope and Twain, labeling *What Is Man?* an "essay" ignores the implications of the dialogue form Twain employs. Even so notable a scholar as Henry Nash Smith, who sets out to discuss "the problems of style and structure Mark Twain faced" (vii), unaccountably refers to *What Is Man?* as a "philosophical treatise" (171). Cummings, for example, looks closely at many of the influences on Twain's *What Is Man?* such as Lecky, Paine, Darwin, and Oliver Wendell Holmes, but analyzes content, not form. Even the fact that Holmes's *Autocrat of the Breakfast Table* is essentially a dialogue receives barely a nod from Cummings in his analysis. Twain found the *form* itself compelling, so one ought not to ignore it.

Twain's dialogue was part of his ongoing religious dialogue, and it is appropriate, then, that the Socratic dialogues were not the only important formal influence on *What Is Man?* The *Shorter Catechism* of the Presbyterian Church is a particular variant of dialogue form that influenced Twain's life from an early age. When he put pen to paper in 1871 to satirize Boss Tweed and the Tammany gang, he entitled it "The Revised Catechism" (Vogelback 69–70). Twain drew on the catechetical form he had memorized in his childhood, changing it for the purposes of satire:

What is the chief end of man?
A. To get rich. (539)

Twain was "brought up, from the cradle, an old-time, boiler-iron, Westminster-Catechism Christian," as he described Mary Baker Eddy's early training, and the catechism form was one that he returned to often (*Christian Science* 356). In "Colloquy between a Slum Child and a Moral Mentor" (circa 1860s/80s), Twain creates a catechetical situation from the first line: "Who made the grass?" (106). Twain similarly structures chapter 14 of *3,000 Years among the Microbes* (1905) after such a situation by including a "clergyman" who quizzes the cholera germ narrator named Huck:

> "You are a Christian."
> "I am."
> "What is a creature?"
> "That which has been created." (495–96)

The exchange parodies the language of the catechism and burlesques the catechetical situation. The late "Little Bessie" dialogues function in a similar way, with the titular character asking questions of the adult, directly parodying certain prompts from the *Shorter Catechism,* such as when Bessie asks, "Mamma, is Christ God?" (43). Along with the Socratic dialogues that bothered Olivia Clemens, the *Shorter Catechism* was one of the important formal influences on *What Is Man?*

In *Problems of Dostoevsky's Poetics,* Mikhail Bakhtin asserts that the dialogue is a "means of seeking truth [that] is counterposed to *official* monologism, which pretends to *possess a ready-made truth*" (110). The form, Bakhtin asserts, is inherently dialogic, even when, as in some dialogues, the speaker tries to create a monologic worldview. Mark Twain's *What Is Man?* follows this pattern. Twain's work dramatizes the attempts by the character the "Old Man" to subvert the monology of the catechism by substituting his own "ready-made truth"; that is, he attempts to substitute his own catechism for the existing one. Twain's *What Is Man?* becomes, as Bakhtin says of such attempts at monologic dialogue, a "catechism" that adopts the "question-and-answer form for training neophytes" (PDP 110). The Old Man's efforts fail, however, as the dialogue *form* forces a dialogue over *content.* The contest between form and content, between dialogue and monologue, is visible at several points in *What Is Man?* ultimately creating a true dialogue. This chapter will demonstrate that Twain obtained his dialogue structure from Socrates and the *Shorter Catechism,* and that the *form* he chose influenced the *content,* the theological debate evident in his work *What Is Man?* The truth that emerges from *What Is Man?* belongs neither to the

Old Man or to Old Man Twain; rather, the truth is a dialogic truth produced by the conflict of warring forms.

THE INFLUENCE OF THE *SHORTER CATECHISM:* "Y. M. IS THAT A NEW GOSPEL?" (169)

It was specifically the conjunction of the *sacred* form with the *dialogue* form that created *What Is Man?* When discussing his dialogue, Twain most often employed language freighted with religious connotations. In letters to friends, in conversations, in many autobiographical writings, and even in the dialogue itself, Twain referred to *What Is Man?* as "my gospel" (e.g., MTE 239–41; *WIM?* 169). In letters to William Dean Howells and the Reverend Joe Twichell, Twain referred to the manuscript as "my Bible" (MTHL II: 689; Paine Letters 2:705). Twain also describes his work as "unfamiliar doctrine," fearing "it would not make a single convert" (MTE 241).

To a great extent, Twain's conception of *What Is Man?* as a "gospel," "Bible," or "doctrine" explains one of the most compelling features of the dialogue. For in *What Is Man?* Twain establishes a catechism for his new gospel. The situation is inherently catechetical, with the Old Man instructing the Young Man. As Josef Andreas Jungmann asserts, the purpose of a catechism is clear: "Catechetics must never lose sight of the fact that catechesis means the transference of the content of Christian doctrine to those who are maturing and that, as a consequence, the task of education cannot be divorced from it" (xii). The purpose of the catechetical *form,* then, is to transfer *content.* The *Shorter Catechism* with its question-and-answer format was something Twain knew intimately from what he called "my Presbyterian Training." It appears as a dialogue, but is in fact monologic, as the "Truth" is not something searched for, but dictated. This is, arguably, the purpose of church doctrine, although in reality the history of the *Shorter Catechism* has been one of vigorous dialogue. Generally, a catechism is a good example of how form has memory and how form itself conveys content. Bakhtin's idea that even bricks have form and thus "express something" is a crucial one. Because bricks have form, they convey meaning, and more complex forms, such as literary genres, likewise "express something" apart from content. "Genres (of literature and speech)," Bakhtin asserts, "throughout the centuries of their life accumulate forms of seeing and interpreting particular aspects of the world" ("Response" 5). The epic form has a certain collection of ways of viewing the world, for example, and so too does the catechetical form. The question-and-answer format is founded on certain assumptions about the nature of truth and the relationship of one person to another. If one vigorously shook a copy of the *Shorter Catechism* until the content fell out and only the form remained, *the content would yet remain*. It would still be the same question-and-answer form, and a person would still have his or her role dictated. There truly is a "law of genre," as Derrida argues. Despite Derrida's attempts to undermine genre as "an authoritarian summons," genre remains the law and provides its own sheriff for enforcement (203). No one, not even Derrida, can deconstruct genre; even his acolytes refer to his work "The Law of Genre" as— what else!—*an essay*. So, too, even without the content, the catechism would still convey its essential theology: Every question has an answer; one is placed (even predestined) in a certain role as either questioner or answerer; a higher power has dictated the form that the discussion will follow. Looked at in this way, one can say that the entire structure of a catechism responds to the question "What Is Man?" and enforces the Calvinist concept of the sovereignty of God as its answer.

Because Twain's Old Man seeks to establish a catechism, really a burlesque catechism, parallel to the traditional one, there are many monologic qualities to *What Is Man?* When Twain first presented his "gospel" to the "Monday Evening Club," he reports that "there was not a man there that didn't scoff at it, jeer at it, revile it, and call it a lie, a thousand times a lie!" (MTE 240). Twain's attitude toward his audience is telling: "those able men were such children, such incompetents, in the presence of an unfamiliar doctrine" (MTE 241). One might say that they were "children" needing catechesis in his new "gospel."

In *What Is Man?* Twain creates a catechetical situation in its own right, but he also patterns his dialogue after the question-and-answer form of the *Shorter Catechism,* mirroring certain questions used in the catechism and even referring to it at one point. While Twain's work is not an encyclopedic treatment of theology, it does share the following elements with the *Shorter Catechism:* The question of man; The Creation; The Fall and Depravity; Infant Salvation (deleted portion); Trinitarian questions (deleted); and Free Will. The form the questions take parallels the form used in the *Shorter Catechism.* The title of Twain's dialogue, for example, parallels the opening question of the catechism, "What is the chief end of man?" "To glorify God and enjoy him forever" is the proper catechetical response. The title Twain selects asks the same sort of question and provides an answer differing only slightly in emphasis.

In five places in the Bible, the question "What is man?" is asked, always in similar contexts. Most frequently, Twain is seen as alluding to Psalms 8:3–4 "When I consider thy heavens, the work of thy fingers, the moon and the stars, which thou has ordained; What is man, that thou art mindful of him? and the son of man, that thou visitest him?" One of the five biblical iterations of the phrase is Paul's quoting of this verse from Psalms in Hebrews 2:6. There is indeed warrant for identifying this particular passage in Psalms as the source for the title, for Twain had quoted it in early 1870 in a letter to his future wife, Olivia Langdon:

> How insignificant we are, with our pigmy little world!—an atom glinting with uncounted myriads of other atom worlds in a broad shaft of light streaming from God's countenance—& yet prating complacently of our speck as the Great World, & regarding the other specks as pretty trifles made to steer our schooners by & inspire the reveries of "puppy" lovers. Did Christ live 33 years in each of the millions & millions of worlds that hold their majestic courses above our heads? . . . I do not see how astronomers can help feeling exquisitely insignificant, for every new page of the Book of the Heavens they open reveals to them more & more that the world we are so proud of is to the universe of careering globes as is one mosquito to the winged & hoofed flocks & herds that darken the air & populate the plains & forests of all the earth. If you killed the mosquito, would it be missed? Verily, What is Man, that he should be considered of God? (MTL 4:12)

The insignificance of humans when compared to the enormity of creation is the text, so to speak, of Reverend Twain's sermon. Likewise, if we look toward the other iterations of the question "What is man?" in the Bible, we see a similar attitude expressed. Later in the book of Psalms, we again hear, "Lord, what *is* man, that thou takest knowledge of him! *or* the son of man, that thou makest account of him!" (144: 3).

The book of Job, however, is the most likely source for the title of *What Is Man?* In Job, the rhetorical device "What is man?" is used twice, both in contexts similar to Psalms and Hebrews. The first is a question by Job, wondering why God would take notice of him. "What *is* man, that thou shouldest magnify him? And that thou shouldest set thine heart upon him?" (7:17). The second iteration is by Eliphaz the

Temanite, later called by Job one of the "forgers of lies . . . physicians of no value" (13:4). Eliphaz the Temanite queries, "What *is* man, that he should be clean? And *he which is* born of a woman, that he should be righteous?" (Job 15:14). In both cases, the question is part of an attempt to understand the relationship between God and man; the answer Twain provides with his allusion differs from the catechetical response, suggesting that our ability as humans to glorify God is strictly limited. Another connection is that, like Twain's work, Job is a philosophical dialogue, even a catechism. "Teach me," Job declares, sounding much like a catechumen seeking enlightenment, "and I will hold my tongue" (6: 24). Twain may have relied on Job for the title to comment on the relationship between teacher and student in a catechetical environment and to establish the form and content his own dialogue would take. The Old Man in Twain's dialogue may, like Eliphaz the Temanite, be a poor teacher.

After the title, Twain opens his dialogue with the question, "What are the materials of which a steam-engine is made?" (125). It seems a strange question to begin with, given that the subject is supposed to be humankind. There is method here, however, and eventually, Twain's Old Man proceeds to connect the analysis of base elements of machine construction with the construction of human beings. In this he follows the *Shorter Catechism* with its questions about the creation of man:

> Q. 9. What is the work of creation?
> A. The work of creation is God's making all things of nothing, by the word of his power, in the space of six days, and all very good.
> Q. 10. How did God create man?
> A. God created man male and female, after his own image, in knowledge, righteousness, and holiness, with dominion over the creatures. (229)

Like *What Is Man?* the catechism approaches the matter of creation first in a general way, following the broad question with one specifically relating the question of creation to *human* creation. The difference, however, is telling. Doctrinally, the discussion of ex nihilo creation magnifies God, and the creation of humans "after his own image" magnifies humanity. The Old Man, in contrast, presents the work of creation as a mechanical process of mining ore, purifying it, and producing a steam engine. While God in Twain's work is depicted somewhat less positively than in the catechism, it is man that is truly disparaged. William Macnaughton rightly notes that the purpose of *What Is Man?* is "to make human pride look ridiculous" (84). In this sense, Twain's work is very like Pope's "Essay on Man" as well as the book of Job, to which it owes its title. The Old Man proceeds to draw an analogy between the construction of a steam engine and the construction of man. From how a steam engine is made, the question turns to "Man the machine—man, the impersonal engine" (128). The Old Man's connection of the creation of a steam engine to the creation of human beings prompts the Young Man to blurt out: "You have arrived at man, now?" (127).

Although it might seem strange to expect Twain to discuss Adam in his dialogue, he in fact introduces the question of Adam at the same rhetorical moment that the *Shorter Catechism* does, immediately following the general questions of creation and the narrowing of focus to the creation of humans. In *What Is Man?* the Young Man raises the question of Adam, maintaining that our common ancestor must be an exception to the Old Man's idea that "[n]o man ever originates anything. All his thoughts, all his impulses, come *from the outside*" (129). As the Young Man contends, "The *first* man had original thoughts, anyway; there was nobody to draw from" (129). The Old Man counteracts this argument by going to the heart of the Eden story, the entrance of Death into the world. This issue covers questions 12–19 in the *Shorter Catechism,* which Twain encapsulates in one long paragraph. The crux of the Old Man's argument is that Adam "had not a shadow of a notion of the difference between good and evil—he had to get the idea *from the outside*. Neither he nor Eve was able to originate the idea that it was immodest to go naked: the knowledge came in with the apple *from the outside*" (130).

Following the discussion of Adam and the Fall of Man, one logically proceeds, as do both *What Is Man?* and the *Shorter Catechism,* to a discussion of total depravity. The catechism asks, "Did all mankind fall in Adam's first transgression?" (230). The affirmative answer does not, however, end the discussion, either in the catechism or in Twain's dialogue. In fact, it leads in both cases to a discussion of what some felt was the worst implication of the Calvinist doctrine of total depravity and one that concerned Twain deeply: Infant Damnation.

Properly speaking, there is no Calvinist doctrine of infant damnation, but rather of infant salvation, and the actual baptism has, in the Presbyterian view, no salvific effect. Whether performed on infant or adult, baptism is a sign only of a grace bestowed by God, not conferred by the ritual. As Calvin puts it, "The only purification which baptism promises is by means of the sprinkling of the blood of Christ" (II:513). Nevertheless, Twain was concerned throughout his entire life about this issue. Such concern may seem peculiar today, but Twain lived in an era that took theology seriously, and it bears repeating that he himself took theology seriously. Contrary to the claims of Sherwood Cummings, who states that "the idea of predestination simply made no impression on him," Twain was deeply involved in the issue (109), for this concept lies at the heart of the question of where unbaptized infants would spend eternity. Twain wrote about the issue many times in his life in such diverse works as the *Connecticut Yankee* manuscript (1889), "Aix-Les-Bains" (1891), "My First Lie and How I Got Out of It" (1899), and his sardonic advice to Paine that when in heaven he should not try to "smuggle water" to the "little unbaptised Presbyterian and Roman Catholic children roasting in the red fires" ("Etiquette" 209). In "Moral and Intellectual Man" (circa 1903), Twain commented that, "Man thinks he is not a fiend. It is because he has not examined the Westminster Catechism which he invented. He and the Polecat.—But it is not fair to class them together, the polecat has not invented a Westminster Catechism."[4]

In *What Is Man?* Twain follows his discussion of Adam with the Young Man's criticism "It is an infamous doctrine," and then proceeds to give all manner of references to babies, not specifically linking them yet to the issue of unbaptized infants. He talks about the "baby born with a billion dollars," "the baby born with nothing" (131), the mother that would "suffer torture to save [her child] from pain; die that it may live" (139), and most tellingly the section entitled "A Little Story" (143–47) and the anecdote from Darwin (181–82) that bring to the forefront the issue of what—according to Twain's understanding of Calvinist doctrine—happens to unbaptized children when they die. As *What Is Man?* exists today, the debate over infant salvation is sublimated, with many oblique references to pagan (and hence unbaptized) children dying. The "God" dialogue, which corresponds to questions 4–8 of the catechism, beginning with "What is God?" was removed by Twain from *What Is Man?* in 1905, as Baender notes. Twain left the direction "NOT TO BE USED" appended to it (See the California Edition of *What Is Man?* Supplement 476). This section contains the most direct reference to the catechism and to the doctrine of Infant Salvation, with the Old Man asking

O.M. Do you believe that God sends unbaptised children to eternal torture by fire?

Y.M. I do not merely believe it, I know it. All Christians know it, and they solemnly state it when they enter upon Church membership.

O.M. Have you friends who have children in hell?

Y.M. Yes, several.

The discussion continues for four pages. It is not quite true that "All Christians know it, and they solemnly state it when they enter upon Church membership," for the doctrine is peculiar to Reformed churches, such as the Presbyterian church, and also to Roman Catholicism, though for different theological reasons. Twain once referred to the doctrine of infant salvation as a "Roman-Catholic-Presbyterian Belief" ("Emendations of the Copy-Text," *Connecticut Yankee* 669). It is also misleading to suggest that the *Shorter Catechism* demands that a "right-hearted Christian sees his unoffending child broiling on the red-hot grates of hell, and proclaims from the housetops that the Author of this unspeakable atrocity is made up all of goodness, mercy and loving-kindness," as the Old Man puts it (482–83). Nevertheless, the Old Man refers directly to the *Catechism* and it is true that in most Presbyterian churches one applying for church membership was examined on these questions. The *Catechism* itself treats the issue in questions 94 and 95, "What is Baptism?" and "To whom is Baptism to be administered?" but it was the convergence of several questions that created—and still creates—a misunderstanding of the doctrine. When the answers to the two questions about baptism, that it is a sacrament of grace and that infants should be baptized, are put into conversation with the earlier questions about Adam and the fall of man, one begins to sense the causes of the controversy. The answer to the latter question from the *Shorter Catechism* reads like Twain's diatribe against the doctrine:

Q. 19. What is the misery of that estate whereinto man fell?
A: All mankind, by their fall, lost communion with God, are under his wrath and curse, and so made liable to all miseries of this life, to death itself, and to the pains of hell forever. (230)

When revising his manuscript in 1905, Twain removed his own treatment of these issues, which he had entitled simply "God," but which might have borne the title used by the *Catechism*'s question, "What is God?" What led him to remove the passage? While it is here that the Old Man states his belief in God, this portion of the dialogue also contains some of the most vitriolic attacks on God (477). It is safe to say that the excised "God" passage demonstrates that Twain's Old Man, if not Old Man Twain himself, does believe in God, he just doesn't like him very much. Was Twain concerned that these passages were too vitriolic even for anonymous publication? The Young Man labels the Old Man's ideas about God "gross blasphemy, and I will not answer you" (482).

Certainly, Twain may have been concerned that his ability to convince his readers might be lessened if he were too savage with their beliefs.

As a practical matter, too, much of the impetus behind the "God" dialogue was removed by a 1903 change in the doctrine of the Presbyterian Church. Debate over the question of infant salvation had raged for years. Several times, the Presbyterian Synods had attempted to amend the doctrine. Twain followed these discussions with interest, writing in "Aix-Les-Bains" that "[i]t was, without doubt, a mistake and a step backward when the Presbyterian Synods of America lately decided, by vote, to leave [God] still embarrassed with the dogma of infant damnation" (4). In 1903, the Presbyterian Church (USA) added a declaratory statement to the Westminster Confession of Faith, stating that "We believe that all dying in infancy are included in the election of grace, and are regenerated and saved by Christ through the Spirit, who works when and where and how he pleases" (216). With this change or clarification of church doctrine, much of the material in the "God" dialogue was rendered moot. Still, removing it left a hole in Twain's dialogue, for he had covered every other "What is _____?" question from the *Shorter Catechism*, such as "What is Man?" "What is Sin?" and so on. The most glaring absence is a discussion of Christ, who is present in the finished dialogue only obliquely. In the excised portion, there is one element following the *Shorter Catechism* that discusses the nature of God and Christ.

> O. M. Are the Savior and God one Person, or two?
> Y. M. One. He is God. (480)

This correlates to the question from the *Shorter Catechism:*

Q. 6. How many Persons are there in the Godhead?

Specifically, this is interesting because Twain, like his source, capitalizes Person, using it in the technical theological sense of "aspect" or "attribute." Calvin, in the *Institutes of the Christian Religion,* defines "Person" as "a subsistence in the Divine essence,—a subsistence which, while related to the other two, is distinguished from them by incommunicable properties" (I: 114). Twain uses this theological term and definition here and, as he follows the *Shorter Catechism* in the form the question takes, one ought to note that the Young Man supplies the correct content, or answer. Leaving out the entire "God" section left a gaping hole that Twain may have intended to later repair, excising some of the discussion of infant salvation, and returning the larger passage to its rightful place in *What Is Man?*

Another excised passage is likewise telling, both for what it reveals of Twain's methods of composition, but also for how the excised passage relates to the entire dialogue. The passage, bearing the title "Further about Training," relies heavily on Twain's reading of Jonathan Edwards's theological treatise *Freedom of the Will*. Twain's Old Man mentions Edwards's volume by name, citing it as an example of poor reasoning and its author as a person with "no more sense of humor than a tombstone" (See the Textual Notes to *What Is Man?* 625–26). Even with such direct references, many critics still insist Twain relied exclusively on his own experiences and intuition rather than research. Typically, then, the intellectual sources of *What Is Man?* are frequently minimized. "It must be insisted," asserts John Frederick in his much-cited work *The Darkened Sky,* "that there is no Calvinism in any accurate sense in Twain's determinism, as has been sometimes suggested" (170). Frederick goes on to mention that "[i]n 1902 Twichell loaned Mark his copy of Jonathan Edwards' *On the Freedom of the Will,* for reasons I can only guess at" (170). Neither Frederick nor anyone else need guess; Twain borrowed the book to consult as he wrote *What Is Man?* Twain tells us plainly, in a letter to Joe Twichell, that reading *Freedom of the Will* gave him "a strange & haunting sense of having been on a three days' tear with a drunken lunatic," yet he still recognized that Edwards "could have written Chapters III & IV of my suppressed Gospel" (Paine, Biography, III: 1157). As he did with his other works, Twain engaged in research while writing *What Is Man?* He borrowed Twichell's copy of *Freedom of the Will* for research, and the "Further about Training" section proves this. Any determinism in Twain's thinking has deep roots in his Calvinist inheritance, and did not crop up with Darwin, Marx, and Freud.

Interestingly, in the excised passage, the Old Man accepts several fundamental premises of Calvinism: the absolute sovereignty of God, election, damnation, and predestination. What he rejects, however, is as important as what he accepts: Free Will. In the *Shorter Catechism,* free will is discussed as the common state of all people, but also as a state that results in sin. The preeminent examples are Adam and Eve in the garden of Eden. The mystery of how the Calvinist concepts of predestination, God's foreknowledge, and human free will work together remains a thorny issue. Twain, with his "free will" versus "free choice" discussion, follows both the *Shorter Catechism* and his readings in Edwards.

Y. M. What is your opinion regarding Free Will?

O. M. That there is no such thing. (199)

The Old Man's rejection of Free Will is crucially a part of the "man as machine" philosophy he propounds. Essentially, the Old Man rejects not the idea that people make no decisions, but that they have any real say in the matter. External conditions cause them inevitably to give or not to give money to a person in need, to choose one profession over another, or to befriend one person over another. The true machine would be a person programmed inevitably to do right and who could do no wrong. Quite the contrary, the Old Man asserts. "The fact that man knows right from wrong proves his *intellectual* superiority·to the other creatures," states the Old Man, "but the fact that he can *do* wrong proves his *moral* inferiority to any creature that *cannot*" (198–99).

In response to his dilemma, the Old Man dispenses with the term "Free Will" entirely, substituting the term "Free Choice," which he defines as "nothing beyond a mere *mental* process" (200). With "Free Choice," one enjoys no "untrammeled power to act as you please," but rather has only the ability to observe the differences among various choices (200). For the Old Man, the point d'appui is a person's "born disposition and the character which has been built around it by training and environment" (200). One should note the passive construction of the Old Man's statement.

If a human "must obey the laws of his construction," so too must the writer of an alternate catechism obey the laws of the genre. Having laid the groundwork for a catechism for a new gospel of man as machine, Twain returns in the end to the catechetical form with a discussion of the soul. Following the section on "Free Will," Twain places another small section entitled "A Difficult Question."

Y. M. Maybe the Me is the Soul?

O. M. Maybe it is. What is the Soul?

Y. M. I don't know.

O. M. Neither does any one else. (205–6)

With this exchange, Twain follows the *Shorter Catechism* closely, using the Old Man to ask the questions and the young man to answer them. At the same time, Twain renders it as conversation, with the Young Man's hesitant "maybe" violating the form—the hallmark of a catechism is spiritual *certainty*. The Old Man repeats the hesitant "maybe," but then follows with the catechetical form we have seen repeatedly throughout the dialogue: "What is the Soul?" The answer, however much it seems like a nonanswer, leading toward inconclusion, really leads to a truly catechetical conclusion by asserting the sovereignty of God.

In the end, too, with a rapid-fire succession of questions, the Old Man catechizes the Young Man, asking question after question that will provoke the response, the solid answer, that emerges from a catechism:

O. M. Who manufactures them, then?
Y. M. God.
O. M. Where does the credit of it belong?
Y. M. To God.
O. M. And the glory of which you spoke, and the applause?
Y. M. To God. (210)

With this conclusion, the Old Man returns to the first answer of the *Shorter Catechism*, "The chief end of man is to glorify God, and to enjoy him forever." Having taken so much away from humanity, from "Man the Machine," the Old Man has to place the glory somewhere; he returned the glory to the God who created Man. Perhaps Twain's burlesquing "new gospel" is in some respects conservative theology, after all, for it responds to the old one, which powerfully reasserts itself through the form the questions take. The Young Man says "I know your whole catalogue of questions, and I could answer every one of them without your wasting the time to ask them" (172). He knows the catalogue because, like those who "solemnly state it when they enter upon Church membership," he has seen it before, memorizing the answers when he learned the catechism. While the Old Man sought to deride humanity, the formal influences of the catechism glorify the creator, producing the same answer to every question: God, God, God.

THE INFLUENCE OF THE SOCRATIC DIALOGUES: "THE UTTERER OF A THOUGHT ALWAYS UTTERS A SECOND-HAND ONE" (*WHAT IS MAN?* 148)

The difference between the beginning of *What Is Man?* and a Socratic dialogue is stark. While Socrates tends to ask probing questions and grill his interlocutor, he is also frequently grilled in turn. In early portions of Twain's dialogue, the Old Man, however, sets the agenda and dominates the discussion. The catechetical purpose of the *Shorter Catechism* is clearly felt in the question-and-answer format of portions of *What Is Man?* leading critics to comment on the lack of true dialogue. Hamlin Hill famously deemed Twain's dialogue "rigged" in the Old Man's favor (133). Carl Dolmetsch, too, avers that "Y. M. never discovers he is playing with loaded dice" (230). Niles Buchanan Thomas, Justin Kaplan, and Chad Rohman all label the dialogue "one-sided" (82; 340; "What" 60). J. Harold Smith delves deeper when he observes that *What Is Man?* is a "Socratic-like dialogue with the Old Man the message-bearer and the Young Man, representing conventional viewpoints, the learner" (166). S. Ramaswamy notes the inequality of the two speakers in *What Is Man?* comparing it to the "Dialogue of the *Guru* and *Sishya*," the teacher and pupil (33).

Twain does not stick to this pattern, however. As the dialogue proceeds, the Old Man and Young Man begin to interact much more dialogically and more naturally, as two *characters* might. This results from aesthetic choices Twain makes that create a true dialogue, in classical Socratic form. Perhaps the most obvious way in which Twain moves from catechism to dialogue is by providing names for the interlocutors. Admittedly, in *What Is Man?* those names are the ultrageneric "Old Man" and "Young Man." Twain may even be making a joking biblical allusion, referring to Ephesians 4:22–24, in which Paul counsels the Ephesians to "put off concerning the former conversation the old man, which is corrupt according to the deceitful lusts" so that they might "put on the new man, which after God is created in righteousness and true holiness." Still, while the "Old Man" and "Young Man" monikers are not as personal as the names in the Socratic dialogues, such as Glaucon, Adeimantus, or Socrates, they are characters. Imagine how different *What Is Man?* would be if it were truly catechetical in form, with successive questions and answers, each relatively distinct and separate from the previous. Twain used such a form numerous times, including two parodies of catechetical situations, "The A B C Lesson" and "The Revised Catechism." The *Shorter Catechism* was never intended to have personality, but rather to allow for the one learning it to step into the catechetical role and provide the correct answers. By contrast, Twain's dialogue becomes a narrative because the names help to create narrative.

Twain creates the Socratic situation, too, by closely patterning his own use of language after Platonic examples. One of the most common devices in dialogue is the use of rejoinders, interjections, and responses to dramatize the dialogue and keep it moving forward. In comparing Twain's dialogue to Platonic examples, this study employs the Jowett translation, the text that Twain owned. Just as one hears echoes of the *Shorter Catechism* in Twain's work, one recognizes many ideas and concepts that Twain obtains from the Socratic dialogues generally and *The Republic* in particular, such as the discussion of "gold men, and tin men, and copper men, and leaden men, and steel men" (*WIM?* 127) that compares to similar discussions in Plato (681, 804–5). Twain was also influenced by the discussion of Platonic "forms" (compare *WIM?* 202–3 to *The Republic* 772). "The Secret History of Eddypus, the World-Empire" that Twain was working on during 1901–2 even as he composed parts of his dialogue contains a clear allusion to the "Myth of the Cave" from book VII of *The Republic* in Twain's tale of "prisoners born and reared in the stench and gloom of a dungeon" who then discovered that there was another world beyond (360). In the deleted "Moral Courage" section, as well, Twain bases the formal aspects of his dialogue on a passage from book III of *The Republic*.

O.M. What is moral courage—a talent, or an acquisition?

Y.M. A talent, of course. It is born in a man, else he is without it.

O.M. Like a talent for mathematics, languages, billiards, poetry, and so on?

Y.M. Yes.

O.M. Can a man have a talent for mathematics and none for poetry, languages and billiards?

Y.M. Certainly. (495)

The Old Man sounds very like Socrates in this exchange. Lastly, there are even bizarre connections in *The Republic* to Twain's ongoing theological interest in infant damnation when Jowett glosses the discussion of "Young children dying almost as soon as they were born" with the phrase "unbaptized infants" (873).

It is the formal influence, however, that is most crucial. Beginning with the description of the setting in the epigraph to *What Is Man?* the formal influence of the Socratic dialogues revolutionizes the monologic contribution of the *Shorter Catechism*.

One of the most basic features of dialogue is the use of "rejoinders," defined by Bakhtin as "the utterances of the interlocutors or partners in dialogue" that facilitate the movement from one speaker to the other (SG 72). Interestingly, of the sixty-nine different rejoinders used by Twain, forty-two of them were used by Socrates in *The Republic*. These run the gamut from those indicating assent and dissent to those that are interrogative. Rejoinders of assent common to both *The Republic* and *What Is Man?* include: yes; indeed; of course; go on; one cannot doubt it; I see; I have; I am not denying it; I suppose not; unquestionably; right; certainly; undoubtedly; explain; perhaps; that is what I fully believe; proceed; I do; Illustrate; and so—; very good; yes, I know it; I think so; true; correct; without a question. Those of dissent include: no; certainly not; I am not convinced; hardly; well, I don't know. Interrogative rejoinders include: whose then? what is that? how do you mean? in what way; why? which one? how? Then what do you mean? what others? what is the difference? Twain may have internalized these important words and phrases, but he may also have compiled lists of them from his reading, as he did so frequently during his writing projects. Twain once wrote "Mother" Fairbanks that "the end & aim of my ambition is to be authentic," and his habitual awareness of the formal attributes of language was part of that mission (MTL 2: 189).[5] When he was writing *The Prince and the Pauper,* for example, he compiled long lists of language that would make his novel sound authentic; it should hardly surprise us to find that he did this for *What Is Man?* Regardless of how he acquired them, the effect is startling, for the rejoinders create an energetic dialogue. They are, as Bakhtin says, "link[s] in the chain of speech communion" (SG 76). As such, they help to unify the dialogue from beginning to end, making the enterprise an authentic dialogue.

Similarly, there are many narrative techniques Twain employs that were probably influenced by his reading of the dialogues. Techniques such as anadiplosis, interruption, and the completion of dangling sentences are crucial to the aesthetic success of *What Is Man?* Like the rejoinders, they interweave the two characters in a realistic, natural dialogue.

> Y.M. Do you really believe that mere public opinion could force a timid and peaceful man to—
> O.M. Go to the wars? Yes—public opinion can force some men to do *anything.*
> Y.M. *Anything?*
> O.M. Yes—anything.
> Y.M. I don't believe that. Can it force a right-principled man to do a wrong thing?
> O.M. Yes.
> Y.M. Can it force a kind man to do a cruel thing?
> O.M. Yes. (137)

Above all, it bears commenting that this dialogue sounds *real*. Twain's goal, here as elsewhere, is authenticity of form that links with authenticity of content. It is not only authentically Socratic, it is authentically human. Notice how the Young Man has taken over the position of questioner but that the Old Man reaches out and completes his sentence, attempting to reclaim the authority denied him by the dialogue form. The repetition of "Anything" by the Young Man turns the Old Man's statement into a question, forcing his interlocutor to repeat his assertion. The Young Man responds by rejecting the response before asking a follow-up question. Twain crafts a truly beautiful dialogue here, as effective as the greatest passages in his Socratic models. In addition, the form has fostered an interaction between the two men that undermines the dogmatic assertions the Old Man is sometimes prone to as he develops a catechism for his "new gospel."

Another significant formal Socratic contribution parallels the influence of the *Shorter Catechism*. The Socratic question uses the form What is *F*? where *F* can be any quantity. This is, again, a very obvious borrowing from Socrates. In the course of *What Is Man?* the Old Man asks such questions as "What is instinct?" (189), "What is thought?" (190), "What is the soul?" (205). These forms are, to quote Bakhtin, "already heavily laden with meaning," and one may answer the questions in two primary ways. One may opt for the catechetical response, thus ending the exchange. A catechism allows for no discussion—nor does it require one. Or, one may do as the Young Man does and engage in an exploration of the question in the way fostered by the Socratic inheritance of this form. The What is *F*? question is a Bakhtinian "brick" that conveys a history of the dispute between two forms of interaction: catechism and dialogue. *What Is Man?* is best understood as a dialogue between the related but warring genres of catechism and dialogue, each asserting a different set of imperatives.

The Socratic elenchus, too, or cross-examination, is crucial to both the Socratic dialogues and *What Is Man?* Gregory Vlastos views the elenchus as central to the Socratic enterprise, defining the cross-examination techniques as essentially a *"search"* (39). "In elenchus," Vlastos maintains, "the prime object is to search for truth," not win an argument (43). An elenchus typically begins when Socrates questions an assertion his interlocutor has made, subjecting it to one probing question after another. There are many examples of the elenchus in *What Is Man?* but one of the most vigorous comes from the section "A Difficult Question."

Y.M. Now when *I* speak of a man, he is *the whole thing in one,* and easy to hold and contemplate.

O.M. That is pleasant and convenient, if true. When you speak of "my body," who is the "my?"

Y.M. It is the "me."

O.M. The body is a property, then, and the Me owns it. Who is the Me?

Y.M. The Me is *the whole thing;* it is a common property; an undivided ownership, vested in the whole entity.

O.M. If the Me admires a rainbow, is it the whole Me that admires it, including the hair, hands, heels and all?

Y.M. Certainly not. It is my *mind* that admires it.

O.M. So *you* divide the Me yourself. Everybody does; everybody must. What, then, definitely, is the Me? (203–4)

This is really great fun. The Old Man's cross-examination reveals the insufficiency of the Young Man's conception, but even as he delivers the judgment "So *you* divide the Me yourself," he proceeds to continue the search by asking further questions. The dialogue continues, as it always does, for one can always ask another question. As Socrates asserts in *The Apology,* seeking truth is the reason for his method, the motive force behind his incessant questioning. Twain's Old Man, too, derides the idea that even the "Seekers after Truth" can ever adequately conclude the search. Like Socrates, the Old Man will continue his questioning.

In *What Is Man?* we encounter just the sorts of elements we might expect to have in an authentic conversation: stories, humor, irritation, impatience, and everything that is human. Vincent Carretta rightly notes that "Twain even tried to imitate the tone of the typical Socratic dialogue with its elements of irony, comedy, and skepticism" (47). The result is a relativity of truth that accounts for the tone that so many have characterized as pleasant, conversational, and, to quote Alexander Jones, "almost jaunty" ("Mark Twain" 2). That relativity is crucial to the influence of the dialogue form. Repeating the tired criticisms of the New Historicists, for whom any aesthetic problem becomes a revealing "tension," Chad Rohman argues that "While *What Is Man?* does exhibit formal problems, its inconsistency of thought may be its strongest feature, indicative of Twain's real thought process, which was often ambivalent and contradictory" ("What" 60). Where one sees confusion, another sees dialogue. The very point of dialogue, its raison d'être, is the exploration of truth's relativity, just as criticism should discuss both aesthetics and ethics, form and content, at one and the same time. Gregory Vlastos brilliantly summarizes the Socratic mission as a "relentless polemic against dogmatism" (52). Ironically, dialogues such as *What Is Man?* are polemics and also antipolemics; dogma asserting the insufficiency of dogma. One could even say that the Socratic dialogue is a form that champions a certain formlessness both of structure and of thought, for the attributes of dialogue militate against dogmatism of both form and content. Far from imposing certain messages or doctrines, its very structure is as free ranging and varied as human conversation; encouraged by form, the content follows in the same indeterminate pattern. Dialogue is, then, antimechanistic, antideterministic, for we cannot know where the dialogue will go and when it might end. It will never *conclude*.

"BE YE NOT TROUBLED . . . THE END SHALL NOT BE YET" (MARK 13:7)

What Is Man? is in a sense a dialogue of forms, a dialogue between a catechism on the one hand and an intellectual inquiry on the other. One proclaims Truth; One explores Truth. Certainly the contribution of the *Shorter Catechism* was great. But Twain did not end there. He put the catechism into dialogue with the Socratic dialogues. The result was—voilà!—dialogue. In a letter to Livy in 1894, Twain described a conversation that changed its tenor abruptly: "At this juncture, dialogue died. Monologue inherited its assets & continued the business at the old stand" (MTHL 2:658). The trajectory of *What Is Man?* is just the opposite, for dialogue drives monologue out of business, setting up shop in its place. *What Is Man?* is good-natured philosophical talk written by a writer who adored talking philosophically. The questions are ubiquitous, but the answers that Mark Twain offers in the end are these: Inquire, Question, Seek the Truth. Perhaps surprisingly, given the Old Man's mechanistic philosophy, the two characters of the dialogue are not in fact Q&A machines. The catechism of the "new gospel" is disrupted both by the *Shorter Catechism*, which asserts traditional truths, and by the Socratic dialogue form, which asserts traditional intellectual inquiry after Truth.

Both the *Shorter Catechism* and the Socratic dialogues create a classical, formal presence along the lines of Krauth's "Proper Mark Twain," for one sees in *What Is Man?* the tug and pull, the dialogue, between conservative and subversive elements. The presence of form "means something" and is a voice for the conservative genres and catechisms of

Twain's "new gospel." Krauth observes that Twain "worried over his place in Victorian American culture and often tried to align himself with it" (4). The dialogue form allowed Twain to be both "aligned" by employing traditional, classic genres and still have the subversive influence that, as Bakhtin observes, the dialogue form allows, encourages, and even demands. Iconostasis and iconoclasm unite in the burlesque persona of the Reverend Mark Twain. Twain's gospel brings not peace but a word, a word that will continue well after *his* dialogue ceases, a dialogue that continues today.

Mark Twain ends his great dialogue *What Is Man?* with the biblical injunction "I beg you not to be troubled," resonating with passages in the books of Matthew, Peter, Acts, and John's "Let not your heart be troubled" (14:1, 14:27). Of course, it is not *too* much to suppose that Twain was alluding to Mark 13:7, creating an emblem of dialogue out of his own identity: "Be ye not troubled . . . the end shall not be yet." After all, during the years he composed *What Is Man?* Twain and Andrew Carnegie jokingly referred to each other as "Saint Mark" and "Saint Andrew" respectively, with Twain sometimes signing his letters "† Mark" (See *What Is Man?* Explanatory Notes 550). The irony of the allusion then gets to the heart of the dialogue form, for the end is not yet, not ever yet. Or, as Socrates states in Plato's great political catechism, *The Republic,* "With these words I was thinking that I had made an end of the discussion; but the end, in truth, proved to be only a beginning" (621).

CHAPTER 7

"PROPHECY WENT OUT WITH THE CHICKEN GUTS"

No. 44, The Mysterious Stranger *and* the Christian Prophetic Tradition

Behold, therefore I will bring strangers upon thee, the terrible of the nations: and they shall draw their swords against the beauty of thy wisdom, and they shall defile thy brightness.
—EZEKIEL 28:7

The dreams are all right enough, but the art of interpreting is lost. 1500 yr ago they were getting to do it so badly it was considered better to depend on chicken-guts & other naturally intelligent sources of prophecy, recognising that when guts can't prophecy it is no use for Ezekiel to go into the business. Prophecy went out with the chicken guts.
—*Mysterious Stranger Manuscripts,* 462–63

HAVING BILLED himself as the *Reverend* Mark Twain and *Saint* Mark at different stages of his career, it should surprise no one that in between those two points Mark Twain compared himself to the *Prophet* Samuel. In "Wit-Inspirations of the 'Two-Year-Olds'" (1870), Twain relates the (obviously) fabricated conversation he had with his father upon the subject of his own naming. The infant rejects the name "Samuel," even though, as his father points out, he was a "prophet."

"What! There was Samuel the prophet. Was not he great and good?"

"Not so very."

"My son! With his own voice the Lord called him."

"Yes, sir, and had to call him a couple of times before he would come!" (405)

The boy's objections notwithstanding, the sketch concludes with Judge Clemens naming his boy "Samuel," another of Twain's *imagined* identities, like his self-ordination as a Reverend or self-canonization as a Saint. In 1865, Twain had experienced such a "call," perhaps, when claiming that he was answering a "'call' to literature, of a low order—i.e. humorous" that would "excite the *laughter* of God's creatures" (MTL 1: 322–23). While Twain was never literally a Reverend Mark Twain or a Saint Mark, he frequently created a theologically inflected identity as a writer. His persona as a prophet, sometimes comic and often serious, encompasses his career, from first to last, with its apex the jeremiad *No. 44, The Mysterious Stranger.*

"PROPHECY: TWO BULL'S EYES OUT OF A POSSIBLE MILLION"[1]

From his earliest days in Hannibal, young Sam Clemens had an intimate understanding of Christian traditions of prophecy, and of their expressions in folk culture. Ernest Tuveson discusses the formative influence of the specifically Christian cultural milieu Twain inhabited, with its knowledge of and belief in traditional biblical prophecies along with the millennial role many believed America would play in them. As discussed in the first chapter, Twain seems to have once accepted millennial prophecies about the Mississippi Valley. Tuveson notes the influence of Presbyterian beliefs in prophecy as well as those of wildcat groups such as the Millerites and Campbellites, noting that in Hannibal, the "millennium, apparently, was one of the liveliest issues in the popular mind" (216).

Early on, Twain was certainly a part of this credulous culture as much as he was apart from it; even as he accepted many folk-prophetic beliefs, he also exploited some of their pseudoscientific expressions for his own amusement. As Twain describes in his *Autobiography,* for several weeks he occupied an envied position as the chief subject of a traveling mesmerist, functioning essentially as a partner in crime to dupe and entertain the townspeople (50–58). More seriously, many people believed that Sam had foreseen the deaths of a schoolmate and of his brother Henry, who died tragically when the steamboat he worked on exploded (HHT 58). Dixon Wecter reports, too, that the "primitive folk belief" of slaves and settlers alike created a milieu that gave credence to ideas of prophetic dreams and second sight (197; see also Twain's *Autobiography* 5, 11). Reportedly, Twain's mother, Jane Lampton Clemens, shared such beliefs in "anything mystic," perhaps transferring them to her children (MTB 14). One can see folkloric and humorous traces of these beliefs after Sam Clemens became Mark Twain in such works as "Earthquake Almanac," in which he pokes fun at the idea of predicting natural events as common as the weather or as cataclysmic as earthquakes. These "prophecies" were printed on October 17, 1865, *after* a major earthquake; like many prophecies it is *retrospectively* prophetic. "The Oldest Inhabitant—The Weather of New England" (1876) is similarly interesting, and it contains both a prophetic and punning riddle from *The Merchant of Venice* ("Who can lose it and forget it? / Who can have it and regret it? / Be interposer 'twixt us *Twain*") and a jocular dismissal of the almanac's "reputation for accurate prophecy" (673–74).[2] Twain also wrote many pieces relating to quasimystic quackery such as "Getting My Fortune Told" (1869) and "Mental Telegraphy" (1891). Even as an old man, Twain was drawn toward prophecy in its various forms. In a letter to William Dean Howells on December 26, 1902, Twain writes of a brush with a pseudoprophet:

> Every day, from the first, Clara has been persecuted & worried & distressed by superstitions born of my Xmas story "Heaven—or hell" darkly divining prophecy in it; & for five months I have been persecuted by superstitions born of Cheiro's prediction of 7 years ago—repeated in London 4 years ago: "In your 68th year you will become—rather suddenly—very rich. . . . This family has joked about Cheiro's prophecy (while carefully keeping it in mind & cherishing it) for 7 years, & so have I—offering it to Mr. Rogers years ago at a heavy discount—but it has troubled me for 5 months now, as it might any old pagan. (MTHL 2:757–58)

This "Cheiro" was one Louis Hamon, a palmist Twain consulted in Europe (MTHL 2: 758–59). Cheiro's forecasts belong to the generic good fortunes provided by any such sham, and he resembles the "peripatetic phrenologist" who was "popular and always welcome" in the Hannibal of Twain's youth (*Autobiography* 65). This phrenologist "was always wise enough to furnish his clients character-charts that would compare favorably with George Washington's" (64–65). Remembering some of the prophetic beliefs of his childhood in the autobiographical notes, "Villagers of 1840–3," Twain tells a story satirizing both the pseudoprophets and the sheep who willingly consent to shearing. Twain inscribes notes on a Mrs. Holiday, who was "Old, but anxious to marry. Always consulting fortune-tellers; always managed to make them understand that she had been promised 3 by the first fraud. They always confirmed the prophecy. She finally died before the prophecies had a full chance" (31). Twain saw the chicanery that was such a part of folk prophecy, but he also at some "old pagan" level was drawn to them, and his works reflect this dualism. Alan Gribben has even shown that while Twain conceded some "possibility of scientific validity" for phrenology, he repeatedly focused on "the exploitations of a gullible public by charlatans" ("Phrenology" 67). In the ultimate irony, Twain prophesied his own death. Born when Halley's comet was high in the sky, Twain often joked that he was born with the comet and would go out with the comet; he did, in fact, die in 1910, the year of the comet's return. In the seventy-six years between the comet's visits, Twain accepted the appeal of prophecies, if not always their legitimacy.

Of his early work, *The Innocents Abroad* (1869) contains Twain's most extensive commentary on prophecy. In this work, Twain devotes most of chapter 38 to a criticism of those who "twist prophecy" to their own ends (325). He expresses particular distaste for his fellow pilgrims, who see in each ruined city in the Holy Land a fulfillment of one prophecy or another. The "infatuated prophecy-enthusiast," Twain contends, abuses the prophecies, overlooking the "ifs" and other conditional language of the original (324). The genre of prophecy, in both high Christian tradition and folkloric forms, is always "essentially related to time," as Bakhtin asserts, always looking to the past or future to criticize the present (RW 235). Nearly every ancient city is in ruins; were all prophesied against? The "prophecy-enthusiast" implicitly assumes so, cites chapter and verse, and proclaims, "How wonderful is prophecy!" (324). Part of Twain's point in this passage and, indeed, in *The Innocents Abroad,* is to suggest that there exists a universal prophecy of decay that will *always* be realized. Some thirty years later, in "Passage from a Lecture" (circa 1900), Twain himself proclaimed a prophecy via the persona of the "distinguished Professor of the Science of Historical Forecast," who foresaw the end of contemporary civilization because "everything perishes" (399–401). In both of these works, separated by decades, Twain derides prophecy, yet employs the prophetic form to criticize the present.

In *The Innocents Abroad,* Twain's criticism is not at all about the concept of prophecy, but really about the uses to which prophecies are put. Hubris is inherent in prophetic interpretation, as Twain observes, but it also makes the original prophet appear ridiculous. One could argue that Twain included the discussion of prophecy in *The Innocents Abroad* to teach his readers the art of interpretation, schooling them in how to read his own book. Repeated references to prophets and their prophecies, however, relate to time and decay. In his analysis of the history of realism, Bakhtin discusses writers like Sir Walter Scott who "could see time in space" ("The *Bildungsroman*" 53). In part, such an ability is to the author's credit, but a landscape with a long history facilitates such an appreciation. The *Quaker City* trip afforded Twain the opportunity to "see time in space" in their true interrelatedness. Prophecy likewise embodies the unity of time and space. "The prophet, like other men, belongs to his time," observes David Lyle Jeffrey, "yet he stands for a terrible moment also outside of temporal order: one foot in the *kronos,* the other in *kairos,* his ear to eternity and mouth toward the city" (26). The genre of prophecy is inherently related to the passing of time, which is visible everywhere on Twain's tour of the Old World and the Holy Land. Twain particularly drew upon Leviticus, Revelation, and the prophets Elijah (435–36), and Elisha (438) in his work because prophecy as a genre conjures the historical panorama he himself hopes to literalize in his own writing.

Not surprisingly, both the traditional forms of Christian prophecy and their more popular expressions play a role in Twain's fiction. Aunt Polly's exclamation in *The Adventures of Tom Sawyer* (1876) remains one of the most pointed of Twain's criticisms of the uses and abuses of prophetic claims: "Tom! The sperrit was upon you! You was a-prophecying—that's what you was doing! Land alive, go on, Tom!" (144). Tom does go on, revealing bit by bit the conversation between Aunt Polly, Mrs. Harper, Mary, and the exemplary Sid that he had overheard when they all thought he was dead. Unaware that he had sneaked back from the island and hidden under her bed, Aunt Polly (naturally) believes that Tom has received a prophetic vision in a dream. Here, however, Tom is less a David who finds "the secret" in a "night vision" (Daniel 2:19) and is more like the false prophets in Jeremiah who "prophesy false dreams . . . and cause my people to err by their lies" (Jeremiah 23:32). Tom cruelly manipulates the beliefs that others have in prophecy to achieve his own ends, and his misuse of prophecy recalls Twain's discussion of false prophecy in Mormonism (see *Roughing It* 546–47).

While Tom's character is worthy of censure, Twain satirizes Aunt Polly, whom we laugh at and pity. She would willingly buy into Tom's lies, twisting them into a prophecy. Similar folk prophecies abound in *Adventures of Huckleberry Finn* (1885). One thinks of Jim, who uses the magical ox's hair-ball to predict Huck's future and warn him "to keep 'way fum de water" (22). The joke is hilarious, for Huck is on the water for most of the novel. Both examples amuse, but they make a statement about the prophetic genre. In each case, characters resort to belief in prophecies when they crave order and stability in a chaotic world. This is very much in keeping with the traditional uses of prophecy. Calvin suggests in his *Institutes* that the prophet had many roles within society, but that one was a "support" role that would sustain the church "until the advent of the Mediator" (II: 426). Similarly, however comic are the prophetic elements in The *Adventures of Tom Sawyer* and *Adventures of Huckleberry Finn,* they testify to an underlying need for the ordering religious vision only a prophet provides.

While Twain employed prophetic elements and forms in work spanning his career, one must say that as he approached the turn of the century, the prophetic genre played an increasingly important role, perhaps in part due to the convergence of uncertainties inherent in Twain's business life, personal life, and within larger society as it picked its way between labor unrest and political upheaval toward the fin de siècle. Prophetic elements abound in *Pudd'nhead Wilson* (1894), for example. There is the reference to the prophet Nathan's trapping of King David in a symbolic narrative, an event related in 2 Samuel 12:7; in Twain's work, this appears when pseudo-Tom "felt as secret murderers are said to feel when the accuser says, 'Thou art the man!'" (969). Prophetic dreams play a significant role in the plot, from the comic (the "colored deacon" who "could not resist a ham when Providence showed him in a dream, or otherwise, where such a thing hung lonesome and longed for some one to love") to the unraveling of the mystery, a "revelation" that comes to David Wilson in a dream (927, 1043). Twain directly refers to biblical prophets, too, with the calendar epigraph of chapter 4 making reference to 2 Kings 2:23–25, a passage describing how children who had mocked Elisha were consumed by bears.

In the last decades of Twain's career, one sees a complete rejection of prophecy as a legitimate theological practice colliding with a simultaneous exploitation of prophetic forms in his own work. In *What Is Man?* (1906), the Old Man affirms his faith in God, saying "I do believe He exists," and is then asked by the Young Man, "And that he has revealed

Himself to man?" To this query the Old Man replies, "By His deeds and works, yes—as we experience them in our persons and see them in Nature. But not in any other way, so far as I know" (477).[3] In *Christian Science* (1907), Twain's assertion is even more blunt: "There *is* no prophecy in our day but history" (321). Most significantly, in "As Concerns Interpreting the Deity" (1905), Twain refers to the Roman use of bird sacrifice and the hubris of such attempts.

> In view of the fact that it takes the Rawlinsons, the Champollions and the Indian experts years and years to dig the meaning out of the modestest little batch of hieroglyphs; and that in interpreting the intentions of God the Roman augurs never scored a single demonstrable success; and that from their day to ours all attempts by men to lay bare to us the mind of the Deity have as signally failed, it seems to me that now is a good time for the interpreting-trade to take a rest. (120)

The basis for Twain's rejection of prophecy is twofold and, despite the intervening thirty-five years, agrees with his commentary in *The Innocents Abroad*. The prophets described in "As Concerns Interpreting the Deity" are of a various sort, but are brethren in their inaccuracy. Stultified by their attempts at interpretation, they are disrespectful to the sovereignty of God. Dismissing their efforts at the "interpreting-trade," Twain derides them as charlatans trying to make money off of something rightly none of their business. In the article written "To the Editor of *American Hebrew*," Twain similarly dismissed what he called "the trick of prophecy" (448).

THE PERSISTENCE OF THE PROPHETIC FORM AND TWAIN'S "PROPHETIC FUNCTION"

His rejection of prophecy notwithstanding, Twain embraced the prophetic *form* in his later years, sometimes for comic purposes, but as frequently as the only suitable vehicle for his own vision of truth. From the late 1890s until his death, Twain moved away from parodic prophecy to what Bakhtin terms the "high, proclamatory genres—of priests, prophets, preachers, judges, leaders, patriarchal fathers, and so forth" ("Notes" 132). In his brilliant "Mark Twain: An Inquiry" (1901), William Dean Howells, who early and often championed Twain's potent cocktail of seriousness and humor, found the "graver and weightier" subject matter of this later period somewhat off-putting, and questioned "whether they are really more important than the lighter things" (350). Howells was always the most perceptive critic of Twain, and while he criticized some of the social commentary and antiimperialist writings of the fin de siècle, he presciently described the "prophetic cast" of Twain's later work, noting the "general recognition of his prophetic function," even while fearing it might overshadow "the humor that has endeared him to mankind" (351). Howells's comments are a stark reversal of his earlier championing of the serious side to his friend's humor. Howells, it seems, felt the pendulum had swung too far toward glorifying the seriousness of purpose and wished to emphasize the humor that was such a part of Twain's genius. Obviously, one must qualify Howells's comments, for Twain always had this "prophetic function," but the humor of such works as "Barnum's First Speech in Congress" belongs to the genre of parodic prophecy, and the humor threatens at times to ride roughshod over the social criticism. Howells's commentary is really a sensitive call for a balanced approach that would "keep Mark Twain what he has always been: a comic force unique in the power of charming us out of our cares and troubles, united with as potent an ethic sense of the duties, public and private, which no man denies in himself without being false to other men" (351). One should not forget that the writer's brief masquerade as the Reverend Mark Twain actually continued in literary form as a burlesque device for the next half century, in one form or another.

Still, one work that reveals this later "prophetic cast" to Twain's work is "Which Was the Dream?" begun in 1897 and never completed. The story begins with an extract from the diary of Mrs. Allison X, a name that surely suggests the "Miss X," whose pseudonymous works included "The Art of Crystal Gazing" (1893), "Hypnotism" (1894), "Second Sight in the Highlands: A Provisional Report by Miss X" (1895), "On the Study of Spiritualisms" (1895), and the collection *Essays in Psychical Research* (1899). So impressed by her work was he that Twain wrote to the English editor who planned to publish the trial transcripts of Joan of Arc, suggesting that he commission Adela M. Goodrich-Freer, otherwise known as "Miss X," to contribute an essay on the "Voices & Prophecies" of St. Joan (See MTHL 2:708–10). It is in this very letter that Twain announces his new writing on a "prime subject," probably one of the various versions of the *Mysterious Stranger Manuscripts* (MTHL 2:710), and Tuckey discusses the influence that Twain's reading of such works as *Phantasms of the Living* had on Twain's thinking (26–27). Jason Horn, too, discusses the influence of William James and the Society for Psy-

chical Research (110–15), as does Susan Gillman (155–59). It was probably Miss X that exerted the greatest influence of this group, for she
focuses on the whole variety of prophecies, both genuine and spurious,
that people have engaged in; her chapter in *Essays in Psychical Research*,
"Saint Columba, The Father of Second Sight," contains a discussion of
prophecies that contributed to Twain's use of such material in *No. 44,
The Mysterious Stranger* and other texts of this later period (295–326). In
these same years, as he wrote "Which Was the Dream?" Twain again
drew on folk elements of prophecy, including a nice touch of romance
between the young Thomas X and his prospective wife, Allison, as they
share an apple and count the seeds to "find out if everything was going
to come out right and we get married" (37). The more serious elements
of the prophetic genre grow from this scene as Thomas and Allison age.
Their daughter, too, hopes that everything will "come out right," but
phrases her hopes and fears in higher Christian tradition: "I only pray
that there may be a God—and a heaven—or SOMETHING BETTER" (50).
In "Which Was the Dream?" Twain includes foretelling the future as a
stock-in-trade of prophecy, but includes also the more significant element of our reaching out toward God and God reaching toward us, a pattern seen, too, in Joan's prophecies in *Personal Recollections of Joan of
Arc*. Jeffrey suggests that "the whole end of Hebrew prophetic texts"
really consists of this primary goal: "to restore conversation with the
original and ultimate Author" (29).

Whether Twain's efforts represent a *personal* effort to connect with
God is impossible to say, but his use of the prophetic form to reconnect
society with God is inherently a form of social criticism, and suggests
Sacvan Bercovitch's apt description of the American jeremiad as "the ritual of a culture on an errand—which is to say, a culture based on a faith
in process" (23). Twain's use of prophecy involves both the faith in the
idea of process and progress, but not necessarily faith in faith itself. In
this unfinished story, a story in process, Twain presents a narrative that
even in its incomplete state grippingly conveys the polarities of faith
versus doubt in a world in which we are demonstrably not prophets. As
Thomas X suggests, "unfortunately none of us can see far ahead; prophecy is not for us. Hence the paucity of suicides" (51). The condition the
prophetic works speak to is precisely this state of unknowing, of hoping amid doubts for "SOMETHING BETTER."

In Bercovitch's description of the prophetic form, he observes that the
form has other imperatives, too, and "the jeremiads included both threat
and hope" (10). The other ingredient, considered from the audience's

viewpoint, is the fear engendered by the threatening rhetoric. Consider this remarkable passage in his *Autobiography* describing a meeting of the tellingly named "Ends of the Earth Club" where the speaker delivered a jingoistic speech concluding with the statement: "We are of the Anglo-Saxon race, and when the Anglo-Saxon wants a thing he just takes it" (346).

> It took those people nearly two minutes to work off their stormy admira-
> tion of that great sentiment; and meanwhile the inspired prophet who had
> discharged it—from his liver or his intestines or his esophagus or wher-
> ever he had bred it—stood there glowing and beaming and smiling and
> issuing rays of happiness from every pore, rays that were so intense that
> they were visible and made him look like the old-time picture in the
> Almanac of the man who stands discharging signs of the zodiac in every
> direction, and so absorbed in happiness, so steeped in happiness, that he
> smiles and smiles and has plainly forgotten that he is painfully and dan-
> gerously ruptured and exposed amidships and needs sewing up right
> away. (346)

Twain casts the entire passage as a jeremiad, from the apocalyptic setting at the "Ends of the Earth Club," to the description of the speaker as an "inspired prophet," to the extended simile comparing the speaker to the picture in the almanac. Here, Twain reverses the prophetic structure, deriding the man's prophesies as gas emanating from some orifice of the body. The parody is itself a jeremiad, and is a form of prophecy. Twain prophesies that such jingoistic imperialism will find its comeuppance. The comparison of the speaker to the almanac man, describing him as "dangerously ruptured and exposed amidships" is a carnival combina-tion of the visual graphic of an "Almanac Man," truss advertisements often found in such almanacs, and language suggesting danger to the military, specifically the navy. As a human figure, too, the "Almanac Man" suggests the *sparagmos* or dissolution of the body in a quasiritu-alistic manner. Unlike the folk-prophetic almanac that Twain derides, his derisive jeremiad recalls Rabbi Abraham Heschel's assertion that prophe-cy engages in "exhortation, not mere prediction" (12). Twain exploits the prophetic form to criticize American and British imperialism, just as he did in many other works later in his life.

Other examples of prophetic jeremiad of this final period in Twain's life include "To the Person Sitting in Darkness" (1901), an antiimperial-ist piece that Twain patterns after Isaiah 42:1, 7. (See also Matthew 4:36

and Micah 7:8.) Twain casts himself again in the role of prophet, building his jeremiad around the two verses, "I have put my spirit upon him: he shall bring forth judgment to the Gentiles" and "To open the blind eyes, to bring out the prisoners from the prison, *and* them that sit in darkness out of the prison house." Similar prophetic structures appear in works such as "Battle Hymn of the Republic (Brought Down to Date)" (circa 1901), a parody of Julia Ward Howe's prophetic hymn, with all its imagery from Revelation. Twain pointedly does not bring the hymn "up" to date, but "down" to date, to fit this depraved world that sings, "As Christ died to make men holy, let men die to make us rich" (475). Another work of the period, "The War Prayer" (1905), features a stranger and prophet figure who strides into a church where the congregation has just prayed for victory in war. The prophet informs the congregants, "I am commissioned of God to put into words the other part of it—that part which the pastor—and also you in your hearts—fervently prayed silently" (654). The silent half of the prayer, of course, is the concomitant loss suffered by their opponents, a loss the prophet details with gruesome specificity. The church setting is crucial, for Twain sends the prophet into the church to deliver this jeremiad, again throwing stones at the church windows *from within,* just as Isaiah, Jeremiah, and Ezekiel did. Twain crafts "The War Prayer" very closely after a work of prophecy, and the purpose is the same as any book of prophecy: call the people back to the right way, *threaten* them with the visions of the present and future, and *compel* them to be better.

"LIFE ITSELF IS ONLY A VISION, A DREAM"

Bernard DeVoto sees Twain writing a "general apocalypse" in his later works (24), and by the time Twain began working on the *Mysterious Stranger Manuscripts,* his interest in the prophetic form was at the highest pitch of his career. Still, one should recall what the point of prophecy is, for the jeremiad as a form seeks to condemn *and* regenerate. It is interesting to note that one feature of prophetic form is the relationship of the author of the text to the Author of everything. Jeffrey notes that the biblical prophet was "so subordinate in authority to his own ultimate Author, that for practical purposes he might more accurately be perceived as a 'non-author'" (21). Twain distanced himself from his last major works. *Personal Recollections of Joan of Arc* was published with the conceit of having been authored by "The Sieur Louis De Conte" and translated by Jean François Alden. The cover page for "3,000 Years among the Microbes" states that the work was "Translated from the Original Microbic by MARK TWAIN" (433). Twain published *What Is Man?* anonymously and asserted he would *never* publish his efforts with the *Mysterious Stranger Manuscripts,* from which he also comically distanced himself with the subtitle, "A Tale Found in a Jug, Translated Freely From the Jug." All of these elements bespeak Twain's fondness for trickery visible in such early works as "The Petrified Man" hoax. Patricia Mandia reads the "translation" reference in "3,000 Years among the Microbes" to suggest that "Twain obviously contrives the form here to emphasize that life, beneath the metaphysical, scientific, and religious systems man contrives, is essentially empty and meaningless" (126–27). Perhaps, however, Twain seeks to connect himself with the authority of the form, for prophetic form is itself preeminently *meaningful.* In its sacred, as distinct from purely literary, manifestations prophecy presupposes a deity for whom to prophesy. As Avraham Oz observes, "prophecy, operating simultaneously on the imaginary and symbolic levels of human response, serves to reassert the necessity of genuine mystery" (57). Oz contends, too, that "[p]rophecy's major rule consists in the existence, somewhere, of a core or a kernel" (58). Ironically, the prophecies of No. 44 reassert the mystery at the heart of prophetic narrative, and the mysterious stranger himself embodies the resurrection of prophecy, mystery, and miracle.

The manuscripts that comprise the *Mysterious Stranger Manuscripts* span the years 1897–1908. Criticism of the texts has been complicated both by the fact that Twain did not complete them and by the fact that Albert B. Paine attempted to. In a botch that one can only ascribe to the kind of editorial hubris that Twain detested, Paine placed the various texts into an editorial grinder to produce what he published in 1916 as *The Mysterious Stranger, A Romance.* In *Mark Twain and Little Satan,* John Tuckey first revealed Paine's editorial work that conflated three manuscripts that, while involving many of the same issues, were in essence different stories. Writing in the introduction to the California edition of the manuscripts, William Gibson bluntly—and accurately— terms Paine's work "an editorial fraud" (1). The editorial history of the texts should not prevent us from discussing them the way Twain left them, focusing primarily on *No. 44, The Mysterious Stranger,* which was the last and longest of the versions and the only one complete, in some sense of the term. *No. 44, The Mysterious Stranger* is also a compelling work because, while it was among the very last projects on which Twain labored, it was in some respects his first "statement." Athough he was at the same time writing his gospel *What Is Man?* and would in fact publish it anonymously, Twain still felt he had never told what was truly in his heart. Writing to Howells in May 1899 from Vienna, Twain voiced his desire to "write a book without reserves . . . right out of my heart" (MTHL 2: 698). This book was several books, the manuscripts that form the collective *Mysterious Stranger Manuscripts,* but was probably specifically the "Schoolhouse Hill" version, which he started in 1898 (Gibson 7). Interestingly, Twain's stated purpose is to "tell what I think of Man, & how he is constructed, & what a shabby poor ridiculous thing he is" (698–99). As with *What Is Man?* Twain censures humanity, but here in the form of a prophecy rather than a catechism. Failing to consider the influence of the form itself, Patricia Mandia sees in these manuscripts a "satire that does not attempt to reform" (102) as does Sholom Kahn, who calls the book "a labor of hate" (179). Prophetic rhetoric threatens people to reform them.

The three texts that comprise the *Mysterious Stranger Manuscripts* indicate Twain's clear conception that his work would adhere to prophetic genre. Formally, Twain refers to *No. 44, The Mysterious Stranger* as a "tale," that is, a sort of story with some element of truth, but without the strict claim of verisimilitude that one sees Twain stressing in such works as "A True Story, Repeated Word for Word Just as I Heard It" (1874) or in his concern with "getting the dialect right" in *Adventures of Huckleberry Finn.* Omens, magicians, sorcerers, black cats, and other paraphernalia of folk prophecy abound in *No. 44, The Mysterious Stranger.* Many such elements surround the character of the sorcerer, Balthasar Hoffman, whose "business suit" consists of a robe "in black velvet starred and mooned and cometed and sun'd with the symbols of his trade in silver, and on his head a conical tower with like symbols glinting from it" (231). At the same time, the work contains repeated references to *biblical* prophets, visions, and dreams. "Balthasar" even suggests the real name of the prophet Ezekiel, "Belshazzar." Ezekiel is referred to numerous times in the manuscript, and Twain may be suggesting the two aspects of prophecy one sees in his earlier work, high Christian tradition and the folkloric prophecies of hucksters. As in his earlier work, Twain derides prophecy, describing people discussing "chat, and gossip, and prophecies, and cards" (266). Placing prophecies between such mundane inconsequentials suggests the practice is sadly fallen from former glory (266). The subtitle "A Tale Found in a Jug, Translated Freely from the Jug" again suggests the prophetic tradition.

Keith Thomas records that the prophecies in the medieval period frequently involved the *found* text narrative: "Very frequently medieval descent was claimed for them by reporting that they had been accidentally discovered in the ruins of some old building, preferably a monastery" (391). Ruined castles, abandoned wells, unearthed pots, ancient cairns, any place or object with some connection to the past offered a purchase with which to approach present and future. Twain patterns his own tale after that prophetic paradigm, but also associates his story with drunkenness, as if this "tale from a jug" came from the drunken visions of a latter-day Jim Blaine; Twain did refer to the joy he took in writing the manuscripts as "an intellectual drunk" (MTHL 2: 698).

If with *What Is Man?* Twain wrote a "new gospel," here he would compose the prophetic books. There is some evidence that Twain was thinking of the *Mysterious Stranger Manuscripts* as a pairing with *What Is Man?* In his working notes for the "School House Hill" incarnation of the stranger motif, he made this notation: "Bible—sermons—dialogues—in *Appendix*" (449). Just as with *What Is Man?* Twain was thinking along theological lines, and in another notation, he wrote "Better get up a Catechism. Yes, 44 will do it. And it is printed: 'Conscience' &c" (445). References to catechisms abound, and Twain even envisioned the "*Devil's Sunday School*" with the "?s & answers of 'Conscience'" from the catechism (447). Considered as examples of prophetic genre, these manuscripts deliver Twain's vision of humanity and its shabbiness. As Twain lamented to Howells in the letter quoted above, "Damn these human beings; if I had invented them I would go hide my head in a bag" (MTHL 2:695). Twain adopts no godlike reference point here toward humans, but certainly he elevates himself above them; somewhere in between God and the rabble, he seems the prophet he writes about. With these associated manuscripts, Twain proposes casting away the tyranny of public opinion and having his say, leading Sholom Kahn to assert that "like any original work of art, 'No. 44' is sui generis" (11). Nothing is ever truly sui generis, however, and the prophetic genre lends itself to a rejection of public opinion and even formal literary expectations; that is, as a genre, prophecy occupies a set of forms and a body of content that acknowledge and celebrate the prophet's right to the unexpected and shocking. Those who read *No. 44, The Mysterious Stranger* expecting to witness a substantive and decisive break from Twain's earlier work will be disappointed, for the manuscripts are—delightfully—the old-time Twain, as tricky and as devoted to prophetic form as ever. Mark Twain's

Mysterious Stranger Manuscripts are most often placed worlds apart from traditional Judeo-Christian belief, but these associated texts are actually in their very bones and sinews quite traditional, both in the form Twain employs and the content immanent to that form.

In *No. 44, The Mysterious Stranger*, the first action following the general description of the place is the scene involving Gretel Marx, who has been studying with a Hussite woman who reveals "God's *real* message," which consists in worshipping "only God" (222). A heretic in the eyes of the church, this woman is a prophet figure, claiming she has access to the "*real* message," while the established church cannot access that esoteric knowledge. Twain's use of John Huss, a martyr of the Reformation, suggests a rejection of those such as Father Adolph who are associated with the hierarchy of the established church. The story begins with a symbolic action, a "Hussite woman," herself a kind of mysterious stranger, coming from outside of the community and claiming privileged knowledge of the creator. Threatened by Father Adolph, who prophesies that the Virgin will punish her, Gretel Marx rejects the Hussite woman in favor of the established church. Just as the priest had predicted, tragedy strikes and Mrs. Marx's horses die. Upon the priest's tip, she purchases a lottery ticket and wins a fortune, just as he had further prophesied. The stupidity of Marx and the townspeople is evident in their reliance on prophecy that consists of chance and coincidence. In the small matters, they see the truth of the prophecy, but miss the larger situation. When Mrs. Marx wins the lottery, it is taken as evidence of the Virgin's favor. Even the narrator, August Feldner, sees in it the lesson that "the Virgin rewards a real repentance," and watches over Mrs. Marx and the village, pointing out that "for reward the Virgin watched over it and took care of it personally, and made it fortunate and prosperous always" (224). In an irony lost on August, the paragraphs immediately following the Virgin's blessing of the village chronicle the many funerals, suicides, and visitations of plague suffered by Eseldorf. The facts are unambiguous, but the villagers in Eseldorf (aptly named Assville) cannot interpret the information correctly.

Against this somnolent backdrop, the character 44 flashes forth. Indeed, his appearance is both mundane and miraculous. He has been compared to many biblical figures: an "unfallen angel" (Gervais 24), *the* fallen angel, Satan (Marotti, Parsons, and many others), Christ (May, Bellamy, and others), and a conflation of God and Satan (Male 43). Perhaps the most astonishing is Dwayne Eutsey's conclusion that "Forty-Four must be God" (48). Donald Malcom, for whom *No. 44, The Mysterious*

Stranger is a "midrashic work, one that calls into question not only Christian precepts, but the nature of the world itself and its basis for existence," sees a largely unconscious Twain constructing his story on the myth of the defeat of a lesser God or "evil Demiurge" to allow August Feldner, the "transcendent being" to achieve his true greatness (43, 52). Shorn of its Gnostic content, Malcom's argument suggests the many analyses of Twain's tale as a Bildungsroman; Joseph Csicsila, for example, so interprets the novel, viewing it as a story of "August's desire to educate himself" (58), and Kahn calls the work "a sort of Bildungsroman" (108). These critics note the importance of August as the object of 44's efforts, but 44's words are more than pedagogical; they are anagogical and prophetic.

While 44 is most commonly identified as Satan by critics, the identification is by no means clear. In the other texts, "Chronicle of the Young Satan" and "Schoolhouse Hill," such an identification finds greater support, but in *No. 44, The Mysterious Stranger,* Twain leaves the identification much more equivocal. Indeed, the 44 character makes little sense viewed as Satan, and quite a bit more sense viewed as Christ, at least if considering him as the ultimate prophet and as the fulfillment of prophecy; in his role as "Prophet, King, and Priest," Christ is both the apex of prophecy and the logical end of the prophetic period (Calvin II: 425–28). If 44 is Christ, it is in his role as prophet, for 44 is the prophet whose presence in the community both enlightens and disturbs. The stranger as prophet has a long history that Twain frequently exploited. Perhaps the most obvious example of the later period is the stranger in "The War Prayer." The role played by the stranger is nearly always a regenerative one, with the stranger calling a community to account for depravity and sin. The critical tendency to view such figures as satanic has more to do with a misunderstanding of the role played by the biblical prophets than it does with Twain's use of them. "The prophet is an iconoclast," observes Rabbi Heschel, "challenging the apparently holy, revered, and awesome. . . . To many a devout believer Jeremiah's words must have sounded blasphemous" (10). In each case, Twain uses the stranger figure not as Christ per se, and certainly not as Satan, but as prophet, offering autognosis and condemnation to the community. In "The Man That Corrupted Hadleyburg" (1899), for example, the stranger's influence changes the town's motto from "Lead us not into temptation" to "Lead us into temptation." This is not to embrace sin, but to embrace an awareness of one's deeply flawed and corrupt nature, the depravity of Calvinist doctrine. That is the work of a prophet. "It is very possible," Michelson suggests, "that Forty-Four's object remains, to the very end, quite the same—not to instruct, but to astound us, to dizzy us" (121). This problematic reading emerges from Michelson's view of the text as governed by a *Deus Ludens,* when in fact the informing genres are those of prophecy and *parodia sacra.* Forty-four's work might begin with astonishment, but this burlesque of the prophetic genre ultimately affirms the educational purpose of the biblical prophets: God's knowledge is his, not yours; do your own work better and know your own place. Although many of Nathaniel Hope Preston's claims are dubious, his analysis of the influence of Jain Indian philosophy on *No. 44, The Mysterious Stranger* is intriguing. The discussion of Indian "prophets" fits into the discussion of Bildungsroman but also links it— appropriately—to the prophetic genre (78). Forty-four is the prophet figure who comes into the community from without, criticizes, disturbs, enlightens, and then departs.[4]

As Matheson notes, Twain employs a "plethora of sleep imagery" in the opening of the work, "suggesting dullness, complacency, and smug, unused intellects" (6). What follows with the arrival of 44, however, is in a sense Twain's "Great Awakening," the eruption of the Reformation and Calvinism into the sleepy Age of Faith. The Hussite's activities signal the arrival of the historical Reformation, and 44 is its prophet. Fleda Brown Jackson is absolutely correct in her analysis of the "celestial imagery" surrounding 44, noting in particular his comparison to comets and the sun (68). The extensive imagery Jackson notes identifies 44 as celestial, but one should stress that the imagery associates 44 with Christ and the biblical prophets. The figure of the stranger noted by Ezekiel in his prophecies has "a likeness as the appearance of fire: from the appearance of his loins even downward, fire; and from his loins even upward, as the appearance of brightness, as the colour of amber" (Ezekiel 8:2; see also 1:27). Similarly, Twain associates 44 with "a great light" and describes his "great transformation scene" as one in which "all his form was clothed in that immortal fire, and flashing like the sun" (390–91). Later, again, "44 stood clothed as with the sun" (399). In addition to Ezekiel, one thinks of Isaiah's chariot of fire. The allusions suggest, too, in the New Testament, the Transfiguration of Christ, with the emphasis on "whiteness"; the allusion to the verse, "his face did shine as the sun, and his raiment was white as the light," suggests 44 as both prophecy and fulfillment of prophecy (Matthew 17:2; see also Luke 9:29, Mark 7:3). The allusions include the book of Revelation, with its description of a figure whose "countenance *was* as the sun shineth" (1:16). Indeed, at several points in his book *Christian Science* (1907), written during the same period as *No. 44, The Mysterious Stranger,* Twain discusses Mary Baker Eddy's claim to be the "woman clothed with the sun" in Revelation 12:1 (see *Christian Science,* 236, 239). Many connections between 44 and Eddy exist, but it would be an exaggeration to claim Eddy as the model for 44, although such a claim is tempting. K. Patrick Ober has suggested that in his manuscript, Twain "carried Eddy's philosophy to its ultimate extreme," in essence contending that the work endorses her philosophy by extending it (220). If Eddy's influence is so profound on *No. 44, The Mysterious Stranger,* it is to provoke burlesque. Twain sandwiches discussion of Eddy and the "Christian Silence dialect" between his criticisms of various methods of interpreting prophecy (383). In both *Christian Science* and *No. 44, The Mysterious Stranger,* one sees Twain's contention that prophecy is part of the past and that those who employ it are charlatans or worse; just as visible, on the other hand, is Twain's reliance on jeremiad as an effective vehicle for his own social commentary.

Perhaps even more than his appearance, 44's most notable feature is his name, and not surprisingly, it has been the subject of many attempted explanations of greater or lesser currency. While Nathaniel Hope Preston suggests that "in making an intentional shift from the value-laden 'Satan' to the unconventional name '44,' he was also inviting a shift away from Judeo-Christian axiology" (98), the most plausible explanations connect the name "44" to the *biblical* associations of the character. Lowrey, for example, uses "metaphysical math" to connect 44's name to Jewish origins; if such a connection exists, however, would it not suggest the Old Testament prophetic genre rather than simply "lyrical form and ironic content"? (101, 110). After all, even the last name "Traum" in earlier versions suggests the "dreams" so common in prophecies. Moreover, the number "4" plays a significant symbolic role in biblical prophecies. Ezekiel 1:5–6, for example, describes the "four living creatures" with the "likeness of a man. And every one had four faces, and every one had four wings" (see also 46:22). The book of Revelation, too, features the four beasts with the four aspects: lion, calf, man, and eagle (4:6–7) and predicts that during the end times only "144,000" will be saved (see 7:4, 14:1, and 14:3). Given that good *Father Peter* is imprisoned and then released, only to be driven insane by 44, it is perhaps significant that A.D. 44 was the year *St. Peter* was imprisoned. In short, two salient facts about 44 impose themselves. One is the surfeit of biblical allusions suggested by the name 44, rather than the contrary. The other is that the name 44 is nearly impossible to interpret, *and that is its most significant point.*

Indeed, 44 complains that humans have "no talent for interpretation," a criticism that he directs toward August with reference to all humans (385). Forty-four discusses the whole variety of means by which God could convey messages to people, paying special attention to "dream-sprites" that "conveyed messages with perfect verbal accuracy" (382). Twain's 44 uses the humorous and dismissive language we have seen in other works involving prophecy, comparing the relative values of dreams versus Western Union telegrams: "He instanced the Joseph-dreams, and gave it as his opinion that if they had gone per Western Union, the lean kine would all have starved to death before the telegrams arrived" (382). The absurd comparison "makes strange" the very idea of prophetic interpretation in the age of the telegraph, yet the criticism is not of the medium, but of the interpreter. Because they have "no talent for interpretation," people are unable to read the prophetic messages. Forty-four's satirical history of prophecy moves to consider the use of augurs, reducing prophecy to the very basic level of trying to comprehend the enormity of God by examining a bird's entrails, "that being the way the Roman Gods had invented to communicate with them when dream-transportation went out and Western Union hadn't come in yet" (385). The subject matter and derisive tone recall Twain's "As Concerns Interpreting the Deity" (1905), written during the same time period. Twain again voices his belief that people have no business attempting to comprehend the mind of God, particularly with such ridiculous means. August's query is the same anyone should ask: "what does a chicken know about the future?" The concept makes the idea of prophecy ridiculous, but suggests, too, why people appeal to prophecy—Twain jokes that we are the "chickens"; lacking the guts to face the future, we resort to divination with chicken guts. Twain humorously rejects the folk traditions of prophecy and also the Christian tradition of prophecies with the "Joseph-dreams" that no longer work, not because God sends no message, but because we are unable to read them. In his working notes, Twain refers most notably to the prophet Ezekiel, linking the failure of the Roman augurs to the end of prophecy:

> The *dreams* are all right enough, but the art of interpreting is lost. 1500 yr ago they were getting to do it so badly it was considered better to depend on chicken-guts & other naturally intelligent sources of prophecy,

recognising that when guts can't prophecy it is no use for Ezekiel to go into the business. Prophecy went out with the chicken guts. (462–63)

Mixing commerce, poultry entrails, and prophetic tradition undermines the seriousness of prophecy as a legitimate theological practice or concern. Like the references to Western Union, the idea of Ezekiel going "into business" establishes a wall between the human world of mundane business affairs and the omnitemporal realm of Deity. Ironically, that is just what prophets do, positioning themselves between the two realms and their distinct time frames.

If, as Calvin asserts, prophecy serves the useful function of keeping the church in "suspense," that is, locating it in time and reminding the inhabitants of what is to come, Twain asserts that we are better off not knowing the future, agreeing with Thomas X. in "Which Was the Dream" that knowing the future would literally kill us. Forty-four is notable among the inhabitants of Eseldorf as one who can foresee the future. He clearly knows everything, and moves easily among all times, so that there exists no real temporal reference point. From Twain's point of view, as indicated by his notes for "The Chronicle of Young Satan," "Satan often draws upon *future* history" (410). Forty-four, too, is a prophet of a Calvinist God yet knows the secrets of predestination: "that which is not forordained will not happen. . . . What is written must happen" (325–26). Still, as Lurye notes, 44 cannot "save" people from their ultimate destiny "just because he knows the future" (566).[5] In contrast to humans, then, 44 has no need for prophecy, for he experiences all times at once; moreover, he willingly embraces human ignorance of the future when he informs August, "I have shut down the prophecy-works" (386). Because he knows the future as well as he knows the past, 44 occupies a position precisely opposite of humankind: the chickens strain their necks to see into the future, but 44 knows everything and knows no fear. In fact, he comes to Earth precisely to dispense with his prophetic power. "I do so love suprises!" he exclaims, continuing to say that "I will let things go their own way, and act as circumstances suggest. Then there will be surprises" (386).

August reacts to 44 out of a human incapacity to comprehend the divine view of creation. For his part, 44 despairs of his project of "enlightening that kind of a mind" with all of its "mental limitations" (331). Chief among those limitations is the belief in time, and 44 derides August, saying "you cut it up and measure it; to your race there is a past, a present and a future" (331). August's language reveals his inability to adopt the divine view when he says that the wonderful banquet of corn-pone, fried chicken, and milk gravy "were non-existent as yet, they were products of the unborn *future!*" (330). The mixture of tenses renders normative the divine view in which time is not "cut," however incapable humans are to understand it or insufficient human language is to explain it. Forty-four's language is accusative as he criticizes the human mind, saying "it doesn't *hold* anything; one cannot pour the starred and shoreless expanses of the universe into a jug!" (332). This "tale found in a jug," then, is in part a jeremiad to reveal the desperate inadequacy of humans compared to divine. One recalls Twain's burlesque sermon against those who presume to explain the mysterious workings of Providence in *Roughing It*. The questions fired at August are intended for every reader: "If—look here: *can't* you extinguish time? *can't* you comprehend eternity? can't you conceive of a thing like that—a thing with *no* beginning—a thing that *always* was?" (332). Sounding much like God speaking from the whirlwind in the book of Job, 44 here reminds August of his place. The point is not, as Rohman suggests, that "what appears to be so, *isn't*" (78). Rather, the truth blinds us, dazzles us, so far separated from it are we and unable, in fact, to contain it. J. Kenneth Van Dover's comment on "The Chronicle of Young Satan," an early version of the manuscripts, holds true for the last version: "most of the 'Chronicle' is devoted to Twain's assaults upon man's ethical pretensions rather than upon the metaphysical reality that underlies them" (194).

In contrast, 44 purposely shuts down his ability to see ahead. The other prophetic function—criticism—remains, with 44 still judging the human race; in fact, accepting the lack of "prophecy-works" on Earth as 44 does is really the main point. Derisive of the human efforts to inquire into deity, 44 is perfectly able to comprehend all time, but decides to embrace the limited view of humanity, at least for a time, and he assures us that it is in its way creative and wonderful. Inspiration, touching mouths, controlling speech, and so on have correlatives in many prophetic works because the divine presence places the words in the prophet's mouth—or shuts that mouth. Thus, we find Jeremiah 1:9, Revelation 22:20. Isaiah 6:5–8, and most obviously Ezekiel 3:26–27, "And I will make thy tongue cleave to the roof of thy mouth, that thou shalt be dumb, and shall not be to them a reprover: for they *are* a rebellious house. But when I speak with thee, I will open thy mouth, and thou shalt say unto them, Thus saith the Lord God" (see also Ezekiel 2:2, 3:24, 33:22). Forty-four frequently puts words into August's mouth, but he just as often prevents him from speaking: "But the words refused to leave my tongue, and I realized that he had applied that mysterious check which had so often shut off a question which I wanted to ask" (333). This "mysterious check" occurs time and again in *No. 44, The Mysterious Stranger,* and 44's practice of directing August either to open his mouth, to close his mouth, or to direct him to say something in particular links the relationship to that of deity and prophet, also effectively conveying the point that not infrequently God directs people to keep their mouths shut: "Be still, and know that I *am* God" (Psalms 46:10).

Within Twain's narrative, the last three chapters work toward a prophetic and apocalyptic conclusion, prophesying a rebirth of a culture of dry bones in two scenes patterned after Ezekiel and Revelation. The prophesied new age is the Reformation within the poetic present of the text, and the predictable result of that historical upheaval applies to Twain's contemporary fin de siècle. *No. 44, The Mysterious Stranger* is, according to Kahn, "an exploration of the confrontation between a fifteenth-century world of practical work in a print shop and the various forms of mystery and miracle associated with the stranger" (93). Despite the setting, which seems to be the modern world encroaching anachronistically on the medieval, the narrative asserts the ancient erupting into the modern and the modern impinging on the ancient. The printing of the Bibles in the shop is one example of this. At the same time that the modern age seems to intrude on the ancient, the obverse occurs. "The printing of Bibles to be sent to Prague in 'No. 44' is instead a tool for the Reformation," Maria Marotti suggests, "and thus represents the taking over of writing by free thought" (124). Marotti is certainly correct that the printing associates the particular time and place with the beginnings of the Reformation, and "free thought," at least as understood in a nineteenth-century context, results. Still, just as the modern influences the ancient, the ancient influences the modern, and the printing of the Bibles asserts the primacy of the biblical texts as a master text, not just as one among many.

Indeed, taken as a whole, the *Mysterious Stranger Manuscripts* create a world in which the prophetic accounts of the past are very much a part of the present. In "The Chronicle of Young Satan," Twain includes a description of a miraculous tree that bears "fruits of many kinds and colors—oranges, grapes, bananas, peaches, cherries, apricots and so on" (168). Generally, the tree relates the story of how petty and selfish humans can be. Even when this tree has divine origins, the "owner" of the land refuses to share, and so is cursed to water the tree every hour of every night, upon pain of death. The tree resembles the vision of the tree in the book of Daniel that "grew, and was strong" and produced fruit for all, but that was ordered cut down by "a watcher and an holy one" (4: 11,13). In Daniel's prophecy, the tree represents Nebuchadnezzar. In Twain's story, the tree represents human selfishness. The tree has other "roots," too. Parsons is far too modest in his essay on the background of Twain's work: "The parent/stock of many of these wondrous trees is perhaps the Tree of Life in the New Jerusalem, 'which bare twelve manner of fruits, and yielded her fruit in every month' (Revelation, 22:2). A definite source of Twain's version probably exists, but I have not discovered it" (64–65). In fact, Parsons is indisputably correct in his identification. In his notes for the manuscripts, Twain wrote the words "New Jerusalem" in the midst of his descriptions of the landscape and a list of Austrian politicians (418). Tuckey connects the Jewish and Christian factions in Vienna to the text Twain was writing (20–22), but it is equally true that Twain was thinking along prophetic lines; the fact that he wrote the words "New Jerusalem" in his working notes indicates he was thinking in terms of prophecy and even the ultimate prophecy, the establishment through Christ's reign of the New Jerusalem.

As *No. 44, The Mysterious Stranger* moves toward its famous conclusion, Twain builds the narrative around events from the books of Ezekiel and Revelation to create a sense of universal human history filled both with horror and humor, the *parodia sacra* writ large. The most notable passage is from the book of Ezekiel, which correlates to the "Mister Bones" section of *No. 44, The Mysterious Stranger*. In Ezekiel, the Lord places the prophet "down in the midst of the valley which *was* full of bones" (37:1). Told to "Prophesy upon these bones," the prophet does, "and as I prophesied, there was a noise, and behold a shaking, and the bones came together, bone to bone" (37:4, 7). As Ezekiel continues to prophesy to the bones, "the sinews and the flesh came upon them" and eventually God breathes from "the four winds" and the "exceeding great army" lives again (37:8–10).

In the "Mr. Bones" section, Twain re-creates the scene from Ezekiel in burlesque, following it immediately with the much more somber "Assembly of the Dead" vision or re-vision of Ezekiel's valley of dry bones. When Mr. Bones comes onto the scene, he announces himself with "a dry, bony noise, such a kl—lackety klackclack, kl—lackety klackclack! . . . I said to myself, 'skeletons a-coming, oh, what shall I do!'" (354). When he arrives, Mr. Bones presents August not with a skeleton, but with a spectacle directly from the minstrel shows of the nineteenth century. Clad in a "clownish and outlandish costume," Mr.

Bones has the exaggerated African features typical of minstrel makeup: "the man's mouth reached clear across his face and was unnaturally red, and had extraordinarily thick lips, and the teeth showed intensely white between them, and the face was as black as night" (354). Even in the comic depiction, however, one senses the biblical syntax, with the repetition of the word "and" in the series, suggesting any number of lines from Revelation. Twain's use of the word "smote" likewise sounds biblical, as do, much more obviously, the "fragments of dry bone" played by the figure.

The biblical-comical elements of *parodia sacra* become less incongruous as Mr. Bones plays for August. Forty-four appears in this guise because August has been depressed, and 44 feels this entertainment would cheer him. Fleda Brown Jackson sees the music in the Mister Bones section as providing "a kind of cathartic musical (creative) salvation" (63). The word "salvation" is rightly chosen. When Mr. Bones sees August and calls out, "*Now* den, Misto' Johnsing, how does yo' corporsosity seem to segashuate!" he is really asking him, "How are you? Are you all right?" (355). The "bastard English" word "corporsosity" makes a joke out of the human fear of becoming a corpse, but as Mr. Bones sings, the language becomes more biblical, and more comforting. August labels his voice "divine" as he sings "Old Folks at Home," and the words "float away toward heaven" (355). August becomes the perfect audience, empathizing completely with the "vision" offered by Mr. Bones (356). Significantly, like the prophecies of Ezekiel on which it is built, the Mr. Bones section is a welter of emotions: sorrow over the lost past and hope for the future.

Sound plays a significant role in the beginning of the "Assembly of the Dead" section of *No. 44, The Mysterious Stranger,* just as it does in the "Mr. Bones" section. The first notable sound is the "*Boom-m-m—boom-m-m—boom-m-m!*" of the clock that, under 44's influence, begins chiming backward (397). Forty-four, August, and even the cat begin talking backward just as time reverses its flight. The scene is one of the most astonishing in Twain's oeuvre, and the aesthetic representation of what is in essence an ethical point is brilliantly done. As time goes backward, all of the "ages of cruelty and captivity and murder and mystery" of the place disappear—are *healed* (388). August, like Ezekiel in the Valley of Dry Bones, observes his Duplicate and "watched its skeleton gather form and solidity; watched it put on flesh and clothes, and all that" (399). Similarly, when the dead begin marching, one hears the "faint clicking sound" and then the "dry sharp clacking" (401). Finally, Twain presents his readers with "the spidery dim forms of thousands of skeletons marching" (401). Twain's army marches into his book straight from the Valley of Dry Bones in Ezekiel. It is surely no accident that Twain portrays his assembly as an army, and that military leaders play a large role in the "Assembly of the Dead." Even his title recalls the sounding of "assembly" in the military, conflating it with the idea of assembling the skeletons from their fragments. Both ideas come from Ezekiel, who "prophesied" to the bones, heard their sound, witnessed their assembly, and then finally recorded that "they lived, and stood up upon their feet, an exceeding great army" (37:10).

Forty-four is certainly not one of the "prophets of doom," as Bercovitch contends (197), nor is this work Twain's "final capitulation to the Great Dark," as Jay Martin judges (196). Forty-four prophesies doom within the context of resurrection, just as Ezekiel does. The chapters leading up to the conclusion of the book follow the dictates of the prophetic genre and look toward resurrection. The conclusion similarly adheres to the prophetic genre, concluding with one final prophecy from 44 to August that, like so many examples of biblical prophecy, relies on dreams:

> "It is true, that which I have revealed to you: there is no God, no universe, no human race, no earthly life, no heaven, no hell. It is all a Dream, a grotesque and foolish dream. Nothing exists but You. And You are but a *Thought*—a vagrant Thought, a useless Thought, a homeless Thought, wandering forlorn among the empty eternities!"
>
> He vanished, and left me appalled; for I knew, and realized, that all he had said was true. (405)

The form itself remains, both the form of our thinking and the form of the work. During the years he composed the *Mysterious Stranger Manuscripts,* Twain also worked on *The Refuge of the Derelicts,* which discusses, among other theological issues, the "minor prophets," with the character George asserting that "it isn't so much *what* a man says that affects us as the *way* he says it" (193–95). The *way* 44 speaks is in the manner of a prophet, even his style following the traditional forms of the genre.[6] Forty-four's words, "It is true, that which I have revealed to you," *sound* like a prophet's words, the style and syntax recalling many passages in the Bible, including "These sayings are faithful and true" (Revelation 22:6). Even 44's words, *"Nothing exists save empty space—and you!"* so seemingly nihilistic, are tame in comparison to Ezekiel's prophecy: "I will make thee a terror, and thou *shalt be* no *more:* though thou be sought for, yet shalt thou never be found again, saith the Lord God" (26:21; see also 28:19). In sum, 44's words are the words of a biblical prophet, and the form reasserts its belief in judgment and regeneration when readers are told to "Dream other dreams, and better!" (404–5). The irony is the irony of the prophets, who routinely tell God's people the same message: God rejects you because of your iniquity; He has sent me, a prophet, out of his love.

No. 44, The Mysterious Stranger was intended to be an unsettling text; building on the prophetic tradition, Twain creates a world in which time stands still, flies backward, and in which forever seems to be now. In an excellent article, Paul Delaney notes the imagery of time in the various manuscripts, claiming that reference to the "'mental and spiritual clock' suggests ways—other than chronological—to measure time" (59). Delaney observes that the narratorial perspective in the end may involve "centuries and centuries," and not just the usual passage of time (59). The temporal shift that accompanies the movement from one type of dream to another is significant, for it is a prophetic vision that emerges, a vision that can take in the whole of time in one experience. Into that world 44 flashes forth to illumine—and disturb—the world. In his analysis of "The Chronicle of Young Satan," Lloyd Daigrepont correctly asserts that the "'enlightenment' or 'awakening' has failed to replace the comforting tranquility of medieval society and faith" (40). As one sees in Twain's fiction so frequently, particularly in his jeremiads, there is little support for equating faith and peace. In fact, Twain used the prophetic form throughout his career specifically because as a genre, prophecy shakes people up—religious folk in particular, witness "The War Prayer" and "The Man That Corrupted Hadleyburg."

The ending adheres to the genre. Rabbi Heschel suggests that the prophet "begins with *a message of doom;* he concludes with *a message of hope*" (12); so it is with Twain. August is in charge of his own destiny within the context of historical and personal reformation (Reformation), but finds it bittersweet. Free from the bonds of an authoritarian church, he is responsible for making his own way through the world. The prophet Ezekiel and dreams feature so prominently in the manuscripts because Twain delivers a final prophecy, as did Ezekiel when he stated, "Therefore ye shall see no more vanity, nor divine divinations" (13:23). In this context, one must reinterpret 44's assertion, "*Life itself is only a vision, a dream*" (404). Indeed, the only "vision" in the world after the Reformation is the personal vision; all the onus is on each individual, as it is for August, who must now become his own prophet; the only "divine divinations" are the "other dreams, and better" he is instructed to dream—and interpret—for himself. Beginning with a cultural studies approach, Frederick Pratter does not get much beyond Twain's text as "working out social anxieties in imaginary, hence harmless, forms" (78). To discuss Twain's writing as "harmless" is to assume, as Pratter does, that literature is inscribed by society, rather than *inscribing society*. In fact, during his own time, many viewed Twain's writing as *harmful*, and he himself viewed his writing as a vocation that was hardly innocuous. *No. 44, The Mysterious Stranger* proposes, as do Twain's other efforts in the genre of prophecy, to reform society, less politically than in some of his earlier pieces on Reconstruction and lynching, but spiritually. If anything, the ending reveals the wondrous creative possibilities of freedom the Reformation offered and offers, while at the same time deeming it an "appalling" freedom. Twain's *No. 44, The Mysterious Stranger* seems a long way from his joking reference to himself as the Prophet Samuel, but like the biblical prophets, Twain called down judgment on his society, offering a qualified hope for the future, for the "SOMETHING BETTER" longed for by the child in "Which Was the Dream?" (50). With the prophetic material in his great, incomplete work of literary prophecy, Twain's character 44 reminds us, as any biblical prophet would, of our ignorant condition, but he tells us, too, that if the "prophecy-works" have shut down, we can follow his example: "I will let things go their own way, and act as circumstances suggest. Then there will be surprises" (386).

{ CONCLUSION }

I was made in His image, but have never been mistaken for Him.
—MARK TWAIN (unpublished notebook 48, 22)

Mr. Howells does not repeat his forms, and does not need to; he can invent fresh ones without limit. It is mainly the repetition over and over again, by the third-rates, of worn and commonplace and juiceless forms that makes their novels such a weariness and vexation to us, I think.
—MARK TWAIN (William Dean Howells 729)

THEOLOGIAN, Missionary, Priest, Preacher, Prophet, Saint, Brother Twain, Holy Samuel, Bishop of New Jersey, and of course the *Reverend* Mark Twain: these ecclesiastical personae must be understood primarily as burlesques of religious literary genres, for in each case their adoption was associated with "the one right form" Twain adopted for his narratives. The writer's poses are antigenres in the sense that Twain employs them to contextualize his criticism of church and society within the very genres by which church and society contextualize themselves.[1]

In a speech introducing Winston Churchill at the Waldorf-Astoria, for example, Twain introduces himself as a "missionary" and refers to "my missionary efforts" on England's behalf, but then uses the authority of this burlesque persona to chastise England: "England sinned in getting into a war in South Africa . . . just as I think we have sinned in crowding ourselves into a war in the Philippines on the same terms" (455). Twain's strategy is a typical one for him. Just as he adopted other ecclesiastical personae to use the immediately recognizable and instantly authoritative theological forms, in this introduction he appears before the group as a missionary. The speech of a missionary before an assembly back in the states is itself a rhetorical subgenre, and one with which the audience was doubtless familiar. Twain exploits the genre's authority to do what missionaries do: report on the state of the world's soul. Twain's introduction thus becomes a missionary's sermon where his world travels and "missionary efforts" allow him to claim that England and America are "kin in sin" (455).

The Reverend Twain's theological dialogue, then, tells us much about his opinion of society, but does not necessarily reveal the state of his own soul. This study has employed an organic approach, uniting attention to form and content and drawing on biographical sources only when the interpretation of the aesthetic object warranted. One can say this: Calvinism is the order "left standing" in Twain's literary life, and he responds on the level of form and content to the ideas found in that stern inheritance. As a writer, Twain frequently adopts the literary forms of traditional Judeo-Christian religion and creates parodies, burlesques, and creative revisions of those forms. Twain never follows these genres religiously, instead reinvigorating what he deems "juiceless forms." Throughout his career, Twain experimented with every form he adopted; he even tried to break the mold of autobiography when writing his own, suggesting to Henry H. Rogers that "the *form* of this book is one of the most memorable literary inventions of the ages" (MTHHR 611).

In re-creating these genres, however, Twain does not, indeed cannot, destroy or supplant their original forms. To do so would destroy his own work, whose genetic code derives from those eternal genres of his disaffection. Indeed, Twain's writings exist in constant dialogue with his literary models and their immanent ideologies; he found inspiration, and literary structures, in the traditional genres associated with religious belief.

{ N O T E S }

Chapter 1

1. To belabor the point, Twain's Calvinism exerts a shaping influence on his writing, both in terms of content and form. The continued influence of Calvinism must therefore be a productive one. Far too many critics are far too dismissive of the influence. For Sherwood Cummings, this "dreadful Calvinism" had no positive influence in Twain's work, and it was Paine's *The Age of Reason* that "converted him" (21). John Frederick describes Twain's Calvinism as "religious baggage" that he lost on his journey (150). Van Wyck Brooks is correct in his thesis only in that Presbyterianism continued to influence Twain, not in his view that Twain "wishes to take vengeance upon the Jehovah of the Presbyterians," a view that has blinded too many critics to the creative role Calvinism plays in Twain's work (233). Brooks and others have made the extent to which Twain rejected Calvinism the mark of aesthetic success. In contrast, critics like William Phipps who see the importance of religion and theology scour his literary works in the attempt to render biographical judgments on what Twain's beliefs may have been. Twain's appropriation of religious form and his use of it for aesthetic ends ought to be the primary scholarly concern.

2. Philip Fanning's *Mark Twain and Orion Clemens: Brothers, Partners, Strangers* is the best biographical analysis of the complex and creative relationship between the two brothers. Chapter 16, "Orion's Excommunication," is especially valuable. See especially Henry Sweets, *The Hannibal, Missouri Presbyterian Church: A Sesquicentennial History*, for an illuminating discussion of the environment both Orion and Sam grew up in (3–5).

3. Eric Eliason's essay, "Curious Gentiles and Representational Authority in the City of the Saints," is highly misleading on the subject of Twain's depictions of Mormonism. Eliason sees a "reluctance to believe stories of Mormon atrocities" in *Roughing It*, citing Twain's depiction of Rockwell, the "destroying angel" (172). Twain makes the point

very clearly that this person is more destroyer than angel, but does not suggest that the stories of his cruelty are without substance. Eliason also writes that Twain "adds an appendix detailing late-breaking information that (correctly) established Mormon participation in the Mountain Meadows Massacre," seeming to imply that Twain attached, but did not write, the appendix and perhaps did not even believe the claims set forth in it (172).

4. See Fulton's discussion of Robinson and others in the first chapter of *Mark Twain in the Margins*.

Chapter 2

1. Ultimately, Twain obtained his conceptions of the grotesque from reality itself, but he was also influenced by Poe, whose work he refers to in chapter 76 of *Roughing It*, by Southwestern humor, and probably also by Rabelais himself, whose work Twain was familiar with at least by the mid-1870s, if not before. In many respects, Twain was the American Rabelais, and when an editor lamented, "O that we had a Rabelais," Twain retorted, "I judged I could furnish him one" (MTNJ 2: 303). Milton Rickels places Twain and Jim Blaine's story firmly in the tradition of grotesque realism of Southwestern humor, which "balances for a moment fear, horror, and disgust at dismemberment and disability against human vitality, inventiveness, and persistent sociability" (160). Similarly, Kenneth Lynn notes that Southwestern humor frequently "began in whimsicality and ended in blasphemy . . . because it was a way of beating the wilderness at its own game, of converting terror into *joie de vivre* and helplessness into an exhilarating sense of power" (27–28). Henry Nash Smith identifies the grotesque elements in Twain's work, yet seems to view their presence as primarily for comic purpose: "Miss Wagner's trouble with the glass eye and the carnivorous carpet machine are not so much brutal as grotesque. Yet it is not easy to share Mark Twain's fondness for this kind of material, which has retained only a minimum comic force" (67).

2. Most scholars believe Twain was referring to chapter 53 in this letter. See the University of California edition, 863.

3. Twain's "Old Times on the Mississippi" features a similar character, Mr. J—, who "could *not* forget anything" (380). Beginning a "vastly funny anecdote about a dog," he would, like Blaine, pile up the details but "the original first mention would be all you had learned about that dog" (381). "A Touching Story of George Washington's Boyhood" (1864) has Twain himself "writing such a long and elaborate introductory" that he neglects to tell "the story itself" (99).

4. Twain's everyday use of providential language during the composition of *Roughing It* is striking. Writing to Orion about selling their "Tennessee Land," Twain urged him to sell. "I wouldn't fool away any time about it. Providence will not deliver another lunatic into our hands if we slight this present evidence of his beneficent care for us" (MTL 4:114). See also his letter to James Redpath, (MTL 4: 435). Throughout his life, Twain subjected Providence to grotesque interpretations. In his *Autobiography,* he again reminds us of the violent reality Providence is used to explain. In 1906, recalling his dismissal from the *San Francisco Morning Call,* Twain invoked Providence: "By my Presbyterian training I knew that the Morning Call had brought disaster upon

itself. I knew the ways of Providence and I knew that this offense would have to be answered for" (AMT 122). And the offense was answered for when the San Francisco earthquake destroyed the *Call* building, *forty years later.*

Chapter 3

1. Numerous scholars have traced the literary influences on the book's structure. Richard Gray notes the work's debt to love stories, Sunday School books, and dime novel westerns (84). Lawrence Howe states that "the form of *Tom Sawyer* is, like 'Old Times,' a kind of bildungsroman-epic hybrid" (73). Franklin Rogers notes the influence of Sunday-school books, but argues that "to conclude that the basic structure of the book comes from model-boy literature is inaccurate" (*Burlesque Patterns* 106). Albert Stone, too, comments that "[a]lthough *Tom Sawyer* originated in Twain's imagination as a burlesque aimed chiefly at bemused adults, the novel develops, after the opening chapters, into something far more ambitious than a lampoon of Good Boys and Bad Boys. Tom himself as a person, the village of St. Petersburg and the values by which it lives, the interaction of boy and adults—these considerations speedily engross the novelist's attention. The result is a movement away from farce toward the classic concerns of the novel, namely the relation of individual to the community, to social class, and to money" (64).

This is not to imply that *all* critics view the work as crafted well. Bernard DeVoto suggests that the book becomes great only by transcending its own artistry, for he questions if "this literature shall or shall not be called art" and concedes that "by some canon of abstract form, the book lacks a perfect adjustment of part to part" (307). Roger Asselineau questioned the "logic and order" of the book, again invoking the conception of Twain as a slipshod writer (58). Henry Nash Smith suggests that the "structural problems of the novel, like those of Mark Twain's earlier books, reflect the instability of his attitudes toward his material" (82). Twain is neither as radical nor as conservative as some would like, so his "attitudes" are labeled unstable; the novel, as distinct from Twain, proposes a synthesis between formal and natural forms of worship.

2. See for example Virginia Wexman, who argues that the "structural pattern" of the work is the bifurcation of the plot into "two clearly separate worlds," one light and one dark, one comic and one tragic (1). Harold Aspiz, too, views the work as "constructed on a loose framework whose major elements include games of death and games of resurrection" (141). Hamlin Hill argues through impressive analysis that the book is both "a ragbag of memories" and yet "not structureless" ("Structure" 392).

3. Clark Griffith actually cites the opening of chapter 4 as the reason a murder was necessary: "And one sees readily enough why Mark Twain requires the scene. During the long Friday-to-Monday weekend set forth in the eight preceding chapters, St. Petersburg had turned entirely too much into a 'tranquil world' where, without a cloud anywhere, the 'sun beamed down like a benediction'" (124). This reading overlooks the fact that the seriousness of the narrative is inherent to this particular passage and that it is not at all tranquil—only man is vile in this idyllic landscape!

Chapter 4

1. Unpublished notebook 31, 12.

2. See the discussion of Twain's use of the incarnational aesthetic as a structural element for many of his longer works in Fulton, *Mark Twain's Ethical Realism*, 18–26.

3. There is some doubt about the dating of the manuscript. The editors of the California edition suggest 1881 as the probable date, citing the last line of the work: "Thus ended the Second Advent, A.D. 1881" (68), but Paine had written "Probably in 1871" on the manuscript (See Tuckey's note to the Califonia edition, 52). Both dates are circumstantial, the former relying on a date in a fictional work, the other relying on an unsupported judgment, probably based on Twain references within the text to his dispute with Reverend Talmage in 1871, as discussed later in this chapter. As for Paine's suggestion, Twain's memory was long, and the piece could have been written any time after his dispute with Talmage. As for the California date, one should note that in some speculative works, Twain used a future date for satirical purpose. One obvious example is his piece satirizing the Szczepanik affair in Austria. Twain wrote the article in 1898, but titled it "From the 'London Times' of 1904," even providing an imaginative byline to clue people in to the spoof, "Chicago, April 1, 1904" (272). As "The Second Advent" is essentially a kind of apocrypha, one cannot assume that 1881 was the date of composition any more than Twain's essay was written in 1904 or that Orwell wrote his novel *1984* in 1984. For decades, Twain toyed with burlesques of Christ's life, making a judgment very difficult to render. Some of his comments embodied in letters illustrate his delight in such burlesque. In a letter to Howells in 1900, Twain wrote, "For England must not fall: it would mean an inundation of Russian & German political degradations which would envelop the globe & steep it in a sort of Middle-Age night & slavery which would last till Christ comes again—which I hope he will not do; he made trouble enough before" (MTHL 2: 716). Similarly, he wrote Howells in 1909, "A stranger came, half an hour ago. I do not quite make out what strangers are for. It would have been so much better for us all if this one had been caught by mistake 19 centuries ago & crucified. Then the other one would have gone free, & that would have had pleasant results for everybody" (MTHL 2: 849).

4. See also Twain's burlesque of Eddy's "The Lord's Prayer—Amended" in *Christian Science*, 316.

Chapter 5

1. Twain continued to have concerns about Catholic temporal dominion. Years later, as he read *The Memoirs of the Duke of Saint-Simon,* Twain made this marginal comment: "The Catholics are moving steadily and surely toward dominion" (Baender 10). Similarly, in his book *Christian Science* (1906), which ostensibly addressed his fears of Mary Baker Eddy, Twain wondered if Christian Science would secretly insinuate itself into power: "Just as Protestantism has smiled and nodded this long time (while the alert and diligent Catholic was slipping in and capturing the public schools), and is now beginning to hunt around for the key when it is too late?" (262). Twain concluded that "after a generation or two," Christian Scientism would "probably divide Chris-

tendom with the Catholic Church" (252). The fear and loathing of Catholicism of Twain's early years remained with him until the end.

2. Twain obviously relied on folktales throughout his career, from the early "Ghost Life on the Mississippi" (1861) to the myriad of folk elements in *The Adventures of Tom Sawyer* (1876), *Adventures of Huckleberry Finn* (1885), and many other works. The structure influenced many works besides *Personal Recollections of Joan of Arc*, and Propp notes that Twain's *Prince and the Pauper* (1881) "is told as a folktale" (*Theory* 8). In 1883, Twain wrote a promising burlesque "1,002^d Arabian Night," replete with Sultan, remarkable births, and a wicked witch (101). Most interesting is Twain's experimentation with the form, for the Sultan repeatedly orders Scherezade to omit the typical elements such as lists, speeches, and so on. In essence, the work burlesques the situation of the Sultan trying to hasten the story while the teller protracts it, and at the same time highlighting the form such stories take. Twain experimented with the related form of the fable, finding it a hospitable means of social criticism. "Some Learned Fables, for Good Old Boys and Girls" (1875) criticizes the use of science to aggrandize human worth, as do the "Goose Fable" (1899–1900) and "The Fable of the Yellow Terror" (1904–1905). "In the Animal's Court" (1905) discusses the idea that, temperamentally, the human mind is "a machine," an idea Twain also explores during the same period in *What Is Man?* (1906). "A Fable" (1909) offers some good advice for Twain scholars with its concluding moral: "you can find in a text whatever you bring" (879).

It is interesting to note that many fairy tale elements appear in Twain's works throughout the 1890s and beyond. One may reasonably suspect that Twain reread fairy tales during this period as research for the "right form" he found for *Personal Recollections of Joan of Arc*. Evidence for such research includes references to Hans Christian Andersen in "Is He Living or Is He Dead?" (109–10). His "Two Little Tales" (1901) is particularly reminiscent of Andersen. Twain's "Five Boons of Life" is literally a fairy tale and features "the good fairy" carrying a basket with "boons" that a person may choose (524).

Chapter 6

1. Alan Gribben's *Mark Twain's Library: A Reconstruction* is the most important resource for documenting the *literary* voices contributing to Twain's writing. See also Fulton's *Mark Twain in the Margins*.

2. What is a dialogue? The dividing line between dialogue and narrative is not always clear. Formal attributes such as the printing of the speakers' names before their comments certainly create the sense that what one is reading is a dialogue. In a dialogue, too, the absence of plot as such, even when narrative is present, contributes to the dialogue form. Some larger works such as "3,000 Years among the Microbes" contain long philosophical dialogues within a larger narrative, such as the cholera germ's discussion with the yellow fever germ named "Benjamin Franklin" or the clergyman germ who begins the dialogue of chapter 14 by a kind of catechism: "You are a Christian?" (495). This study follows Bakhtin in including catechism and parodies of catechisms as special examples of the dialogue form.

3. See Fulton, "Following the 'Compass of Fact': Rethinking Mark Twain's Composing Process," the first chapter of *Mark Twain in the Margins,* 1–28.

4. See an edition of "Moral and Intellectual Man" in Joe Fulton, "The Lost Manuscript Conclusion to Mark Twain's 'Corn-Pone Opinions': An Editorial History and an Edition of the Restored Text."

5. See the discussion in Fulton, *Mark Twain's Ethical Realism: The Aesthetics of Race, Class, and Gender,* 30–31.

Chapter 7

1. See "More Maxims of Mark," 946.

2. E. S. Fussell views Twain's "interests in mental telepathy, spiritualism and dreams" as connected to a "solipsistic position" (96). John E. Becker provides an interesting discussion of *Adventures of Huckleberry Finn* as prophecy, but treats it as an example of prophecy "woven through the narrative" (139). Becker's analysis is ultimately unsatisfying, for he views prophecy in literature as "the result of habits of reflection taught us ultimately by the traditions of biblical prophecy" (131). Doubtless, this is true, but then one may see prophecy *everywhere;* it is much more legitimate to track an author's use of prophetic elements by the traces we find along the way and to cite such evidence as providing warrant for a deeper analysis. Jon Powell's analysis of Twain's use of the book of Jeremiah in "A True Story" and *Adventures of Huckleberry Finn* is much more substantive. Vivienne Perkins likewise has a very useful study, but again issues of genre are largely unexamined. Perkins believes the story "founders artistically" because Twain experiences "two contradictory impulses," that of "love" and "scorn" for humanity (42). These impulses are hardly "mutually exclusive," as she suggests, and are united in the jeremiad of the prophet (43). Geismar's *Mark Twain: An American Prophet* deals very generally with Twain as a "prophet," and considers the formal implications of such an identification not at all. The small volume *False Prophets* by James Martin Gillis contains a chapter on Mark Twain, but the content is so dismissive of Twain as a man concerned about religious issues that we should be forgiven for being dismissive of the book and its slight content. Veneta Nielsen's discussion of Twain as a "savage prophet" is oddly compelling, but ultimately written in so obscure and arcane a fashion (mirroring, one imagines, Sibylline prophecy) that it remains a useless oddity. Much more satisfying is Ernest Tuveson's discussion of Twain in *Redeemer Nation: The Idea of America's Millennial Role.* Tuveson discusses *Connecticut Yankee* as an example of an apocalyptic and millennial narrative, casting light on many issues in that novel, particularly the ending (215–31). Finally, in *Mark Twain and the Bible,* Allison Ensor states that "the writings of the Old Testament prophets, he seems to have neglected almost entirely" (99). As this chapter demonstrates, Twain's knowledge of the prophetic works was impressive.

3. While it is true that in his re-vision of the Apostle's Creed (1880s), Twain immediately follows his affirmative statement, "I believe in God Almighty" with the qualification, "I do not believe He has ever sent a message to man by anybody, or delivered one to him by word of mouth, or made Himself visible to mortal eyes at any time or in any place," it is equally true that he knew a great deal about the prophets and

their prophecies, and wrote about them a great deal for a person who supposedly discounted them (56).

4. Specific sources for the various *Mysterious Stranger Manuscripts* are many and are ably discussed by Carroll Laverty, who traces in particular the influence of Jane Taylor's story "The Mysterious Stranger," which was included as a selection in the McGuffey Readers. Laverty points out that Twain's work "might be considered a satirical expansion of Jane Taylor's moral little tale" (18). Coleman Parsons also chronicles many other sources very usefully in "The Background of *The Mysterious Stranger*."

5. The translation from Lurye is my own.

6. A close genetic connection exists between *The Refuge of the Derelicts* and the *Mysterious Stranger Manuscripts,* in terms of research, subject matter, and genre. Satan features in both sets of texts, as do discussions of prophets and certain historical information like Medieval folklore about priests tricking the devil into building bridges (cf. *The Refuge of the Derelicts,* 194; "The Chronicle of Young Satan," 39–40; and *No. 44, The Mysterious Stranger,* 225–27).

Conclusion

1. To sort these personae out for the interested reader, this list is appended. Twain called himself a theologian in "Was the World Made for Man?" (101); a missionary in "Introducing Winston S. Churchill" (454–55); a preacher in, among other places, his *Autobiography* (273); prophet in "Wit-Inspirations of the 'Two-Year-Olds'" (405), and in many other venues; saint in his correspondence with Andrew Carnegie; Brother in "Further of Mr. Mark Twain's Important Correspondence" (160); "Holy Samuel" was the nickname given him by Susan Crane, his sister-in-law, whom he called "Saint Sue" (MFMT 59–60); Priest and Bishop of New Jersey in "The Secret History of Eddypus, the World-Empire" (318–19); and the Reverend Mark Twain in the *Alta California* letters (MTMB 113–15).

⊰ WORKS CITED ⊱

Alsen, Eberhard. "The Futile Pursuit of Truth in Twain's 'What Is Man?' and Anderson's 'The Book of the Grotesque.'" *Mark Twain Journal* 17.3 (1974): 12–14.

Andersen, Hans Christian. "How to Cook Soup upon a Sausage Pin." *The Complete Fairy Tales and Stories*. Trans. Erik Christian Haugaard. New York: Doubleday and Company, 1974. 516–27.

Anonymous. Review. *Personal Recollections of Joan of Arc. Methodist Review* 78 (1896): 845–46.

———. Review. *Roughing It. Manchester Guardian* (March 6, 1872): 7.

———. Review. *Roughing It. Overland Monthly and Out West Magazine*. 8.6 (June 1872): 580–81.

———. *Willy Graham Or, The Disobedient Boy*. Philadelphia: American Sunday-School Union, 1844.

Arac, Jonathan. "Why Does No One Care about the Aesthetic Value of *Huckleberry Finn*?" *New Literary History* 30 (1999): 769–84.

Arthur, T. S. *Ten Nights in a Bar-Room. And What I Saw There*. Chicago: M. A. Donohue and Co., nd.

Aspiz, Harold. "Tom Sawyer's Games of Death." *Studies in the Novel* 27 (1995): 141-53.

Asselineau, Roger. *The Literary Reputation of Mark Twain from 1910 to 1950*. Westport, CN: Greenwood Press, 1971 (1954).

Baender, Paul. Introduction. *What Is Man? And Other Philosophical Writings*. Berkeley: University of California Press, 1973: 1–34.

Bakhtin, Mikhail. "Author and Hero in Aesthetic Activity." Trans. Vadim Liapunov. *Art and Answerability: Early Philosophical Essays by M. M. Bakhtin*. Austin: University of Texas Press, 1990. 4–56.

———. "The *Bildungsroman* and Its Significance in the History of Realism (Toward a Historical Typology of the Novel)." *Speech Genres and Other Late Essays*. Trans. Vern W. McGee. Ed. Caryl Emerson and Michael Holquist. Austin: University of Texas Press, 1986. 10–59.

———. "Discourse in the Novel." Trans. Caryl Emerson and Michael Holquist. *The Dialogic Imagination*. Austin: University of Texas Press, 1981. 259–422.

———. "Forms of Time and Chronotope in the Novel." Trans. Caryl Emerson and Michael Holquist. *The Dialogic Imagination*. Austin: University of Texas Press, 1981. 84–258.

———. "From Notes Made in 1970–71." Trans. Vern W. McGee. *Speech Genres and Other Late Essays*. Austin: University of Texas Press, 1986. 132–58.

———. "From the Prehistory of Novelistic Discourse." Trans. Caryl Emerson and Michael Holquist. *The Dialogic Imagination*. Austin: University of Texas Press, 1981. 41–83.

———. "The Problem of Content, Material, and Form in Verbal Art." Trans. Kenneth Brostrom. *Art and Answerability: Early Philosophical Essays by M. M. Bakhtin*. Austin: University of Texas Press, 1990. 257–325.

———. "The Problem of Speech Genres." Trans. Vern W. McGee. *Speech Genres and Other Late Essays*. Austin: University of Texas Press, 1986. 60–102.

———. *Problems of Dostoevsky's Poetics*. Trans. Caryl Emerson. Minneapolis: University of Minnesota Press, 1984.

———. *Rabelais and His World*. Trans. Helene Iswolsky. Bloomington: Indiana University Press, 1984.

———. "Response to a Question from the *Novy Mir* Editorial Staff." Trans. Vern W. McGee. *Speech Genres and Other Late Essays*. Austin: University of Texas Press, 1986. 1–9.

———. "Toward a Methodology for the Human Sciences." Trans. Vern W. McGee. *Speech Genres and Other Late Essays*. Austin: University of Texas Press, 1986. 159–72.

Bakhtin, M. M., and P. N. Medvedev. *The Formal Method in Literary Scholarship: A Critical Introduction to Sociological Poetics*. Trans. Albert J. Wehrle. Cambridge: Harvard University Press, 1985.

Bassett, John E. "*Roughing It:* Authority through Comic Performance." *Mark Twain: An Anthology of Recent Criticism*. Ed. Prafulla Kar. Dehli: Pencraft International, 1992. 90–103.

Becker, John E. "Twain: The Statements was Interesting but Tough." *Poetic Prophecy in Western Literature*. Ed. Jan Wojcik and Raymond-Jean Frontain. Rutherford, NJ: Fairleigh Dickinson University Press, 1984. 131–42.

Beidler, Philip D. "Realistic Style and the Problem of Context in *The Innocents Abroad* and *Roughing It*." *American Literature* 52 (1980): 33–49.

Bellamy, Gladys Carmen. *Mark Twain as a Literary Artist*. Norman: University of Oklahoma Press, 1950.

Bercovitch, Sacvan. *The American Jeremiad*. Madison: University of Wisconsin Press, 1978.

Berkove, Lawrence. "The Trickster God in *Roughing It*." *Thalia* 18 (1998): 21–30.

Bird, John. "The Chains of Time: Temporality in *Huckleberry Finn*." *Texas Studies in Literature and Language* 32 (1990): 262–76.

Blair, Walter. *Mark Twain and Huck Finn*. Berkeley: University of California Press, 1960.

———. "On the Structure of *Tom Sawyer*." *Modern Philology* 37 (1939): 75–88.

Bradley, Ruth Mary. "The Making of Mark Twain's *Personal Recollections of Joan of Arc.*" Ph.D. Dissertation. University of California, Los Angeles, 1970.

Branch, Edgar Marquess. Introduction. *Early Tales and Sketches, Volume 1, 1851–1864.* Ed. Edgar M. Branch and Robert H. Hirst. Berkeley: University of California Press, 1979. 1–57.

Bridgman, Richard. *Traveling in Mark Twain.* Berkeley: University of California Press, 1987.

Brodwin, Stanley. "History and Martyrological Tragedy: The Jewish Experience in Sholem Asch and André Schwarz-Bart." *Twentieth Century Literature* 40 (1994): 72–91.

———. "Mark Twain and the Myth of the Daring Jest." *The Mythologizing of Mark Twain.* Ed. Sara de Saussure Davis and Philip D. Beidler. Tuscaloosa: University of Alabama Press, 1984. 136–57.

———. "Mark Twain's Theology: The Gods of a Brevet Presbyterian." *The Cambridge Companion to Mark Twain.* Ed. Forrest Robinson. New York: Cambridge University Press, 1995. 220–48.

Brooks, Cleanth. "New Criticism." *Princeton Encyclopedia of Poetry and Poetics.* Enlarged Ed. Alex Preminger, Frank J. Warnke, and O. B. Hardison, Jr. Princeton: Princeton University Press, 1974. 567–68.

Brooks, Van Wyck. *The Ordeal of Mark Twain.* Cleveland: Meridian, 1965 (1920).

Brunvand, Jan Harold. "Western Folk Humor in *Roughing It.*" *The Western Folklore Conference: Selected Papers.* Ed. Austin E. Fife. Logan: Utah State University Press, 1964. 53–65.

Budd, Louis J. *Mark Twain: Social Philosopher.* Columbia: University of Missouri Press, 2001 (1962).

Bush, Harold K., Jr. "'A Moralist in Disguise': Mark Twain and American Religion." *A Historical Guide to Mark Twain.* Ed. Shelley Fisher Fishkin. New York: Oxford University Press, 2002. 55–94.

Byers, John R. "A Hannibal Summer: The Framework of *The Adventures of Tom-Sawyer.*" *Studies in American Fiction* 8 (1980): 81–88.

Calvin, John. *Institutes of the Christian Religion.* 2 vols. Trans. Henry Beveridge. Grand Rapids, MI: William B. Eerdmans, 1981.

Cardwell, Guy. Notes. *The Innocents Abroad.* The Innocents Abroad *and* Roughing It. New York: Library of America, 1984. 1001–14.

Caron, James E. "The Comic *Bildungsroman* of Mark Twain." *Modern Language Quarterly* 50 (1989): 145–72.

Carretta, Vincent. "The Roots of Mark Twain's Pessimism in *What Is Man?*" *Cithara* 18.1 (1978): 46–60.

Chase, Richard. *The American Novel and Its Tradition.* New York: Doubleday, 1957.

Clemens, Clara. *My Father, Mark Twain.* New York: Harper, 1931.

Coulombe, Joseph L. *Mark Twain and the American West.* Columbia: University of Missouri Press, 2003.

Covici, Pascal, Jr. *Mark Twain's Humor: The Image of a World.* Dallas, TX: Southern Methodist University Press, 1962.

Cox, James M. *Mark Twain: The Fate of Humor.* Princeton: Princeton University Press, 1966.

Csicsila, Joseph. "Life's Rich Pageant: The Education of August Feldner in Mark Twain's *No. 44, The Mysterious Stranger.*" *Studies in American Humor* 3.4 (1997): 54–67.

Cummings, Sherwood. *Mark Twain and Science: Adventures of a Mind.* Baton Rouge: Louisiana State University Press, 1988.

Daigrepont, Lloyd M. "Mark Twain and the Descent into Consciousness: *The Chronicle of Young Satan.*" *CEA Critic* 63 (2001): 39–45.

Delahaye, Père H. *The Legends of the Saints: An Introduction to Hagiography.* Trans. V. M. Crawford. South Bend: University of Notre Dame Press, 1961.

Delaney, Paul. "The Dissolving Self: The Narrators of Mark Twain's *Mysterious Stranger* Fragments." *Journal of Narrative Technique* 6 (1976): 51–65.

Derrida, Jacques. "La Loi du genre/The Law of Genre." *Glyph* 7. Baltimore: Johns Hopkins University Press, 1980. 176–232.

DeVoto, Bernard. *Mark Twain's America.* Boston: Little, Brown, and Company, 1932.

Dolmetsch, Carl. *"Our Famous Guest": Mark Twain in Vienna.* Athens: University of Georgia Press, 1992.

Donoghue, Denis. "Teaching Literature: The Force of Form." *New Literary History* 30 (1999): 5–24.

Duncan, Jeffrey L. "The Empirical and the Ideal in Mark Twain." *PMLA* 95 (1980): 201–12.

Eichenbaum, Boris. "Literary Environment." *Readings in Russian Poetics: Formalist and Structuralist Views.* Trans. I. R. Titunik, ed. Ladislav Matejka and Krystyna Pomorska. Chicago: Dalkey Archive Press, 2002. 56–65.

———. "O. Henry and the Theory of the Short Story." *Readings in Russian Poetics: Formalist and Structuralist Views.* Trans. I. R. Titunik, ed. Ladislav Matejka and Krystyna Pomorska. Chicago: Dalkey Archive Press, 2002. 227–70.

———. "The Theory of the 'Formal Method.'" *Russian Formalist Criticism: Four Essays.* Trans. Lee T. Lemon and Marion J. Reis. Lincoln: University of Nebraska Press, 1965. 99–139.

Eliason, Eric A. "Curious Gentiles and Representational Authority in the City of the Saints." *Religion and American Culture: A Journal of Interpretation* 11 (2001): 155–90.

Emerson, Everett. "Mark Twain's Quarrel with God." *Order in Variety: Essays and Poems in Honor of Donald E. Stanford.* Ed. R. W. Crump. Newark: University of Delaware Press, 1991. 32–48.

Ensor, Allison. *Mark Twain and the Bible.* Lexington: University of Kentucky Press, 1969.

Eutsey, Duane. "Mark Twain's Attitudes toward Religion: Sympathy for the Devil, or Radical Christianity?" *Religion and Literature* 31 (1999): 45–64.

Fanning, Philip Ashley. *Mark Twain and Orion Clemens: Brothers, Partners, Strangers.* Tuscaloosa: University of Alabama Press, 2003.

Fatout, Paul. *Mark Twain in Virginia City.* Bloomington: Indiana University Press, 1964.

Feinstein, George. "Mark Twain's Idea of Story Structure." *American Literature* 18 (1946): 160–63.

Ferris, George T. "Mark Twain." *Appleton's Journal* 12.276 (July 4, 1874): 15–18.

Folks, Jeffrey J. "Twain and the Garden of the World: Cultural Consolidation on the American Frontier." *Southern Quarterly* 39 (2001): 82–95.

Frederick, John T. *The Darkened Sky: Nineteenth-Century American Novelists and Religion.* Notre Dame: University of Notre Dame Press, 1969.

Fulton, Joe B. "The Lost Manuscript Conclusion to Mark Twain's 'Corn-Pone Opinions': An Editorial History and an Edition of the Restored Text." *American Literary Realism* 37 (2005): 238–58.

———. *Mark Twain's Ethical Realism: The Aesthetics of Race, Class, and Gender.* Columbia: University of Missouri Press, 1997.

———. *Mark Twain in the Margins:* The Quarry Farm *and* A Connecticut Yankee in King Arthur's Court. Tuscaloosa: University of Alabama Press, 2000.

Fussell, E. S. "The Structural Problem of *The Mysterious Stranger.*" *Studies in Philology* 49 (1952): 95–104.

Geismar, Maxwell. *Mark Twain: An American Prophet.* Boston: Houghton Mifflin, 1970.

Gerber, John C. Introduction. *The Adventures of Tom Sawyer. The Adventures of Tom Sawyer; Tom Sawyer Abroad; Tom Sawyer, Detective.* Ed. John C. Gerber, Paul Baender, and Terry Firkins. Berkeley: University of California Press, 1980.

———. "The Adventures of Tom Sawyer." *The Mark Twain Encyclopedia.* Ed. J. R. LeMaster and James D. Wilson. New York: Garland Publishing Co., 1993. 12–15.

Gervais, Ronald J. "'The Mysterious Stranger': The Fall as Salvation." *Philological Association of the Pacific Coast* 5 (1970): 24–33.

Gibson, William M. Introduction. *Mark Twain's Mysterious Stranger Manuscripts.* Berkeley: University of California Press, 1969. 1–34.

Gillis, James Martin. *False Prophets.* Freeport, NY: Books for Libraries Press, 1969 (1925).

Gillman, Susan. *Dark Twins: Imposture and Identity in Mark Twain's America.* Chicago: University of Chicago Press, 1989.

Gilman, Sander. *The Parodic Sermon in European Perspective: Aspects of Liturgical Parody from the Middle Ages to the Twentieth Century.* Wiesbaden: Franz Steiner, 1974.

Gogol, Nicolai. "The Nose." *The Overcoat and Other Tales of Good and Evil.* Trans. David Magarshack. New York: W. W. Norton, 1965. 203–32.

Goodrich-Freer, Adela (Miss X). *Essays in Psychical Research.* London: George Redway, 1899.

Gray, Richard. "Kingdom and Exile: Mark Twain's Hannibal Books." *American Fiction: New Readings.* Ed. Richard Gray. London: Vision, 1983. 80–99.

Greimas, A.-J. *Structural Semantics: An Attempt at a Method.* Trans. Daniele McDowell, Ronald Schleifer, and Alan Velie. Lincoln: University of Nebraska Press, 1983.

Gribben, Alan. "'I Detest Novels, Poetry and Theology': Origin of a Fiction Concerning Mark Twain's Reading." *Tennessee Studies in Literature* 22 (1977): 154–61.

———. "'I Did Wish Tom Sawyer Was There': Boy-Book Elements in *Tom Sawyer* and *Huckleberry Finn.*" *One Hundred Years of Huckleberry Finn: The Boy, His Book, and American Cutlure.* Ed. Robert Sattelmeyer and J. Donald Crowley. Columbia: University of Missouri Press, 1985. 149–70.

———. *Mark Twain's Library: A Reconstruction.* 2 vols. Boston: G. K. Hall, 1980.

———. "Mark Twain, Phrenology, and the 'Temperaments': A Study of Pseudoscientific Influence." *American Quarterly* 24 (1972): 45–68.

Griffith, Clark. *Achilles and the Tortoise: Mark Twain's Fictions*. Tuscaloosa: University of Alabama Press, 1998.

Grimm, Jakob and Wilhelm. "Brier Rose." *Grimms' Tales for Young and Old: The Complete Stories*. Trans. Ralph Manheim. Garden City, NY: Doubleday and Company, 1977. 175–78.

———. "The Cat and the Mouse Set Up Housekeeping." *Grimms' Tales for Young and Old: The Complete Stories*. Trans. Ralph Manheim. Garden City, NY: Doubleday and Company, 1977. 6–8.

Halverson, John. "Patristic Exegesis: A Medieval *Tom Sawyer*." *College English* 27 (1965): 50–55.

Harnsberger, Caroline Thomas. *Mark Twain's Views of Religion*. Evanston, IL: Schori Press, 1961.

Harris, Susan K. *Mark Twain's Escape from Time: A Study of Patterns and Images*. Columbia: University of Missouri Press, 1982.

———. Narrative Structure in Mark Twain's *Joan of Arc*." *Journal of Narrative Technique* 12 (1982): 48–56.

Hays, John Q. *Mark Twain and Religion: A Mirror of American Eclecticism*. Ed. Fred Rodewald. New York: Peter Lang, 1989.

Heschel, Rabbi Abraham J. *The Prophets*. New York: Harper and Row, 1962.

Highet, Gilbert. *The Classical Tradition: Greek and Roman Influences on Western Literature*. New York: Oxford University Press, 1949.

Hill, Hamlin. "The Composition and the Structure of *Tom Sawyer*." *American Literature* 32 (1961): 379–392.

———. "Mark Twain's *Roughing It:* The End of the American Dream." *American Renaissance and American West*. Ed. Christopher Durer. Laramie: University of Wyoming Press, 1982. 3–13.

Holland, Jeffrey R. "Soul-Butter and Hog Wash: Mark Twain and Frontier Religion." *"Soul-Butter and Hog Wash" and Other Essays on the American West*. Ed. Thomas G. Alexander. Provo, UT: Brigham Young University Press, 1978. 6–32.

Hone, William. *The Three Trials of William Hone for Publishing Three Parodies*. London: William Hone, 1818.

Horn, Jason. *Mark Twain and William Jame:. Crafting a Free Self*. Columbia: University of Missouri Press, 1996.

Howard, June. *Form and History in American Literary Naturalism*. Chapel Hill: University of North Carolina Press, 1985.

Howe, Lawrence. *Mark Twain and the Novel: The Double-Cross of Authority*. New York: Cambridge University Press, 1998.

Howells, William Dean. "Mark Twain: An Inquiry." *William Dean Howells as Critic*. Ed. Edwin H. Cady. Boston: Routledge and Kegan Paul, 1973. 337–51.

———. Review. *Roughing It*. *Atlantic* 29 (June 1872): 754–55.

Hudson, Father Daniel. "Review of *A Connecticut Yankee in King Arthur's Court*." *Ave Maria* 30 (1890): 116.

———. "Review of *Personal Recollections of Joan of Arc*." *Ave Maria* 75 (1912): 729.

Irwin, Terence. *Plato's Ethics*. New York: Oxford University Press, 1995.

Jackson, Fleda Brown. "Reconciliation and Optimism in Twain's 'Mysterious Stranger' Manuscripts." *CLA Journal* 35 (1991): 57–71.

Jakobson, Roman. "The Dominant." *Language in Literature*. Ed. Krystyna Pomorska and Stephen Rudy. Cambridge: Harvard University Press, 1987. 41–46.

———. *Main Trends in the Science of Language*. New York: Harper and Row, 1974.

James, Henry. "The Figure in the Carpet." *Henry James: Major Stories and Essays*. New York: Library of America College Edition, 1999. 276–312.

James, William. *Pragmatism*. Amherst, NY: Prometheus, 1991.

Jeffrey, David Lyle. *People of the Book: Christian Identity and Literary Culture*. Grand Rapids, MI: William B. Eerdmans Publishing, 1996.

Jones, Alexander E. "Heterodox Thought in Mark Twain's Hannibal." *Arkansas Historical Quarterly* 10 (1951): 244–57.

———. "Mark Twain and the Determinism of *What Is Man?*" *American Literature* 29 (1957): 1–17.

Jones, Howard Mumford. *Belief and Disbelief in American Literature*. Chicago: University of Chicago Press, 1967.

Jungmann, Josef Andreas. *Handing on the Faith: A Manual of Catechetics*. Trans. A. N. Fuerst. New York: Herder and Herder, 1959.

Kahn, Sholom J. *Mark Twain's "Mysterious Stranger": A Study of the Manuscript Texts*. Columbia: University of Missouri Press, 1978.

Kaplan, Amy. *The Social Construction of American Realism*. Chicago: University of Chicago Press, 1988.

Kaplan, Justin. *Mr. Clemens and Mark Twain*. New York: Simon and Schuster, 1966.

Kayser, John R., and John Fitzgerald. "Modern Republicanism and the Education of Achilles: An Interpretation of *Tom Sawyer*." *Connotations* 5 (1995–96): 228–39.

Kratins, Ojars. "The Middle English *Amis and Amiloun:* Chivalric Romance or Secular Hagiography?" *PMLA* 81 (1966): 347–54.

Krauth, Leland. *Proper Mark Twain*. Athens: University of Georgia Press, 1999.

Laverty, Carroll D. "The Genesis of *The Mysterious Stranger*." *Mark Twain Quarterly* 7 (1947): 15–19.

Lee, Robert Edson. *From West to East: Studies in the Literature of the American West*. Urbana: University of Illinois Press, 1966.

Lévi-Strauss, Claude. "Structure and Form: Reflections on a Work by Vladimir Propp." In Vladimir Propp, *Theory and History of Folklore*. Trans. Ariadna Y. Martin and Richard P. Martin and Several Others. Ed. Anatoly Liberman. Minneapolis: University of Minnesota Press, 1984. 167–88.

———. "The Structural Study of Myth." *Journal of American Folklore* 68 (1955): 428–44.

Lorch, Fred. "Adrift for Heresy." *Palimpsest* 10 (1929): 372–80.

Lowrey, Robert E. "Imagination and Redemption: 44 in the Third Version of *The Mysterious Stranger*." *Southern Review* 18 (1982): 100–110.

Lurye, I. C. "M. Bulgakov I Mark Tven." *Seriya Literatury I Izika* 46.6 (1987): 564–71.

Lynn, Kenneth S. *Mark Twain and Southwestern Humor*. Westport, CN: Greenwood Press, 1972.

Macnaughton, William R. *Mark Twain's Last Years as a Writer*. Columbia: University of Missouri Press, 1979.

Maik, Thomas A. *A Reexamination of Mark Twain's "Joan of Arc"* Lewiston, NY: Edwin Mellen Press, 1992.

Mailloux, Steven. *Rhetorical Power.* Ithaca: Cornell University Press, 1989.

Malcom, Donald. "Mark Twain's Gnostic Old Age: Annihilation and Transcendence in 'No. 44, the Mysterious Stranger.'" *American Literary Realism* 28 (1996): 41–58.

Male, Roy R. *Enter, Mysterious Stranger.* Norman: University of Oklahoma Press, 1979.

Mandia, Patricia M. *Comedic Pathos: Black Humor in Twain's Fiction.* Jefferson, NC: McFarland, 1991.

Margolis, Stacey. "*Huckleberry Finn;* or, Consequences." *PMLA* 116 (2001): 329–43.

Markels, Julian. "Negotiating an Audience for American Exceptionalism: *Redburn* and *Roughing It.*" *Reciprocal Influences: Literary Production, Distribution, and Consumption in America.* Ed. Steven Fink and Susan S. Williams. Columbus: Ohio State University Press, 1999. 139–50.

Marotti, Maria Ornella. *The Duplicating Imagination: Twain and the Twain Papers.* University Park: Pennsylvania State University Press, 1990.

Marsh, Joss. *Word Crimes: Blasphemy, Culture, and Literature in Nineteenth-Century England.* Chicago: University of Chicago Press, 1998.

Martin, Jay. *Harvests of Change: American Literature, 1865–1914.* Englewood Cliffs, NJ: Prentice Hall, 1967.

Matheson, Terence J. "The Devil and Philip Traum: Twain's Satiric Purposes in *The Mysterious Stranger.*" *Markham Review* 12 (1982): 5–11.

May, John R. "The Gospel According to Philip Traum: Structural Unity in 'The Mysterious Stranger.'" *Studies in Short Fiction* 8 (1971): 411–22.

McKeon, Michael. *The Origins of the English Novel, 1600–1740.* Baltimore: Johns Hopkins University Press, 1987.

McWilliams, Jim. *Mark Twain in the* St. Louis Post-Dispatch, *1874–1891.* Troy, NY: Whitson Publishing Company, 1997.

Medvedev, P. N., and M. M. Bakhtin. *The Formal Method in Literary Scholarship: A Critical Introduction to Sociological Poetics.* Trans. Albert J. Wehrle. Cambridge: Harvard University Press, 1985.

Meindl, Dieter. *American Fiction and the Metaphysics of the Grotesque.* Columbia: University of Missouri Press, 1996.

Melton, Jeffrey Alan. "The Wild Teacher of the Pacific Slope: Mark Twain, Travel Books, and Instruction." *Thalia* 16 (1996): 46–52.

Michelson, Bruce. "Deus Ludens: The Shaping of Mark Twain's *Mysterious Stranger.*" *Modern Critical Views: Mark Twain.* Ed. Harold Bloom. New York: Chelsea House, 1986. 107–21.

———. "Ever Such a Good Time: The Structure of Mark Twain's *Roughing It.*" *American Literature in Belgium.* Ed. Gilbert Debusscher. Amsterdam: Rodopi, 1988. 27–41.

Miller, Victoria Thorpe. "*Personal Recollections of Joan of Arc* in Today's Classroom." *Making Mark Twain Work in the Classroom.* Ed. James S. Leonard. Durham, NC: Duke University Press, 1999. 55–64.

Mitchell, Lee Clark. "Verbally *Roughing It:* The West of Words." *Nineteenth-Century Literature* 44 (1989): 67–92.

Morson, Gary Saul. "Parody, History, and Metaparody." *Rethinking Bakhtin: Extensions and Challenges.* Eds. Gary Saul Morson and Caryl Emerson. Evanston, IL:

Northwestern University Press, 1989. 63–86.

Mott, Bertram, Jr. "Twain's Joan: A Divine Anomaly." *Etudes Anglaises* 23 (1970): 245–55.

Nadeau, Lionel Carl. "Mark Twain's *Joan of Arc*—An Analysis of the Background and Original Sources." Ed.D. Dissertation. Ball State University, 1979.

Nielsen, Veneta. "The Savage Prophet; or, Who's Afraid of Samuel Twain?" *Proceedings of the Utah Academy of Sciences, Arts and Letters* 43 (1966): 1–7.

Obenzinger, Hilton. *American Palestine: Melville, Twain, and the Holy Land Mania.* Princeton: Princeton University Press, 1999.

Ober, K. Patrick. *Mark Twain and Medicine: "Any Mummery Will Cure."* Columbia: University of Missouri Press, 2003.

O'Connor, Flannery. "Some Aspects of the Grotesque in Southern Fiction." *Flannery O'Connor. Collected Works.* New York: Library of America, 1988. 813–21.

Oriard, Michael. "From Tom Sawyer to Huckleberry Finn: Toward Godly Play." *Studies in American Fiction* 8 (1980): 183–202.

Oz, Avraham. *The Yoke of Love: Prophetic Riddles in "The Merchant of Venice."* Newark: University of Delaware Press, 1995.

Paine, Albert Bigelow. *Mark Twain, A Biography.* 3 vols. New York: Chelsea House, 1980.

Parker, Hershel. *Flawed Texts and Verbal Icons: Literary Authority in American Fiction.* Evanston, IL: Northwestern University Press, 1984.

Parsons, Coleman O. "The Background of *The Mysterious Stranger.*" *American Literature* 32 (1960): 55–74.

Perkins, Vivienne. "The Trouble with Satan: Structural and Semantic Problems in the *Mysterious Stranger.*" *Gypsy Scholar* 3 (1975): 37–43.

Phipps, William E. *Mark Twain's Religion.* Macon, GA: Mercer University Press, 2003.

Plato. *The Republic.* Trans. B. Jowett. *The Dialogues of Plato.* 2 vols. New York: Random House, 1937 (1892). 1: 591–879.

Powell, Jon. "Trouble and Joy from 'A True Story' to *Adventures of Huckleberry Finn:* Mark Twain and the Book of Jeremiah." *Studies in American Fiction* 20.2 (1992): 145–54.

Pratter, Frederick E. "The Mysterious Traveler in the Speculative Fiction of Howells and Twain." *America as Utopia.* Ed. Kenneth M. Roemer. New York: Burt Franklin and Company, 1981. 78–90.

Preston, Nathaniel Hope. "'Oh, Flower of Eastern Silence': The Influence of Indian Religion on American Fiction, 1882–1933." Ph.D. dissertation. University of Tennessee, Knoxville, May 1999.

Propp, Vladimir. *Morphology of the Folktale.* Trans. Laurence Scott. 2nd rev. ed. Austin: University of Texas Press, 1968.

———. *Theory and History of Folklore.* Trans. Ariadna Y. Martin and Richard P. Martin and Several Others. Ed. Anatoly Liberman. Minneapolis: University of Minnesota Press, 1984.

Ramaswamy, S. "Mark Twain's *What Is Man?*—An Indian View." *Mark Twain and Nineteenth Century American Literature.* Ed. E. Nageswara Rao. Hyderabad, India: American Studies Research Centre, 1993. 27–36.

Rickels, Milton. "The Grotesque Body of Southwestern Humor." *Critical Essays on*

American Humor. Ed. William Bedford Clark and W. Craig Turner. Boston: G. K. Hall, 1984. 155–66.

Ricoeur, Paul. *Time and Narrative.* Vol. 1. Trans. Kathleen McLaughlin and David Pellauer. Chicago: University of Chicago Press, 1983.

———. *Time and Narrative.* Vol. 2. Trans. Kathleen McLaughlin and David Pellauer. Chicago: University of Chicago Press, 1985.

Robinson, Forrest G. *In Bad Faith: The Dynamics of Deception in Mark Twain's America.* Cambridge: Harvard University Press, 1986.

———. "The Innocent at Large: Mark Twain's Travel Writing." *The Cambridge Companion to Mark Twain.* Ed. Forrest Robinson. New York: Cambridge University Press, 1995. 27–51.

Rogers, Franklin R. Introduction. *Mark Twain Satires and Burlesques.* Berkeley: University of California Press, 1967. 1–16.

———. *Mark Twain's Burlesque Patterns, as Seen in the Novels and Narratives, 1855–1885.* Dallas: Southern Methodist University Press, 1960.

Rohman, Chad. "'Searching for the fructifying dew of truth': 'Negative Evidence' and Epistemological Uncertainty in Mark Twain's *No. 44, The Mysterious Stranger.*" *American Literary Realism* 31 (1999): 72–88.

———. "What *Is* Man? Mark Twain's Unresolved Attempt to Know." *Nineteenth Century Studies* 15 (2001): 57–72.

Rosenberger, Edward G. "An Agnostic Hagiographer." *Catholic World* 127 (1928): 717–23.

Ross, Kenneth. Personal Interview. July 24, 2001.

Rubin, Louis D., Jr. "Tom Sawyer and the Use of Novels." *American Quarterly* 9 (1957): 209–16.

Saxon, A. H. *P. T. Barnum: The Legend and the Man.* New York: Columbia University Press, 1989.

Schrager, Cynthia D. "Mark Twain and Mary Baker Eddy: Gendering the Transpersonal Subject." *American Literature* 70 (1998): 29–62.

Seelye, John. "What's in a Name: Sounding the Depths of Tom Sawyer." *Sewanee Review* 90 (1982): 408–29.

Shanahan, Lawrence Bernard. "Mark Twain's *Personal Recollections of Joan of Arc:* The Sentimental Tradition and the Ambivalent Reality." Ph.D. dissertation, University of Wisconsin, 1972.

Shklovsky, Viktor. *A Sentimental Journey.* Trans. Richard Sheldon. Ithaca: Cornell University Press, 1970.

———. *Theory of Prose.* Trans. Benjamin Sher. Elmwood Park, IL: Dalkey Archive Press, 1990.

The Shorter Catechism. Book of Confessions. Louisville, KY: Geneva Press, 1996. 229–41.

Shurr, William H. *Rappaccini's Children: American Writers in a Calvinist World.* Lexington: University Press of Kentucky, 1981.

Simpson, Lewis. Review. *What Is Man? and Other Philosophical Writings* by Mark Twain. Ed. Paul Baender. *American Literature* 45 (1974): 617–18.

Skandera-Trombley, Laura E. "Mark Twain's Cross-Dressing Oeuvre." *College Literature* 24.2 (1997): 82–96.

Smiley, Jane. "Say It Ain't So, Huck: Second Thoughts on Mark Twain's 'Masterpiece.'" *Harper's Magazine* (January 1996): 61–67.

Smith, Henry Nash. *Mark Twain: The Development of a Writer.* Cambridge: Harvard University Press, 1962.

Smith, J. Harold. *Mark Twain: Rebel Pilgrim.* New York: Heath Cote Publishing Group, 1973.

Spengemann, William C. *Mark Twain and the Backwoods Angel: The Matter of Innocence in the Works of Samuel L. Clemens.* Kent, OH: Kent State University Press, 1966.

Stahl, John Daniel. "American Myth in European Disguise: Fathers and Sons in *The Prince and the Pauper.*" *American Literature* 58 (1986): 203–16.

———. "Mark Twain's 'Slovenly Peter' in the Context of Twain and German Culture." *Lion and the Unicorn* 20.2 (1996): 166–80.

Stone, Albert E., Jr. *The Innocent Eye: Childhood in Mark Twain's Imagination.* New Haven: Yale University Press, 1961.

Sweets, Henry H. *The Hannibal, Missouri Presbyterian Church: A Sesquicentennial History.* Hannibal: Presbyterian Church of Hannibal, 1984.

Tanner, Tony. *The Reign of Wonder: Naivety and Reality in American Literature.* New York: Harper and Row, 1965.

Thomas, Keith. *Religion and the Decline of Magic.* New York: Charles Scribner's Sons, 1971.

Thomas, Niles Buchanan. *A Study of the Determinism of Mark Twain: Selected Novels, 1885–1910, and "What Is Man?* M.A. thesis. Auburn University: June 3, 1969.

Toby, B. B. "Review of *Roughing It.*" *San Francisco Morning Call.* April 28, 1872. 1.

Tomashevsky, Boris. "Thematics." *Russian Formalist Criticism: Four Essays.* Ed. Lee T. Lemon and Marion J. Reis. Norman: University of Oklahoma Press, 1964. 61–95.

Tompkins, Jane. *Sensational Designs: The Cultural Work of American Fiction 1790–1860.* New York: Oxford University Press, 1985.

Towers, Tom. "'Hateful Reality': The Failure of the Territory in *Roughing It.*" *Western American Literature* 9 (1974): 3–15.

———. "'I Never Thought We Might Want to Come Back': Strategies of Transcendence in *Tom Sawyer.*" *Modern Fiction Studies* 21 (1976): 509–20.

Tuckey, John S. *Mark Twain and Little Satan: The Writing of "The Mysterious Stranger."* West Lafayette, IN: Purdue University Studies, 1963.

———. "Mark Twain's Later Dialogue: The 'Me' and the Machine." *American Literature* 41 (1970): 532–42.

Tumbleson, Raymond. *Catholicism in the English Protestant Imagination: Nationalism, Religion, and Literature, 1660–1745.* Cambridge: Cambridge University Press, 1998.

Tuveson, Ernest Lee. *Redeemer Nation: The Idea of America's Millennial Role.* Chicago: University of Chicago Press, 1968.

Twain, Mark. [Samuel Clemens]. "The A B C Lesson." *Mark Twain in Eruption.* Ed. Bernard DeVoto. New York: Harper and Brothers, 1940. 105–6.

———. "About Magnanimous-Incident Literature." *Mark Twain. Collected Tales, Sketches, Speeches, and Essays, 1852–1890.* New York: Library of America, 1992. 703–9.

———. "About Smells." *What Is Man? and Other Philosophical Writings.* Ed. Paul Baender. Berkeley: University of California Press, 1973. 48–50.

————. "Adam's Soliloquy." *Mark Twain: Collected Tales, Speeches, and Essays, 1891–1910.* New York: Library of America, 1992. 635–41.

————. *Adventures of Huckleberry Finn.* Berkeley: University of California Press, 2003.

————. *The Adventures of Tom Sawyer. The Adventures of Tom Sawyer; Tom Sawyer Abroad; Tom Sawyer,Detective.* Ed. John Gerber, Paul Baender, and Terry Firkins. Berkeley: University of California Press, 1980. 31–237.

————. "Aix-Les-Bains." *Collected Tales, Sketches, Speeches, and Essays, 1891–1910.* New York: Library of America, 1992. 1–14.

————. *The American Claimant.* New York: Gabriel Wells, 1923.

————. "The Autobiography of a Damned Fool." *Mark Twain's Satires and Burlesques.* Ed. Franklin R. Rogers. Berkeley: University of California Press, 1967. 134–64.

————. *The Autobiography of Mark Twain.* Ed. Charles Neider. New York: Harper Perennial, 1959, 1990.

————. "Barnum's First Speech in Congress." *Mark Twain: Collected Tales, Sketches, Speeches, and Essays, 1852–1890.* New York: Library of America, 1992. 210–13.

————. "Battle Hymn of the Republic (Brought Down to Date)." *Mark Twain: Collected Tales, Sketches, Speeches, and Essays, 1891–1910.* New York: Library of America, 1992. 474–75.

————. "Boy's Manuscript." *The Adventures of Tom Sawyer. The Adventures of Tom Sawyer; Tom Sawyer Abroad; Tom Sawyer, Detective.* Ed. John C. Gerber, Paul Baender, and Terry Firkins. Berkeley: University of California Press, 1980. 420–51.

————. "The Chinese Temple." *Early Tales and Sketches, Volume 2, 1864–1865.* Ed. Edgar M. Branch and Robert H. Hirst. Berkeley: University of California Press, 1981. 44.

————. *Christian Science. What Is Man? and Other Philosophical Writings.* Ed. Paul Baender. Berkeley: University of California Press, 1973. 215–397.

————. "Christian Spectator." *Early Tales and Sketches, Volume 2, 1864–1865.* Ed. Edgar M. Branch and Robert H. Hirst. Berkeley: University of California Press, 1981. 394–95.

————. "The Christmas Fireside. For Good Little Boys and Girls. By Grandfather Twain. The Story of the Bad Little Boy That Bore a Charmed Life." *Early Tales and Sketches, Volume 2, 1864–1865.* Ed. Edgar M. Branch and Robert H. Hirst. Berkeley: University of California Press, 1981. 407–10.

————. "The Chronicle of Young Satan." *Mark Twain's Mysterious Stranger Manuscripts.* Berkeley: University of California Press, 1969. 35–174.

————. "Clairvoyant." *Hannibal, Huck and Tom.* Ed. Walter Blair. Berkeley: University of California Press, 1969. 61–66.

————. "Colloquy between a Slum Child and a Moral Mentor." *Mark Twain's Fables of Man.* Ed. John S. Tuckey. Berkeley: University of California Press, 1972. 106–9.

————. "Concerning Copyright." *Collected Tales, Sketches, Speeches, and Essays, 1891–1910.* New York: Library of America, 1992. 627–34.

————. "Concerning 'Martyrs' Day.'" *Mark Twain's Fables of Man.* Ed. John S. Tuckey. Berkeley: University of California Press, 1972. 303–7.

————. "As Concerns Interpreting the Deity." *What Is Man and Other Philosophical Writings.* Ed. Paul Baender. Berkeley: University of California Press, 1973. 109–20.

————. *A Connecticut Yankee in King Arthur's Court.* Ed. Bernard L. Stein. Berkeley: University of California Press, 1979.

————. "Consistency." *Mark Twain. Collected Tales, Sketches, Speeches, and Essays, 1852–1890.* New York: Library of America, 1992. 909–16.

————. "A Couple of Sad Experiences." *Mark Twain. Collected Tales, Sketches, Speeches, and Essays, 1852–1890.* New York: Library of America, 1992. 388–95.

————. "The Dervish and the Offensive Stranger." *Collected Tales, Sketches, Speeches, and Essays, 1891–1910.* New York: Library of America, 1992. 547–49.

————. "Dialogue on the Philippines." Mark Twain Project. University of California, Berkeley. 1902–3.

————. "Dinner Speech in Montreal." *Mark Twain: Collected Tales, Sketches, Speeches, and Essays, 1852–1890.* New York: Library of America, 1992. 776–80.

————. "Earthquake Almanac." *Early Tales and Sketches, Volume 2, 1864–1865.* Berkeley: University of California Press, 1981. 298–99.

————. "Edward Mills and George Benton: A Tale." *Mark Twain: Collected Tales, Sketches, Speeches, and Essays, 1852–1890.* New York: Library of America, 1992. 747–52.

————. "An Encounter with an Interviewer." *Collected Tales, Sketches, Speeches, and Essays, 1852–1890.* New York: Library of America, 1992. 583–87.

————. "Etiquette for the Afterlife: Advice to Paine." *The Bible According to Mark Twain: Writings on Heaven, Eden, and the Flood.* Ed. Howard G. Baetzhold and Joseph B. McCullough. Athens: University of Georgia Press, 208–10.

_____. "Eve's Diary." *Mark Twain: Collected Tales, Sketches, Speeches, and Essays, 1891–1910.* New York: Library of America, 1992. 695–709.

_____. "Eve Speaks." *Mark Twain: Collected Tales, Sketches, Speeches, and Essays, 1891–1910.* New York: Library of America, 1992. 710–12.

_____. "Extracts from Adam's Diary." *Mark Twain: Collected Tales, Sketches, Speeches, and Essays, 1891–1910.* New York: Library of America, 1992. 98–108.

————. "A Fable." *Mark Twain: Collected Tales, Sketches, Speeches, and Essays, 1891–1910.* New York: Library of America, 1992. 877–79.

————. "The Fable of the Yellow Terror." *Mark Twain's Fables of Man.* Ed. John S. Tuckey. Berkeley: University of California Press, 1972. 426–29.

————. "Female Suffrage." *Mark Twain: Collected Tales, Sketches, Speeches, and Essays, 1852–1890.* New York: Library of America, 1992. 224–27.

————. "The Five Boons of Life." *Mark Twain: Collected Tales, Sketches, Speeches, and Essays, 1891–1910.* New York: Library of America, 1992. 524–26.

————. "From the 'London Times' of 1904." *Collected Tales, Sketches, Speeches, and Essays, 1891–1910.* New York: Library of America, 1992. 273–83.

————. "Further of Mr. Mark Twain's Important Correspondence." *Early Tales and Sketches, Volume 2, 1864–1865.* Berkeley: University of California Press, 1981. 159–62.

————. "Getting My Fortune Told." *Mark Twain: Collected Tales, Sketches, Speeches, and Essays, 1852–1890.* New York: Library of America, 1992. 325–28.

————. "Ghost Life on the Mississippi." *The Works of Mark Twain. Early Tales and Sketches, Volume 1, 1851–1864.* Ed. Edgar M. Branch and Robert H. Hirst. Berkeley: University of California Press, 1979. 147–51.

———. "Goose Fable." *Mark Twain's Fables of Man.* Ed. John S. Tuckey. Berkeley: University of California Press, 1972. 150–51.

———. "Hellfire Hotchkiss." *Mark Twain's Satires and Burlesques.* Ed. Franklin R. Rogers. Berkeley: University of California Press, 1967. 175–203.

———. "A Helpless Situation." *Collected Tales, Sketches, Speeches, and Essays, 1891–1910.* New York: Library of America, 1992. 687–91.

———. "Henry Irving." *Mark Twain's Speeches: The Writings of Mark Twain, Vol. XXVIII* (Definitive ed., 37 vols.). New York: Gabriel Wells, 1923. 193–94.

———. "How to Tell a Story." *Mark Twain. Collected Tales, Sketches, Speeches, and Essays, 1891–1910.* New York: Library of America, 1992. 201–6.

———. "In the Animal's Court." *What Is Man? and Other Philosophical Writings.* Ed. Paul Baender. Berkeley: University of California Press, 1973. 121–23.

———. "The Indignity Put upon the Remains of George Holland by the Rev. Mr. Sabine." *Mark Twain. Collected Tales, Sketches, Speeches, and Essays, 1852–1890.* New York: Library of America, 1992. 517–21.

———. *The Innocents Abroad.* Mark Twain: *The Innocents Abroad and Roughing It.* New York: Library of America, 1984. 1–523.

———. "The International Lightning Trust." *Mark Twain's Fables of Man.* Ed. John S. Tuckey. Berkeley: University of California Press, 1972. 80–104.

———. "Introducing Winston S. Churchill." *Mark Twain. Collected Tales, Sketches, Speeches, and Essays, 1891–1910.* New York: Library of America, 1992. 454–55.

———. "Is He Living or Is He Dead?" *Mark Twain. Collected Tales, Sketches, Speeches, and Essays, 1891–1910.* New York: Library of America, 1992. 109–17.

———. "Letters from the Earth." *What Is Man and Other Philosophical Writings.* Ed. Paul Baender. Berkeley: University of California Press, 1973. 401–54.

———. *Life on the Mississippi. Mississippi Writings.* Ed. Guy Cardwell. New York: Library of America, 1982. 217–616.

———. "Little Bessie." *Mark Twain's Fables of Man.* Ed. John S. Tuckey. Berkeley: University of California Press, 1972. 34–44.

———. "The Man That Corrupted Hadleyburg." *Mark Twain: Collected Tales, Sketches, Speeches, and Essays, 1891–1910.* New York: Library of America, 1992. 390–438.

———. "Man's Place in the Animal World." *What Is Man and Other Philosophical Writings.* Ed. Paul Baender. Berkeley: University of California Press, 1973. 80–89.

———. *Mark Twain-Howells Letters: The Correspondence of Samuel L. Clemens and William Dean Howells, 1872–1910.* Ed. Henry Nash Smith and William M. Gibson. 2 vols. Cambridge: Harvard University Press, 1960.

———. *Mark Twain in Eruption.* Ed. Bernard DeVoto. New York: Harper and Brothers, 1922.

———. *Mark Twain's Correspondence with Henry Huttleston Rogers.* Ed. Lewis Leary. Berkeley: University of California Press, 1969.

———. *Mark Twain's Fables of Man.* Ed. John S. Tuckey. Berkeley: University of California Press, 1972.

———. *Mark Twain's Letters.* 2 vols. Ed. Albert Bigelow Paine. New York: Harper, 1917.

———. *Mark Twain's Letters, Volume 1: 1853–1866.* Ed. Edgar Marquess Branch,

Michael B. Frank, and Kenneth M. Sanderson. Berkeley: University of California Press, 1988.

———. *Mark Twain's Letters, Volume 2: 1867–1868.* Ed. Harriet Elinor Smith and Richard Bucci. Berkeley: University of California Press, 1990.

———. *Mark Twain's Letters, Volume 3: 1869.* Ed. Victor Fischer and Michael B. Frank. Berkeley: University of California Press, 1992.

———. *Mark Twain's Letters, Volume 4: 1870–1871.* Eds. Victor Fischer and Michael B. Frank. Berkeley: University of California Press, 1995.

———. *Mark Twain's Letters, Volume 5: 1872–1873.* Ed. Lin Salamo and Harriet Elinor Smith. Berkeley: University of California Press, 1997.

———. *Mark Twain's Letters, Volume 6: 1874–1875.* Ed. Michael B. Frank and Harriet Elinor Smith. Berkeley: University of California Press, 2002.

———. *Mark Twain's Letters to His Publishers, 1867–1894.* Ed. Hamlin Hill. Berkeley: University of California Press, 1967.

———. *Mark Twain's Mysterious Stranger Manuscripts.* Berkeley: University of California Press, 1969.

———. *Mark Twain's Notebooks and Journals, Volume 1: 1855–1873.* Ed. Frederick Anderson, Michael B. Frank, and Kenneth M. Sanderson. Berkeley: University of California Press, 1975.

———. *Mark Twain's Notebooks and Journals, Volume 2: 1877–1883.* Ed. Frederick Anderson, Lin Salamo, and Bernard L. Stein. Berkeley: University of California Press, 1975

———. *Mark Twain's Notebooks and Journals, Volume 3: 1883–1891.* Eds. Robert Pack Browning, Michael Frank, and Lin Salamo. Berkeley: University of California Press, 1979.

———. *Mark Twain's Travels with Mr. Brown.* New York: Alfred A. Knopf, 1940.

———. "Mental Telegraphy." *Mark Twain: Collected Tales, Sketches, Speeches, and Essays, 1891–1910.* New York: Library of America, 1992. 30–48.

———. "Mr. Beecher and the Clergy." *Mark Twain. Collected Tales, Sketches, Speeches, and Essays, 1852–1890.* New York: Library of America, 1992. 291–95.

———. "More Maxims of Mark." *Mark Twain: Collected Tales, Sketches, Speeches, and Essays, 1891–1910.* New York: Library of America, 1992. 939–47.

———. "My Late Senatorial Secretaryship." *Mark Twain. Collected Tales, Sketches, Speeches, and Essays, 1852–1890.* New York: Library of America, 1992. 257–61.

———. "The New Chinese Temple." [August 19, 1864]. *Early Tales and Sketches, Volume 2, 1864–1865.* Ed. Edgar M. Branch and Robert H. Hirst. Berkeley: University of California Press, 1981. 41–43.

———. "The New Chinese Temple." [August 23, 1864]. *Early Tales and Sketches, Volume 2, 1864–1865.* Ed. Edgar M. Branch and Robert H. Hirst. Berkeley: University of California Press, 1981. 45–46.

———. "The New Wildcat Religion." *The Washoe Giant in San Francisco.* Ed. Franklin Walker. San Francisco: George Fields, 1938. 133–34.

———. *No. 44, The Mysterious Stranger. Mark Twain's Mysterious Stranger Manuscripts.* Berkeley: University of California Press, 1969. 221–405.

———. "Old Times on the Mississippi." *Classic American Autobiographies.* Ed. William Andrews. New York: Mentor Books, 1992. 328–412.

————. "The Oldest Inhabitant—the Weather of New England." *Mark Twain: Collected Tales, Sketches, Speeches, and Essays, 1852–1890*. New York: Library of America, 1992. 673–76.

————."On Foreign Critics." *Collected Tales, Sketches, Speeches, and Essays, 1852–1890*. New York: Library of America, 1992. 942–44.

————. "Our Stock Remarks." *Early Tales and Sketches, Volume 1, 1851–1864*. Ed. Edgar M. Branch and Robert H. Hirst. Berkeley: University of California Press, 1979. 176.

————. "Passage from a Lecture." *Mark Twain's Fables of Man*. Ed. John S. Tuckey. Berkeley: University of California Press, 1972. 399–402.

————. *Personal Recollections of Joan of Arc. Historical Romances*. New York: Library of America, 1994. 541–970.

————. *The Prince and the Pauper*. Ed. Victor Fischer and Lin Salamo. Berkeley: University of California Press, 1979.

————. *Pudd'nhead Wilson. Mississippi Writings*. New York: Library of America, 1982. 915–1056.

————. "The Recurrent Major and Minor Compliment." *Mark Twain's Fables of Man*. Ed. John S. Tuckey. Berkeley: University of California Press, 1972. 430–33.

————. "Reflections on the Sabbath." *What Is Man and Other Philosophical Writings*. Ed. Paul Baender. Berkeley: University of California Press, 1973. 39–41.

————. *The Refuge of the Derelicts. Mark Twain's Fables of Man*. Ed. John S. Tuckey. Berkeley: University of California Press, 1972. 157–248.

————. "A Reminscence of Artemus Ward." *Mark Twain. Collected Tales, Sketches, Speeches, and Essays, 1852–1890*. New York: Library of America, 1992. 231–34.

————. "The Revised Catechism." *Collected Tales, Sketches, Speeches, and Essays, 1852–1890*. New York: Library of America, 1992. 539–40.

————. *Roughing It*. Ed. Harriet Elinor Smith and Edgar Marquess Branch. Berkeley: University of California Press, 1993.

————. "Saint Joan of Arc." *Collected Tales, Sketches, Speeches, and Essays, 1891–1910*. New York: Library of America, 1992. 584–96.

————. "Schoolhouse Hill." *Mark Twain's Mysterious Stranger Manuscripts*. Berkeley: University of California Press, 1969. 175–220.

————. "The Second Advent." *Mark Twain's Fables of Man*. Ed. John S. Tuckey. Berkeley: University of California Press, 1972. 53–68.

————. "The Secret History of Eddypus, the World-Empire." *Mark Twain's Fables of Man*. Ed. John S. Tuckey. Berkeley: University of California Press, 1972. 318–82.

————. *Slovenly Peter [Der Struwwelpeter]*. Translated into English Jingles from the Original German of Dr. Heinrich Hoffman. New York: Marchbanks Press, 1935.

————. "Some Learned Fables for Good Old Boys and Girls." *Mark Twain. Collected Tales, Sketches, Speeches, and Essays, 1852–1890*. New York: Library of America, 1992. 611–31.

————. "The Stock Broker's Prayer." [Attributed]. *Mark Twain in Virginia City*. Ed. Paul Fatout. Bloomington: Indiana University Press, 1964. 93.

————. "The Story of the Good Little Boy Who Did Not Prosper." *Mark Twain. Collected Tales, Sketches, Speeches, and Essays, 1852–1890*. New York: Library of America, 1992. 374–78.

————. "The Story of Mamie Grant, the Child-Missionary." *Mark Twain's Satires and Burlesques.* Ed. Franklin Rogers. Berkeley: University of California Press, 1967.

————. "A Sunday in Carson." *Early Tales and Sketches, Volume 1, 1851–1864.* Ed. Edgar M. Branch and Robert H. Hirst. Berkeley: University of California Press, 1979. 222.

————. "Supernatural Impudence." *Early Tales and Sketches, Volume 2, 1864–1865.* Ed. Edgar M. Branch and Robert H. Hirst. Berkeley: University of California Press, 1981. 47–48.

————. "1002d Arabian Night." *Mark Twain's Satires and Burlesques.* Ed. Franklin R. Rogers. Berkeley: University of California Press, 1967. 88–133.

————. "Three Statements of the Eighties." *What Is Man and Other Philosophical Writings.* Ed. Paul Baender. Berkeley: University of California Press, 1973. 56–59.

————. "3,000 Years among the Microbes." *Mark Twain's "Which Was the Dream" and Other Symbolic Writings of the Later Years.* Ed. John S. Tuckey. Berkeley: University of California Press, 1968. 430–553.

————. "To the Editor of the Editor of the American Hebrew." *Mark Twain's Fables of Man.* Ed. John S. Tuckey. Berkeley: University of California Press, 1972. 446–48.

————. "To the Person Sitting in Darkness." *Mark Twain: Collected Tales, Sketches, Speeches, and Essays, 1891–1910.* New York: Library of America, 1992. 457–73.

————. "Tom Sawyer's Conspiracy." *Mark Twain's Hannibal, Huck and Tom.* Ed. Walter Blair. Berkeley: University of California Press, 1969. 152–242.

————. "The 'Tournament' in A.D. 1870." *Mark Twain: Collected Tales, Sketches, Speeches, and Essays, 1852–1890.* New York: Library of America, 1992. 418–20.

————. "A Touching Story of George Washington's Boyhood." *Early Tales and Sketches, Volume 2, 1864–1865.* Ed. Edgar M. Branch and Robert H. Hirst. Berkeley: University of California Press, 1981. 95–99.

————. "A True Story." *Mark Twain. Collected Tales, Sketches, Speeches, and Essays, 1852–1890.* New York: Library of America, 1992. 578–82.

————. "Two Little Tales." *Mark Twain: Collected Tales, Sketches, Speeches, and Essays, 1891–1910.* New York: Library of America, 1992. 496–506.

————. "The United States of Lyncherdom." *Mark Twain: Collected Tales, Sketches, Speeches, and Essays, 1891–1910.* New York: Library of America, 1992. 479–86.

————. Unpublished notebook 31 [Old 26], August 1891–July 1892. Mark Twain Papers TS, University of California at Berkeley.

————. Unpublished notebook 37 [Old 29], January–April 1896. Mark Twain Papers TS, University of California at Berkeley.

————. Unpublished notebook 42 [Old 323], June 1897–March 1900. Mark Twain Papers TS, University of California at Berkeley.

————. Unpublished notebook 46 [Old 36], 1903–1904. Mark Twain Papers TS, University of California at Berkeley.

————. Unpublished notebook 47 [Old 37], 1904. University of California at Berkeley.

————. Unpublished notebook 48 [Old 38], 1905–1908. Mark Twain Papers TS, University of California at Berkeley.

————. "Villagers of 1840–3." *Hannibal, Huck and Tom.* Ed. Walter Blair. Berkeley: University of California Press, 1969. 28–40.

————. "The War Prayer." *Mark Twain: Collected Tales, Sketches, Speeches, and Essays 1891–1910.* New York: Library of America, 1992. 652–55.

———. "Was the World Made for Man?" *What Is Man? And Other Philosophical Writings.* Ed. Paul Baender. Berkeley: University of California Press, 1973. 101–6.

———. *What Is Man? What is Man? and Other Philosophical Writings.* Ed. Paul Baender. Berkeley: University of California Press, 1973. 124–214.

———. "Which Was It?" *Mark Twain's "Which Was the Dream" and Other Symbolic Writings of the Later Years.* Ed. John S. Tuckey. Berkeley: University of California Press, 1968. 179–429.

———. "Which Was the Dream?" *Mark Twain's "Which Was the Dream" and Other Symbolic Writings of the Later Years.* Ed. John S. Tuckey. Berkeley: University of California Press, 1968. 33–73.

———. "The Winner of the Medal." *The Twainian* 2.8 n.s. (1943): 1–4.

———. "Wit-Inspirations of the 'Two-Year-Olds.'" *Mark Twain: Collected Tales, Sketches, Speeches, and Essays, 1852–1890.* New York: Library of America, 1992. 403–6.

Tynjanov, Jurij. "On Literary Evolution." *Readings in Russian Poetics: Formalist and Structuralist Views.* Ed. Ladislav Matejka and Krystyna Pomorska. Chicago: Dalkey Archive Press, 2002. 66–78.

Uncle Madison. *The Polite Boy. With Illustrations. By Uncle Madison.* Boston: James M. Usher, ca.1860.

Uruburu, Paula M. *The Gruesome Doorway: An Analysis of the American Grotesque.* New York: Peter Lang, 1987.

Van Dover, J. Kenneth. "Mark Twain's Final Phase: 'The Mysterious Stranger.'" *Samuel L. Clemens: A Mysterious Stranger. Tubingen Essays in Celebration of the Mark Twain-Year 1985.* Ed. Hans Borchers and Daniel E. Williams. Frankfurt: Verlag Peter Lang, 1986. 187–203.

Vlastos, Gregory. "The Socratic Elenchus." *Plato 1: Metaphysics and Epistemology. Oxford Readings in Philosophy.* Ed. Gail Fine. New York: Oxford University Press, 1999. 36–63.

Vogelback, Arthur L. "Mark Twain and the Tammany Ring." *PMLA* 70 (1955): 69–77.

Waggoner, Hyatt Howe. "Science in the Thought of Mark Twain." *American Literature* 8 (1937): 357–70.

Wagner-Martin, Linda. Afterword. *What Is Man?* New York: Oxford University Press, 1996. 1–10.

Wallace, John. "The Case against Huck Finn." *Satire or Evasion? Black Perspectives on Huckleberry Finn.* Ed. James S. Leonard, Thomas A. Tenney, and Thadious M. Davis. Durham, NC: Duke University Press, 1992. 16–24.

Walsh, John K. "French Epic Legends in Spanish Hagiography: The *Vida de San Ginés* and the *Chanson de Roland.*" *Hispanic Review* 50 (1982): 1–16.

Webb, Walter Prescott. *The Great Plains.* New York: Grosset and Dunlap, 1931.

Wecter, Dixon. *Sam Clemens of Hannibal.* Boston: Houghton Mifflin, 1952.

Welleck, René, and Austin Warren. *Theory of Literature.* New York: Harvest/MJB, 1977.

West, Victor Royce. *Folklore in the Works of Mark Twain.* Lincoln, NE: n.p., 1930.

The Westminster Confession of Faith. Book of Confessions. Part 1 of the Constitution of the Presbyterian Church (U.S.A.). Louisville, KY: Geneva Press, 1996. 173–225.

Wexman, Virginia. "The Role of Structure in *Tom Sawyer* and *Huckleberry Finn*." *American Literary Realism* 6 (1973): 1–11.

Wilson, James D. "Religious and Esthetic Vision in Mark Twain's Early Career." *Canadian Review of American Studies* 17 (1986): 155–72.

Wolff, Cynthia Griffin. "*The Adventures of Tom Sawyer:* A Nightmare Vision of American Boyhood." *Modern Critical Views: Mark Twain.* Ed. Harold Bloom. New Haven: Chelsea House, 1986. 93–105.

Zlatic, Thomas D. "The 'Seeing Eye' and the 'Creating Mouth': Literacy and Orality in Mark Twain's *Joan of Arc*." *CLIO* 21 (1992): 285–304.

Zwarg, Christina. "Woman as Force in Twain's *Joan of Arc:* The Unwordable Fascination." *Criticism* 27 (1985): 57–72.

∤ INDEX ∤